SURVEYS OF ECONOMIC THEORY

Volume III

In the same series

*

SURVEYS OF ECONOMIC THEORY

Resource Allocation

PREPARED FOR
THE AMERICAN ECONOMIC ASSOCIATION
AND
THE ROYAL ECONOMIC SOCIETY

VOLUME III
SURVEYS IX–XIII

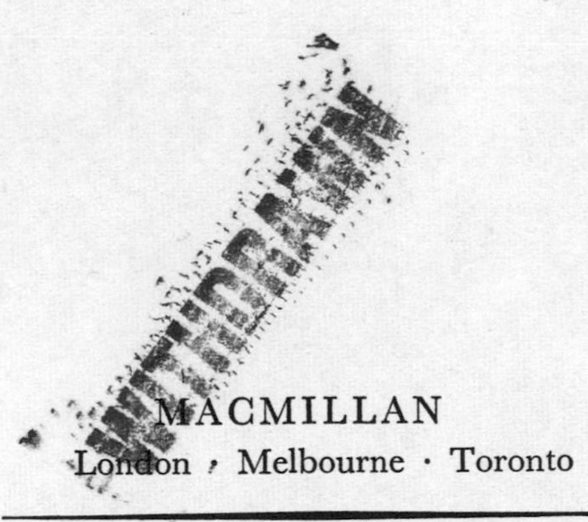

MACMILLAN
London · Melbourne · Toronto

ST MARTIN'S PRESS
New York
1966

MACMILLAN AND COMPANY LIMITED
Little Essex Street London WC2
also Bombay Calcutta Madras Melbourne

THE MACMILLAN COMPANY OF CANADA LIMITED
70 Bond Street Toronto 2

ST MARTIN'S PRESS INC
175 Fifth Avenue New York NY 10010

Library of Congress Catalog Card No: 65–26933

PRINTED IN GREAT BRITAIN

CONTENTS

FOREWORD

THE surveys printed in this volume and the two accompanying volumes in the series have been produced by the American Economic Association and the Royal Economic Society with the encouragement and financial support of the Rockefeller Foundation, and were first published in the *American Economic Review* and the *Economic Journal* respectively. The initiative in their planning and preparation was taken by the late Professor Norman Buchanan when he was Director for the Social Sciences at the Foundation. The purpose of the surveys cannot be better described than in the memorandum which he prepared for submission to the councils of the two bodies which is printed below.

The American Economic Association and the Royal Economic Society have collaborated throughout in the planning of the surveys in order that the two series should so far as possible be complementary to each other. They have also been fully informed of the similar series of surveys being published by *Econometrica* and have taken account of those also in making their plans.

The problems of publication were already in Professor Buchanan's mind when he wrote his memorandum. The two bodies both reached the same conclusion—that, to reach the widest audience, initial publication within the covers of the *American Economic Review* and the *Economic Journal* was most effective. But at the same time the two bodies have agreed that the surveys should also be made more readily available to students and research-workers and teachers in volumes of convenient size, planned in a single series on the basis of subject matter rather than of national origin. It was agreed that they should be printed for the two societies by the printers of the *Economic Journal*, using the type already set up for those surveys in the *Economic Journal* series. In order to make the whole series available as cheaply as possible to all students, the two societies have contributed to the cost of printing the American series in the style of the *Economic Journal*. They have received also very valuable help and advice from Messrs. Macmillan, publishers for the joint venture.

It is the belief of the two societies that this series of surveys, admirably prepared for them by the authors whom they have chosen, will fulfil in great degree the objectives set out by Professor Buchanan and enthusiastically accepted by all concerned. Since Professor Buchanan wrote his memorandum the flow of economic literature has continued to increase and the need for such reviews has grown even greater.

As development of economics continues, new surveys will unquestionably be needed. When the time comes for this the two societies will again consider together the need to carry such surveys further.

PREFACE

THE PURPOSE OF THESE SURVEYS

MEMORANDUM BY

NORMAN S. BUCHANAN

of the Rockefeller Foundation

I

Increasing concern has been expressed in many quarters over the swelling volume of published products of research in the social sciences. Books pile up at an alarming rate. Scientific journals and monographs have increased at an even greater rate. With many more social scientists and more abundant research funds from public and private sources, these trends are likely to be accelerated.

Unlike some other sciences and the law, the social sciences have so far not evolved any effective way of meeting the problem of keeping track of what is being published, where, on what topics, with what significance. Consequently, important contributions often go long unnoticed; there is duplication of effort, while at the same time important topics in research are neglected. Perhaps the most serious consequence, however, is that social scientists are increasingly becoming narrow specialists in some small segment of a particular subdivision of anthropology, economics, political science or sociology.

Scarcely less serious than the narrowing areas of competence of the best social scientists are two other problems. First, the task of training the on-coming generations of social scientists with any semblance of breadth and depth is becoming more and more difficult in all the social science disciplines. Those teaching the graduate courses acknowledge that increasingly their offerings fall far short of what they would wish because, on the one hand, they themselves find it impossible to be intimately acquainted with all the work in their aspect of the discipline to make a wise selection of subject-matter and emphasis for the graduate course and because, on the other hand, the time allotted to them within the whole graduate programme is far too short. In economics, for example, a poll of those individuals offering graduate work for the Ph.D. at any large university as to how much work *should* be required to provide " reasonably adequate " Ph.D. programme would, if summed, raise the duration of the Ph.D. programme by at least a factor of two. In other words, eight to ten years instead of the present four to five.

The second problem arises in those many countries where the social sciences heretofore have been neglected or only slightly recognised as fields of serious study. Nowadays, however, the leaders in these countries realise their need for skilled economists, statisticians, sociologists, etc., that such persons cannot be imported from the more developed countries in adequate numbers, and that therefore they must train their own people in the social sciences. Moreover, once trained they must be able to keep *au courant* in their specialities. Yet both the training and the keeping up present enormous problems in these countries because there are no effective means available for doing so. To try to stock the libraries and to subscribe to the important scientific journals would be far too costly and usually wholly impractical on other grounds.

Thus, the cascade of published research in the social sciences in books and journals would appear to raise important problems in three directions, viz., for the established and promising social scientists, for graduate training in the social sciences, for the development of social sciences in the under-developed countries.

II

Other sciences have encountered and partially overcome the problem just described for the social sciences. Two approaches have been used: first, a systematic abstracting programme for the journal literature, and secondly, a carefully planned sequence of analytical review-articles authored by the best specialists. The quality of the persons doing the abstracting and writing the review-articles determines the worth of these ventures.

For the social sciences at the present juncture it seems unwise to attempt the abstracting approach. This is inevitably a large, costly and uncertain undertaking, which is not made more appealing by the experience of the ill-fated *Social Science Abstracts.* The analytical-review approach, however, seems to hold certain promise. What is here proposed is set forth in terms of economics, though presumably the comments made below would apply equally to the other social sciences.

III

The bulk of the most important work in economics is in English, and the American Economic Association and the Royal Economic Society are large and effective professional societies. Their journals, the *American Economic Review* and the *Economic Journal*, have a circulation of approximately 11,000 and 8,000. These two associations, with their excellent journals with a world-wide circulation, seem the logical bodies to undertake the systematic review-article programme. Such articles could be included in the journals or made *separate* to be distributed to their subscribers.

How could such a programme be organised? Several points seem to be relevant here. First, the present editors should not be asked to undertake this task as an added burden. They need an advisory committee—which perhaps need meet *in camera* only rarely, if at all—to designate what branches of the science are ripe for a review-article and who would be the best person to do it. Second, once the topic and author are selected, the chairman of the committee, perhaps most suitably the editor of the journal, should be able to offer a proper honorarium to the prospective author. Such an honorarium, along with the scientific recognition in being solicited to do a difficult but important task, should assure that the best-qualified persons would accept the assignments. Third, since both the *A.E.R.* and the *E.J.* are already declining perhaps three-quarters of the manuscripts submitted to them, the pressure on space is severe. Hence the review-articles would mean adding to the total pages published and so to the total costs, perhaps about as much as the honorarium. Fourth, if the two professional associations were to undertake this proposal the two topic–author advisory committees should keep in close touch to avoid duplication. This could be easily arranged.

If the above proposal has merit, a grant-in-aid to each of the associations would allow the plan to be tried out. At the outset, perhaps, no more than two review-articles should be tried annually. As experience accumulated, this could be increased.

IX

THEORIES OF DECISION-MAKING IN ECONOMICS AND BEHAVIOURAL SCIENCE

By

HERBERT A. SIMON[1]

Recent years have seen important new explorations along the boundaries between economics and psychology. For the economist, the immediate question about these developments is whether they include new advances in psychology that can fruitfully be applied to economics. But the psychologist will also raise the converse question—whether there are developments in economic theory and observation that have implications for the central core of psychology. If economics is able to find verifiable and verified generalisations about human economic behaviour, then these generalisations must have a place in the more general theories of human behaviour to which psychology and sociology aspire. Influence will run both ways.[2]

I. How Much Psychology Does Economics Need?

How have psychology and economics gotten along with little relation in the past? The explanation rests on an understanding of the goals towards which economics, viewed as a science and a discipline, has usually aimed.

Broadly speaking, economics can be defined as the science that describes and predicts the behaviour of several kinds of economic man—notably the consumer and the entrepreneur. While perhaps literally correct, this definition does not reflect the principal focus in the literature of economics. We usually classify work in economics along two dimensions: (*a*) whether it is concerned with industries and the whole economy (macroeconomics) or with individual economic actors (microeconomics); and (*b*) whether it strives to describe and explain economic behaviour (descriptive economics), or to guide decisions either at the level of public policy (normative

[1] The author is Professor of Administration at the Carnegie Institute of Technology. This paper draws heavily upon earlier investigations with his colleagues in the Graduate School of Industrial Administration, carried out in library, field and laboratory, under several grants from the Ford Foundation for research on organisations. He is especially indebted to Julian Feldman, whose wide-ranging exploration of the so-called binary choice experiment [25] has provided an insightful set of examples of alternative approaches to a specific problem of choice. For bibliographical references see pp. 26–28.

[2] The influence of economics upon recent work in the psychology of higher mental processes is well illustrated by Bruner, Goodnow and Austin [14, Ch. 3 and 4]. In this work, game theory is used to throw light on the processes of concept formation.

macroeconomics) or at the level of the individual consumer or businessman (normative microeconomics).

The profession and literature of economics have been largely preoccupied with normative macroeconomics. Although descriptive macroeconomics provides the scientific base for policy prescription, research emphases have been determined in large part by relevance to policy (*e.g.*, business cycle theory). Normative microeconomics, carried forward under such labels as " management science," " engineering economics " and " operations research," is now a flourishing area of work having an uneasy and ill-defined relations with the profession of economics, traditionally defined. Much of the work is being done by mathematicians, statisticians, engineers and physical scientists (although many mathematical economists have also been active in it).[1]

This new area, like the old, is normative in orientation. Economists have been relatively uninterested in descriptive microeconomics—understanding the behaviour of individual economic agents—except as this is necessary to provide a foundation for macroeconomics. The normative microeconomist " obviously " doesn't need a theory of human behaviour: he wants to know how people *ought* to behave, not how they *do* behave. On the other hand, the macroeconomist's lack of concern with individual behaviour stems from different considerations. First, he assumes that the economic actor is rational, and hence he makes strong predictions about human behaviour without performing the hard work of observing people. Second, he often assumes competition, which carries with it the implication that only the rational survive. Thus, the classical economic theory of markets with perfect competition and rational agents is deductive theory that requires almost no contact with empirical data once its assumptions are accepted.[2]

Undoubtedly there is an area of human behaviour that fits these assumptions to a reasonable approximation, where the classical theory with its assumptions of rationality is a powerful and useful tool. Without denying the existence of this area, or its importance, I may observe that it fails to include some of the central problems of conflict and dynamics with which economics has become more and more concerned. A metaphor will help to show the reason for this failure.

Suppose we were pouring some viscous liquid—molasses—into a bowl of very irregular shape. What would we need in order to make a theory of the form the molasses would take in the bowl? How much would we have to know about the properties of molasses to predict its behaviour under

[1] The models of rational decision-making employed in operations research are surveyed in Churchman, Ackoff and Arnoff [16]; Bowman and Fetter [11]; and Vazsonyi [69].

[2] As an example of what passes for empirical " evidence " in this literature, I cite pp. 22–23 of Friedman's *Essays in Positive Economics* [27], which will amaze anyone brought up in the empirical tradition of psychology and sociology, although it has apparently excited little adverse comment among economists.

the circumstances? If the bowl were held motionless, and if we wanted only to predict behaviour in equilibrium, we would have to know little, indeed, about molasses. The single essential assumption would be that the molasses, under the force of gravity, would minimise the height of its centre of gravity. With this assumption, which would apply as well to any other liquid, and a complete knowledge of the environment—in this case the shape of the bowl—the equilibrium is completely determined. Just so, the equilibrium behaviour of a perfectly adapting organism depends only on its goal and its environment; it is otherwise completely independent of the internal properties of the organism.

If the bowl into which we were pouring the molasses were jiggled rapidly, or if we wanted to know about the behaviour before equilibrium was reached, prediction would require much more information. It would require, in particular, more information about the properties of molasses: its viscosity, the rapidity with which it " adapted " itself to the containing vessel and moved towards its " goal " of lowering its centre of gravity. Likewise, to predict the short-run behaviour of an adaptive organism, or its behaviour in a complex and rapidly changing environment, it is not enough to know its goals. We must know also a great deal about its internal structure and particularly its mechanisms of adaptation.

If, to carry the metaphor a step farther, new forces, in addition to gravitational force, were brought to bear on the liquid, we would have to know still more about it even to predict behaviour in equilibrium. Now its tendency to lower its centre of gravity might be countered by a force to minimise an electrical or magnetic potential operating in some lateral direction. We would have to know its relative susceptibility to gravitational and electrical or magnetic force to determine its equilibrium position. Similarly, in an organism having a multiplicity of goals, or afflicted with some kind of internal goal conflict, behaviour could be predicted only from information about the relative strengths of the several goals and the ways in which the adaptive processes responded to them.

Economics has been moving steadily into new areas where the power of the classical equilibrium model has never been demonstrated, and where its adequacy must be considered anew. Labour economics is such an area, oligopoly or imperfect competition theory another, decision-making under uncertainty a third and the theory of economic development a fourth. In all of these areas the complexity and instability of his environment becomes a central feature of the choices that economic man faces. To explain his behaviour in the face of this complexity, the theory must describe him as something more than a featureless, adaptive organism; it must incorporate at least some description of the processes and mechanisms through which the adaptation takes place. Let us list a little more concretely some specific problems of this kind:

(*a*) The classical theory postulates that the consumer maximises utility.

Recent advances in the theory of rational consumer choice have shown that the existence of a utility function, and its characteristics, if it exists, can be studied empirically.

(*b*) The growing separation between ownership and management has directed attention to the motivations of managers and the adequacy of the profit-maximisation assumption for business firms. So-called human relations research has raised a variety of issues about the motivation of both executives and employees.

(*c*) When, in extending the classical theory, the assumptions of perfect competition were removed, even the definition of rationality became ambiguous. New definitions had to be constructed, by no means as " obvious " intuitively as simple maximisation, to extend the theory of rational behaviour to bilateral monopoly and to other bargaining and outguessing situations.

(*d*) When the assumptions of perfect foresight were removed, to handle uncertainty about the environment, the definition of rationality had to be extended in another direction to take into account prediction and the formation of expectations.

(*e*) Broadening the definition of rationality to encompass goal conflict and uncertainty made it hard to ignore the distinction between the objective environment in which the economic actor " really " lives and the subjective environment that he perceives and to which he responds. When this distinction is made, we can no longer predict his behaviour—even if he behaves rationally—from the characteristics of the objective environment; we also need to know something about his perceptual and cognitive processes.

We shall use these five problem areas as a basis for sorting out some recent explorations in theory, model building and empirical testing. In Section II we will examine developments in the theory of utility and consumer choice. In Section III we will consider somewhat parallel issues relating to the motivation of managers. In Section IV we will deal with conflict of goals and the phenomena of bargaining. In Section V we will survey some of the work that has been done on uncertainty and the formation of expectations. In Section VI we will explore recent developments in the theory of human problem-solving and other higher mental processes, and see what implications these have for economic decision-making.

II. The Utility Function

The story of the re-establishment of cardinal utility, as a consequence of the introduction of uncertainty into the theory of choice, is well known.[1] When Pareto and Slutsky had shown that the theory of consumer demand

[1] Ward Edwards [23] provides an account of these developments from the psychologist's point of view; Chapter 2 of Luce and Raiffa [43] is an excellent introduction to the " new " utility theory. Arrow [5] contains a non-mathematical survey of this and related topics.

could be derived from the properties of indifference curves, without postulating a cardinal utility function underlying these curves, it became fashionable to regard utility as an ordinal measure—a ranking of alternatives by preference. Indeed, it could be shown that only ordinal utility had operational status—that the experiments that had been proposed, and even tried in a couple of instances, to measure an individual's utilities by asking him to choose among alternatives could never distinguish between two cardinal utility functions that were ordinally equivalent—that differed only by stretchings and contractions of the unit of measurement.

It was shown by von Neumann and Morgenstern, as a by-product of their development of the theory of games, that if the choice situation were extended to include choices among uncertain prospects—among lottery tickets, say—cardinal utilities could be assigned to the outcomes in an unequivocal way.[1] Under these conditions, if the subject's behaviour was consistent, it was possible to measure cardinally the utilities that different outcomes had for him.

A person who behaved in a manner consistent with the axioms of choice of von Neumann and Morgenstern would act so as to maximise the expected value—the average, weighted by the probabilities of the alternative outcomes of a choice—of his utility. The theory could be tested empirically, however, only on the assumption that the probabilities assigned to the alternatives by the subject were identical with the "objective" probabilities of these events as known to the experimenter. For example, if a subject believed in the gamblers' fallacy, that after a run of heads an unbiased coin would be more likely to fall tails, his choices might appear inconsistent with his utility function, while the real difficulty would lie in his method of assigning probabilities. This difficulty of "subjective" versus "objective" probability soon came to light when attempts were made to test experimentally whether people behaved in accordance with the predictions of the new utility theory. At the same time it was discovered that the problem had been raised and solved thirty years earlier by the English philosopher and mathematician Frank Ramsey.[2] Ramsey had shown that, by an appropriate series of experiments, the utilities and subjective probabilities assigned by a subject to a set of uncertain alternatives could be measured simultaneously.

Empirical Studies

The new axiomatic foundations of the theory of utility, which show that it is possible at least in principle to determine empirically whether people "have" utility functions of the appropriate kind, have led to a rash of

[1] The second edition of von Neumann and Morgenstern [50] contains the first rigorous axiomatic demonstration of this point.

[2] Ramsey's important essay [57] was sufficiently obscure that it was overlooked until the ideas were rediscovered independently by de Finetti [26]. Valuable notes on the history of the topic together with a thorough formal treatment will be found in the first five chapters of Savage [58].

choice experiments. An experimenter who wants to measure utilities, not merely in principle but in fact, faces innumerable difficulties. Because of these difficulties, most experiments have been limited to confronting the subjects with alternative lottery tickets, at various odds, for small amounts of money. The weight of evidence is that, under these conditions, most persons choose in a way that is reasonably consistent with the axioms of the theory—they behave as though they were maximising the expected value of utility and as though the utilities of the several alternatives can be measured.[1]

When these experiments are extended to more "realistic" choices—choices that are more obviously relevant to real-life situations—difficulties multiply. In the few extensions that have been made, it is not at all clear that the subjects behave in accordance with the utility axioms. There is some indication that when the situation is very simple and transparent, so that the subject can easily see and remember when he is being consistent, he behaves like a utility maximiser. But as the choices become a little more complicated—choices, for example, among phonograph records instead of sums of money—he becomes much less consistent [21, Ch. 3] [47].[2]

We can interpret these results in either of two ways. We can say that consumers "want" to maximise utility, and that if we present them with clear and simple choices that they understand they will do so. Or we can say that the real world is so complicated that the theory of utility maximisation has little relevance to real choices. The former interpretation has generally appeared more attractive to economists trained in classical utility theory and to management scientists seeking rules of behaviour for normative microeconomics; the latter to behavioural scientists interested in the description of behaviour.

Normative Applications

The new utility theory has provided the formal framework for much recent work in mathematical statistics—*i.e.*, statistical decision theory.[3] Similarly (it would be accurate to say "synonymously"), this framework provides the basis for most of the normative models of management science and operations research designed for actual application to the decision-making problems of the firm.[4] Except for some very recent developments, linear programming has been limited to decision-making

[1] Some of the empirical evidence is reviewed in [23]. A series of more recent empirical studies is reported in Davidson and Suppes [21].

[2] Some more recent experiments [57a], show a relatively high degree of transitivity. A. G. Papandreou, in a publication I have not yet seen (University of California Publications in Economics) also reports a high degree of transitivity.

[3] The systematic development of statistics as decision theory is due largely to A. Wald [70] on the basis of the earlier work of J. Neyman and E. Pearson. Savage [58] carries the development further, erecting the foundations of statistics solidly on utility and probability theory.

[4] This work relates, of course, to profit maximisation and cost minimisation rather than utility maximisation, but it is convenient to mention it at this point. See [11] [16] [69].

under certainty, but there have been far-reaching developments of dynamic programming dealing with the maximisation of expected values of outcomes (usually monetary outcomes) in situations where future events can be predicted only in terms of probability distributions.[1]

Again, there are at least two distinct interpretations that can be placed on these developments. On the one hand, it can be argued: " Firms would like to maximise profits if they could. They have been limited in doing so by the conceptual and computational difficulties of finding the optimal courses of action. By providing powerful new mathematical tools and computing machines, we now enable them to behave in the manner predicted by Alfred Marshall, even if they haven't been able to in the past." Nature will imitate art and economic man will become as real (and as artificial) as radios and atomic piles.

The alternative interpretation rests on the observation that, even with the powerful new tools and machines, most real-life choices still lie beyond the reach of maximising techniques—unless the situations are heroically simplified by drastic approximations. If man, according to this interpretation, makes decisions and choices that have some appearance of rationality, rationality in real life must involve something simpler than maximisation of utility or profit. In Section VI we will see where this alternative interpretation leads.

The Binary Choice Experiment

Much recent discussion about utility has centred around a particularly simple choice experiment. This experiment, in numerous variants, has been used by both economists and psychologists to test the most diverse kinds of hypotheses. We will describe it so that we can use it as a common standard of comparison for a whole range of theories and empirical studies.[2]

We will call the situation we are about to describe the *binary choice* experiment. It is better known to most game theorists—particularly those located not far from Nevada—as a two-armed bandit; and to most psychologists as a partial reinforcement experiment. The subject is required, in each of a series of trials, to choose one or the other of two symbols—say, plus or minus. When he has chosen he is told whether his choice was " right " or " wrong," and he may also receive a reward (in psychologist's language, a reinforcement) for " right " choices. The experimenter can arrange the schedule of correct responses in a variety of ways. There may be a definite pattern, or they may be randomised. It is not essential that one and only one response be correct on a given trial: the experimenter may determine that both or neither will be correct. In the latter case the

[1] Arrow, Harris and Marschak [3] were among the first to treat inventory decisions dynamically. A general treatment of the theory of dynamic programming will be found in Bellman [9].

[2] My understanding of the implications of the binary choice experiment owes much to conversations with Julian Feldman, and to his unpublished work on the experiment. See also Bush and Mosteller [15], particularly Chapter 13.

subject may or may not be informed whether the response he did not choose would have been correct.

How would a utility-maximising subject behave in the binary choice experiment? Suppose that the experimenter rewarded " plus " on one-third of the trials, determined at random, and " minus " on the remaining two-thirds. Then a subject, provided that he believed the sequence was random and observed that minus was rewarded twice as often as plus, should always, rationally, choose minus. He would find the correct answer two-thirds of the time, and more often than with any other strategy.

Unfortunately for the classical theory of utility in its simplest form few subjects behave in this way. The most commonly observed behaviour is what is called *event matching*.[1] The subject chooses the two alternatives (not necessarily at random) with relative frequencies roughly proportional to the relative frequencies with which they are rewarded. Thus, in the example given, two-thirds of the time he would choose minus, and as a result would make a correct response, on the average, in 5 trials out of 9 (on two-thirds of the trials in which he chooses minus, and one-third of those in which he chooses plus).[2]

All sorts of explanations have been offered for the event-matching behaviour. The simplest is that the subject just doesn't understand what strategy would maximise his expected utility; but with adult subjects in a situation as transparent as this one, this explanation seems far-fetched. The alternative explanations imply either that the subject regards himself as being engaged in a competitive game with the experimenter (or with " nature " if he accepts the experimenter's explanation that the stimulus is random), or that his responses are the outcome of certain kinds of learning processes. We will examine these two types of explanation further in Sections IV and V respectively. The important conclusion at this point is that even in an extremely simple situation, subjects do not behave in the way predicted by a straightforward application of utility theory.

Probabilistic Preferences

Before we leave the subject of utility, we should mention one recent important development. In the formalisations mentioned up to this point, probabilities enter only into the estimation of the consequences that will follow one alternative or another. Given any two alternatives, the first is definitely preferable to the second (in terms of expected utility), or the second to the first, or they are strictly indifferent. If the same pair of alternatives is presented to the subject more than once he should always prefer the same member of the pair.

[1] An example of data consistent with event-matching behaviour is given on p. 283 of [15].

[2] Subjects tend to choose the more highly rewarded alternative slightly more frequently than is called for by event matching. Hence, the actual behaviour tends to be some kind of average between event matching and the optimal behaviour. See [15, Ch. 13].

One might think this requirement too strict—that, particularly if the utility attached to one alternative were only slightly greater or less than that attached to the other, the subject might vacillate in his choice. An empirical precedent for such vacillation comes not only from casual observation of indecision but from analogous phenomena in the psychophysical laboratory. When subjects are asked to decide which of two weights is heavier, the objectively heavier one is chosen more often than the lighter one, but the relative frequency of choosing the heavier approaches one-half as the two weights approach equality. The probability that a subject will choose the objectively heavier weight depends, in general, on the ratio of the two weights.

Following several earlier attempts, a rigorous and complete axiom system for a utility theory incorporating probabilistic preferences has been constructed recently by Duncan Luce [cf. 43, App. 1]. Although the theory weakens the requirements of consistency in preference, it is empirically testable, at least in principle. Conceptually, it provides a more plausible interpretation of the notion of "indifference" than does the classical theory.

III. The Goals of Firms

Just as the central assumption in the theory of consumption is that the consumer strives to maximise his utility, so the crucial assumption in the theory of the firm is that the entrepreneur strives to maximise his residual share—his profit. Attacks on this hypothesis have been frequent.[1] We may classify the most important of these as follows:

(*a*) The theory leaves ambiguous whether it is short-run or long-run profit that is to be maximised.

(*b*) The entrepreneur may obtain all kinds of "psychic incomes" from the firm, quite apart from monetary rewards. If he is to maximise his utility, then he will sometimes balance a loss of profits against an increase in psychic income. But if we allow "psychic income" the criterion of profit maximisation loses all of its definiteness.

(*c*) The entrepreneur may not care to maximise, but may simply want to earn a return that he regards as satisfactory. By sophistry and an adept use of the concept of psychic income, the notion of seeking a satisfactory return can be translated into utility maximising but not in any operational way. We shall see in a moment that "satisfactory profits" is a concept more meaningfully related to the psychological notion of aspiration levels than to maximisation.

(*d*) It is often observed that under modern conditions the equity owners and the active managers of an enterprise are separate and distinct groups of people, so that the latter may not be motivated to maximise profits.

[1] For a survey of recent discussions see Papandreou [55].

(*e*) Where there is imperfect competition among firms, maximising is an ambiguous goal, for what action is optimal for one firm depends on the actions of the other firms.

In the present section we shall deal only with the third of these five issues. The fifth will be treated in the following section; the first, second and fourth are purely empirical questions that have been discussed at length in the literature; they will be considered here only for their bearing on the question of satisfactory profits.

Satisficing versus Maximising

The notion of satiation plays no role in classical economic theory, while it enters rather prominently into the treatment of motivation in psychology. In most psychological theories the motive to act stems from *drives*, and action terminates when the drive is satisfied. Moreover, the conditions for satisfying a drive are not necessarily fixed, but may be specified by an aspiration level that itself adjusts upward or downward on the basis of experience.

If we seek to explain business behaviour in the terms of this theory we must expect the firm's goals to be not maximising profit, but attaining a certain level or rate of profit, holding a certain share of the market or a certain level of sales. Firms would try to "satisfice" rather than to maximize.[1]

It has sometimes been argued that the distinction between satisficing and maximising is not important to economic theory. For in the first place the psychological evidence on individual behaviour shows that aspirations tend to adjust to the attainable. Hence in the long run, the argument runs, the level of aspiration and the attainable maximum will be very close together. Second, even if some firms satisficed, they would gradually lose out to the maximising firms, which would make larger profits and grow more rapidly than the others.

These are, of course, precisely the arguments of our molasses metaphor, and we may answer them in the same way that we answered them earlier. The economic environment of the firm is complex, and it changes rapidly; there is no *a priori* reason to assume the attainment of long-run equilibrium. Indeed, the empirical evidence on the distribution of firms by size suggests that the observed regularities in size distribution stem from the statistical equilibrium of a population of adaptive systems rather than the static equilibrium of a population of maximisers.[2]

Models of satisficing behaviour are richer than models of maximising behaviour, because they treat not only of equilibrium but of the method of reaching it as well. Psychological studies of the formation and change

[1] A comparison of satisficing with maximising models of decision-making can be found in [64, Ch. 14]. Katona [40] has independently made similar comparisons of economic and psychological theories of decision.

[2] Simon and Bonini [66] have constructed a stochastic model that explains the observed data on the size distributions of business firms.

of aspiration levels support propositions of the following kinds.[1] (*a*) When performance falls short of the level of aspiration, search behaviour (particularly search for new alternatives of action) is induced. (*b*) At the same time, the level of aspiration begins to adjust itself downward until goals reach levels that are practically attainable. (*c*) If the two mechanisms just listed operate too slowly to adapt aspirations to performance, emotional behaviour—apathy or aggression, for example—will replace rational adaptive behaviour.

The aspiration level defines a natural zero point in the scale of utility—whereas in most classical theories the zero point is arbitrary. When the firm has alternatives open to it that are at or above its aspiration level the theory predicts that it will choose the best of those known to be available. When none of the available alternatives satisfies current aspirations the theory predicts qualitatively different behaviour: in the short run, search behaviour and the revision of targets; in the longer run, what we have called above emotional behaviour, and what the psychologist would be inclined to call neurosis.[2]

Studies of Business Behaviour

There is some empirical evidence that business goals are, in fact, stated in satisficing terms.[3] First, there is the series of studies stemming from the pioneering work of Hall and Hitch that indicates that businessmen often set prices by applying a standard mark-up to costs. Some economists have sought to refute this fact, others to reconcile it—if it is a fact—with marginalist principles. The study of Earley [22a, pp. 44–70] belongs to the former category, but its evidence is suspect because the questions asked of businessmen are leading ones—no one likes to admit that he would accept less profit if he could have more. Earley did not ask his respondents how they determined marginal cost and marginal revenue, how, for example, they estimated demand elasticities.

Another series of studies derived from the debate over the Keynesian doctrine that the amount of investment was insensitive to changes in the rate of interest. The general finding in these studies has been that the rate of interest is not an important factor in investment decisions [24] [39, Ch. 11] [71].

More recently, my colleagues, Cyert and March, have attempted to test the satisficing model in a more direct way [19]. They found in one

[1] A standard psychological reference on aspiration levels is [42]. For applications to economics, see [61] and [45] (in the latter, consult the index under "aspiration levels").

[2] Lest this last term appear fanciful I should like to call attention to the phenomena of panic and broken morale, which are well known to observers of the stock market and of organisations but which have no reasonable interpretation in classical utility theory. I may also mention that psychologists use the theory described here in a straightforward way to produce experimental neurosis in animal and human subjects.

[3] A comprehensive bibliography of empirical work prior to 1950 will be found in [37]. Some of the more recent work is [19] [24] [39, Ch. 11].

industry some evidence that firms with a declining share of market strove more vigorously to increase their sales than firms whose shares of the market were steady or increasing.

Aspirations in the Binary Choice Experiment

Although to my knowledge this has not been done, it would be easy to look for aspiration-level phenomena in the binary choice experiment. By changing the probabilities of reward in different ways for different groups of subjects, we could measure the effects of these changes on search behaviour—where amount of search would be measured by changes in the pattern of responses.

Economic Implications

It has sometimes been argued that, however realistic the classical theory of the firm as a profit maximiser, it is an adequate theory for purposes of normative macroeconomics. Mason, for example, in commenting on Papandreou's essay on " Problems in the Theory of the Firm " [55, pp. 183–222] says, " The writer of this critique must confess a lack of confidence in the marked superiority, *for purposes of economic analysis*, of this newer concept of the firm over the older conception of the entrepreneur." The italics are Mason's.

The theory of the firm is important for welfare economics—*e.g.*, for determining under what circumstances the behaviour of the firm will lead to efficient allocation of resources. The satisficing model vitiates all the conclusions about resource allocation that are derivable from the maximising model when perfect competition is assumed. Similarly, a dynamic theory of firm sizes, like that mentioned above, has quite different implications for public policies dealing with concentration than a theory that assumes firms to be in static equilibrium. Hence, welfare economists are justified in adhering to the classical theory only if: (*a*) the theory is empirically correct as a description of the decision-making process; or (*b*) it is safe to assume that the system operates in the neighbourhood of the static equilibrium. What evidence we have mostly contradicts both assumptions.

IV. Conflict of Interest

Leaving aside the problem of the motivations of hired managers, conflict of interest among economic actors creates no difficulty for classical economic theory—indeed, it lies at the very core of the theory—so long as each actor treats the other actors as parts of his " given " environment, and doesn't try to predict their behaviour and anticipate it. But when this restriction is removed, when it is assumed that a seller takes into account the reactions of buyers to his actions, or that each manufacturer predicts the behaviours of his competitors—all the familiar difficulties of imperfect competition and oligopoly arise.[1]

The very assumptions of omniscient rationality that provide the basis for deductive prediction in economics when competition is present lead to ambiguity when they are applied to competition among the few. The central difficulty is that rationality requires one to outguess one's opponents, but not to be outguessed by them, and this is clearly not a consistent requirement if applied to all the actors.

Game Theory

Modern game theory is a vigorous and extensive exploration of ways of extending the concept of rational behaviour to situations involving struggle, outguessing and bargaining. Since Luce and Raiffa [43] have recently provided us with an excellent survey and evaluation of game theory, I shall not cover the same ground here.[2] I concur in their general evaluation that, while game theory has greatly clarified the issues involved, it has not provided satisfactory solutions. Not only does it leave the definition of rational conduct ambiguous in all cases save the zero-sum two-person game, but it requires of economic man even more fantastic reasoning powers than does classical economic theory.[3]

Power and Bargaining

A number of exploratory proposals have been put forth as alternatives to game theory—among them Galbraith's notion of countervailing power [30] and Schelling's bargaining theory [59] [60]. These analyses draw at least as heavily upon theories of power and bargaining developed initially to explain political phenomena as upon economic theory. They do not lead to any more specific predictions of behaviour than do game-theoretic approaches, but place a greater emphasis upon description and actual observation, and are modest in their attempt to derive predictions by deductive reasoning from a few " plausible " premises about human behaviour.

At least four important areas of social science and social policy, two of them in economics and two more closely related to political science, have as their central concern the phenomena of power and the processes of bargaining: the theory of political parties, labour-management relations, international politics and oligopoly theory. Any progress in the basic theory applicable to one of these is certain to be of almost equal importance to the

[1] There is by now a voluminous literature on the problem. The difficulties in defining rationality in competitive situations are well stated in the first chapter of von Neumann and Morgenstern [50].

[2] Chapters 5 and 6 of [43] provide an excellent survey of the attempts that have been made to extend the theory of games to the kinds of situations most relevant to economics.

[3] In a forthcoming volume on *Strategy and Market Structure,* Martin Shubik approaches the topics of imperfect competition and oligopoly from the standpoint of the theory of games.

others. A growing recognition of their common concern is evidenced by the initiation of a new cross-disciplinary journal, *Journal of Conflict Resolution.*

Games against Nature

While the binary choice experiment is basically a one-person game, it is possible to interpret it as a " game against nature," and hence to try to explain it in game-theoretic terms. According to game theory, the subject, if he believes in a malevolent nature that manipulates the dice against him, should minimax his expected utility instead of maximising it. That is, he should adopt the course of action that will maximise his expected utility under the assumption that nature will do her worst to him.

Minimaxing expected utility would lead the subject to call plus or minus at random and with equal probability, regardless of what the history of rewards has been. This is something that subjects demonstrably do not do.

However, it has been suggested by Savage [58] and others that people are not as interested in maximising utility as they are in minimising regret. " Regret " means the difference between the reward actually obtained and the reward that could have been obtained with perfect foresight (actually, with perfect hindsight!). It turns out that minimaxing regret in the binary choice experiment leads to event-matching behaviour [64, Ch. 16]. Hence, the empirical evidence is at least crudely consistent with the hypothesis that people play against nature by minimaxing regret. We shall see, however, that event-matching is also consistent with a number of other rules of behaviour that seem more plausible on their face; hence we need not take the present explanation too seriously—at least I am not inclined to do so.

V. The Formation of Expectations

While the future cannot enter into the determination of the present, expectations about the future can and do. In trying to gain an understanding of the saving, spending and investment behaviour of both consumers and firms, and to make short-term predictions of this behaviour for purposes of policy-making, economists have done substantial empirical work as well as theorising on the formation of expectations.

Empirical Studies

A considerable body of data has been accumulated on consumers' plans and expectations from the Survey of Consumer Finances, conducted for the Board of Governors of the Federal Reserve System by the Survey Research Centre of the University of Michigan [39, Ch. 5]. These data, and similar data obtained by others, begin to give us some information on the expectations of consumers about their own incomes, and the predictive value of their expenditure plans for their actual subsequent behaviour. Some large-scale attempts have been made, notably by Modigliani and Brumberg

[48, pp. 388–436] and, a little later, by Friedman [28] to relate these empirical findings to classical utility theory. The current empirical research on businessmen's expectations is of two main kinds:

1. Surveys of businesmen's own forecasts of business and business conditions in the economy and in their own industries [24, pp. 165–88] [29, pp. 189–98]. These are obtained by straightforward questionnaire methods that assume, implicitly, that businessmen can and do make such forecasts. In some uses to which the data are put, it is also assumed that the forecasts are used as one basis for businessmen's actions.

2. Studies of business decisions and the role of expectations in these decisions—particularly investment and pricing decisions. We have already referred to studies of business decisions in our discussion of the goals of the firm.[1]

Expectations and Probability

The classical way to incorporate expectations into economic theory is to assume that the decision-maker estimates the joint probability distribution of future events.[2] He can then act so as to maximise the expected value of utility or profit, as the case may be. However satisfying this approach may be conceptually, it poses awkward problems when we ask how the decision-maker actually estimates the parameters of the joint probability distribution. Common sense tells us that people don't make such estimates, nor can we find evidence that they do by examining actual business forecasting methods. The surveys of businessmen's expectations have never attempted to secure such estimates, but have contented themselves with asking for point predictions—which, at best, might be interpreted as predictions of the means of the distributions.

It has been shown that under certain special circumstances the mean of the probability distribution is the only parameter that is relevant for decision—that even if the variance and higher moments were known to the rational decision-maker, he would have no use for them.[3] In these cases the arithmetic mean is actually a certainty equivalent, the optimal decision turns out to be the same as if the future were known with certainty. But the situations where the mean is a certainty equivalent are, as we have said, very special ones, and there is no indication that businessmen ever ask whether the necessary conditions for this equivalence are actually met in practice. They somehow make forecasts in the form of point predictions and act upon them in one way or another.

The " somehow " poses questions that are important for business-cycle theory, and perhaps for other problems in economics. The way in which

[1] See the references cited [12, p. 160].

[2] A general survey of approaches to decision-making under uncertainty will be found in [2] and in [43, Ch. 13].

[3] The special case in which mean expectations constitute a certainty equivalent is treated in [62]. An alternative derivation, and fuller discussion is given by Theil [67, Ch. 8, sect. 6].

expectations are formed may affect the dynamic stability of the economy, and the extent to which cycles will be amplified or damped. Some light, both empirical and theoretical, has recently been cast on these questions. On the empirical side, attempts have been made: (*a*) to compare businessmen's forecasts with various " naïve " models that assume the future will be some simple function of the recent past, and (*b*) to use such naïve models themselves as forecasting devices.

The simplest naïve model is one that assumes the next period will be exactly like the present. Another assumes that the change from present to next period will equal the change from last period to present; a third, somewhat more general, assumes that the next period will be a weighted average of recent past periods. The term " naïve model" has been applied loosely to various forecasting formulae of these general kinds. There is some affirmative evidence that business forecasts fit such models. There is also evidence that elaboration of the models beyond the first few steps of refinement does not much improve prediction; see, for example, [20]. Arrow and his colleagues [4] have explored some of the conditions under which forecasting formulae will, and will not, introduce dynamic instability into an economic system that is otherwise stable. They have shown, for example, that if a system of multiple markets is stable under static expectations it is stable when expectations are based on a moving average of past values.

The work on the formation of expectations represents a significant extension of classical theory. For, instead of taking the environment as a " given," known to the economic decision-maker, it incorporates in the theory the processes of acquiring knowledge about that environment. In doing so, it forces us to include in our model of economic man some of his properties as a learning, estimating, searching, information-processing organism [65].

The Cost of Information

There is one way in which the formation of expectations might be reincorporated in the body of economic theory: by treating information-gathering as one of the processes of production, so to speak, and applying to it the usual rules of marginal analysis. Information, says price theory, should be gathered up to the point where the incremental cost of additional information is equal to the incremental profit that can be earned by having it. Such an approach can lead to propositions about optimal amounts of information-gathering activity and about the relative merits of alternative information-gathering and estimating schemes.[1]

This line of investigation has, in fact, been followed in statistical decision

[1] Fundamental and applied research are examples of economically significant information-gathering activities. Griliches [34] has recently made an attempt to estimate the economic return from research on hybrid corn.

theory. In sampling theory we are concerned with the optimal size of sample (and in the special and ingenious case of sequential sampling theory, with knowing when to stop sampling), and we wish to evaluate the efficiencies of alternative sampling procedures. The latter problem is the simpler, since it is possible to compare the relative costs of alternative schemes that have the same sampling error, and hence to avoid estimating the value of the information.[1] However, some progress has been made also towards estimating the value of improved forecast accuracy in situations where the forecasts are to be used in applying formal decision rules to choice situations.[2]

The theory of teams developed by Marschak and Radner is concerned with the same problem (see, *e.g.*, [46]). It considers situations involving decentralised and interdependent decision-making by two or more persons who share a common goal and who, at a cost, can transmit information to each other about their own actions or about the parts of the environment with which they are in contact. The problem then is to discover the optimal communication strategy under specified assumptions about communication costs and payoffs.

The cost of communication in the theory of teams, like the cost of observations in sampling theory, is a parameter that characterises the economic actor, of the relation of the actor to his environment. Hence, while these theories retain, in one sense, a classical picture of economic man as a maximiser, they clearly require considerable information about the characteristics of the actor, and not merely about his environment. They take a long stride towards bridging the gap between the traditional concerns of economics and the concerns of psychology.

Expectations in the Binary Choice Experiment

I should like to return again to the binary choice experiment, to see what light it casts on the formation of expectations. If the subject is told by the experimenter that the rewards are assigned at random, if he is told what the odds are for each alternative *and if he believes the experimenter*, the situation poses no forecasting problem. We have seen, however, that the behaviour of most subjects is not consistent with these assumptions.

How would sequential sampling theory handle the problem? Each choice the subject makes now has two consequences: the immediate reward he obtains from it, and the increment of information it provides for predicting the future rewards. If he thinks only of the latter consequences he is faced with the classical problem of induction: to estimate the probability that an event will occur in the future on the basis of its frequency of occurrence in the past. Almost any rule of induction would require a rational (maximising) subject to behave in the following general manner: to sample

[1] Modern treatments of sampling theory, like Cochran [17], are based on the idea of minimising the cost of obtaining a fixed amount of information.

[2] For the theory and application to macroeconomics, see Theil [67, Ch. 8, sects. 5 and 6].

the two alternatives in some proportion to estimate the probability of reward associated with each; after the error of estimate had been reduced below some bound, always to choose the alternative with the higher probability of reward. Unfortunately, this does not appear to be what most subjects do.

If we give up the idea of maximisation, we can make the weaker assumption that the subject is adaptive—or learns—but not necessarily in any optimal fashion. What do we mean by adaptation or learning? We mean, gradually and on the basis of experience responding more frequently with the choice that, in the past, has been most frequently rewarded. There is a whole host of rules of behaviour possessing this characteristic. Postulate, for example, that at each trial the subject has a certain probability of responding "plus," and the complementary probability of responding "minus." Postulate further that when he makes a particular response the probability of making the same response on the next trial is increased if the response is rewarded and decreased if the response is not rewarded. The amount of increment in the response probability is a parameter characterising the learning rate of the particular subject. Almost all schemes of this kind produce asymptotic behaviours, as the number of trials increases, that are approximately event-matching in character.

Stochastic learning models, as the processes just described are usually called, were introduced into psychology in the early 1950s by W. K. Estes and Bush and Mosteller [15] and have been investigated extensively since that time. The models fit some of the gross features of the observed behaviours—most strikingly the asymptotic probabilities—but do not explain very satisfactorily the fine structure of the observations.

Observation of subjects in the binary choice experiment reveals that usually they not only refuse to believe that (or even to act as if) the reward series were random, but in fact persist over many trials in searching for systematic patterns in the series. To account for such behaviour, we might again postulate a learning model, but in this case a model in which the subject does not react probabilistically to his environment, but forms and tests definite hypotheses about systematic patterns in it. Man, in this view, is not only a learning animal; he is a pattern-finding and concept-forming animal. Julian Feldman [25] has constructed theories of this kind to explain the behaviour of subjects in the binary choice experiment, and while the tests of the theories are not yet completed, his findings look exceedingly promising.

As we move from maximising theories, through simple stochastic learning theories, to theories involving pattern recognition our model of the expectation-forming processes and the organism that performs it increases in complexity. If we follow this route we reach a point where a theory of behaviour requires a rather elaborate and detailed picture of the rational actor's cognitive processes.

VI. Human Cognition and Economics

All the developments we have examined in the preceding four sections have a common theme: they all involve important modifications in the concept of economic man and, for the reasons we have stated, modifications in the direction of providing a fuller description of his characteristics. The classical theory is a theory of a man choosing among fixed and known alternatives, to each of which is attached known consequences. But when perception and cognition intervene between the decision-maker and his objective environment this model no longer proves adequate. We need a description of the choice process that recognises that alternatives are not given but must be sought; and a description that takes into account the arduous task of determining what consequences will follow on each alternative [63, Ch. 5] [64, Part 4] [14].

The decision-maker's information about his environment is much less than an approximation to the real environment. The term " approximation " implies that the subjective world of the decision-maker resembles the external environment closely, but lacks, perhaps, some fineness of detail. In actual fact, the perceived world is fantastically different from the " real " world. The differences involve both omissions and distortions, and arise in both perception and inference. The sins of omission in perception are more important than the sins of commission. The decision-maker's model of the world encompasses only a minute fraction of all the relevant characteristics of the real environment, and his inferences extract only a minute fraction of all the information that is present even in his model.

Perception is sometimes referred to as a " filter." This term is as misleading as " approximation," and for the same reason: it implies that what comes through into the central nervous system is really quite a bit like what is " out there." In fact, the filtering is not merely a passive selection of some part of a presented whole, but an active process involving attention to a very small part of the whole and exclusion, from the outset, of almost all that is not within the scope of attention.

Every human organism lives in an environment that generates millions of bits of new information each second, but the bottleneck of the perceptual apparatus certainly does not admit more than 1,000 bits per second, and probably much less. Equally significant omissions occur in the processing that takes place when information reaches the brain. As every mathematician knows, it is one thing to have a set of differential equations, and another thing to have their solutions. Yet the solutions are logically implied by the equations—they are "all there," if we only knew how to get to them! By the same token, there are hosts of inferences that *might* be drawn from the information stored in the brain that are not in fact drawn. The consequences implied by information in the memory become known only through active information-processing, and hence through active selection of particular problem-solving paths from the myriad that might have been followed.

In this section we shall examine some theories of decision-making that take the limitations of the decision-maker and the complexity of the environment as central concerns. These theories incorporate some mechanisms we have already discussed—for example, aspiration levels and forecasting processes—but go beyond them in providing a detailed picture of the choice process.

A real-life decision involves some goals or values, some facts about the environment and some inferences drawn from the values and facts. The goals and values may be simple or complex, consistent or contradictory; the facts may be real or supposed, based on observation or the reports of others; the inferences may be valid or spurious. The whole process may be viewed, metaphorically, as a process of "reasoning," where the values and facts serve as premises, and the decision that is finally reached is inferred from these premises [63]. The resemblance of decision-making to logical reasoning is only metaphorical, because there are quite different rules in the two cases to determine what constitute "valid" premises and admissible modes of inference. The metaphor is useful because it leads us to take the individual *decision premise* as the unit of description, hence to deal with the whole interwoven fabric of influences that bear on a single decision —but without being bound by the assumptions of rationality that limit the classical theory of choice.

Rational Behaviour and Role Theory

We can find common ground to relate the economist's theory of decision-making with that of the social psychologist. The latter is particularly interested, of course, in social influences on choice, which determine the *role* of the actor. In our present terms a role is a social prescription of some, but not all, of the premises that enter into an individual's choices of behaviour. Any particular concrete behaviour is the resultant of a large number of premises, only some of which are prescribed by the role. In addition to role premises there will be premises about the state of the environment based directly on perception, premises representing beliefs and knowledge and idiosyncratic premises that characterise the personality. Within this framework we can accommodate both the rational elements in choice, so much emphasised by economics, and the non-rational elements to which psychologists and sociologists often prefer to call attention.

Decision Premises and Computer Programs

The analysis of choice in terms of decision premises gives us a conceptual framework for describing and explaining the process of deciding. But so complex is the process that our explanations of it would have remained schematic and hypothetical for a long time to come had not the modern digital computer appeared on the scene. The notion of decision premise can be translated into computer terminology, and when this translation has been accomplished, the digital computer provides us with an instrument for simulating human decision processes—even very complex ones—and hence for testing empirically our explanations of those processes [53].

A fanciful (but only slightly fanciful) example will illustrate how this might be done. Some actual examples will be cited presently. Suppose we were to construct a robot incorporating a modern digital computer and to program (*i.e.*, to instruct) the robot to take the role of a business executive in a specified company. What would the program look like? Since no one has yet done this, we cannot say with certainty, but several points are fairly clear. The program would not consist of a list of prescribed and proscribed behaviours, since what an executive does is highly contingent on information about a wide variety of circumstances. Instead, the program would consist of a large number of *criteria* to be applied to possible and proposed courses of action, of routines for *generating* possible courses of action, of computational procedures for *assessing* the state of the environment and its implications for action, and the like. Hence, the program—in fact, a role prescription—would interact with information to produce concrete behaviour adapted to the situation. The elements of such a program take the form of what we have called decision premises, and what the computer specialists would call instructions.

The promise of constructing actual detailed descriptions of concrete roles and decision processes is no longer, with the computer, a mere prospectus to be realised at some undefined future date. We can already provide actual examples, some of them in the area of economics.

1. *Management Science*. In the paragraphs on normative applications in Section II we have already referred to the use of such mathematical techniques as linear programming and dynamic programming to construct formal decision processes for actual situations. The relevance of these decision models to the present discussion is that they are not merely abstract " theories " of the firm, but actual decision-making devices. We can think of any such device as a simulation of the corresponding human decision-maker, in which the equations and other assumptions that enter into the formal decision-making procedure correspond to the decision premises—including the role prescription—of the decision-maker.

The actual application of such models to concrete business situations brings to light the information-processing tasks that are concealed in the assumptions of the more abstract classical models [65, pp. 51–2]:

(1) The models must be formulated so as to require for their application only data that are obtainable. If one of the penalties, for example, of holding too small inventories is the loss of sales, a decision model that proposes to determine optimal inventory levels must incorporate a procedure for putting a dollar value on this loss.

(2) The models must call only for practicable computations. For example, several proposals for applying linear programming to certain factory scheduling problems have been shown to be impracticable because, even with computers, the computation time is too great. The task of decision theory (whether normative or descriptive) is to find alternative techniques—probably only approximate—that demand much less computation.

(3) The models must not demand unobtainable forecast information. A procedure that would require a sales department to estimate the third moment of next month's sales distribution would not have wide application as either description or prescription, to business decision-making.

These models, then, provide us with concrete examples of roles for a decision-maker described in terms of the premises he is expected to apply to the decision—the data and the rules of computation.

2. *Engineering Design*. Computers have been used for some years to carry out some of the analytic computations required in engineering design—computing the stresses, for example, in a proposed bridge design. Within the past two years ways have been found to program computers to carry out synthesis as well as analysis—to evolve the design itself.[1] A number of companies in the electrical industry now use computers to design electric motors, transformers and generators, going from customer specifications to factory design without human intervention. The significance of this for our purpose here is that the synthesis programs appear to simulate rather closely the processes that had previously been used by college-trained engineers in the same design work. It has proved possible to write down the engineers' decision premises and inference processes in sufficient detail to produce workable computer programs.

3. *Human Problem Solving*. The management science and engineering design programs already provide examples of simulation of human decision-making by computer. It may be thought that, since in both instances the processes are highly arithmetical, these examples are relevant to only a very narrow range of human problem-solving activity. We generally think of a digital computer as a device which, if instructed in painful detail by its operator, can be induced to perform rather complicated and tedious arithmetical operations. More recent developments require us to revise these conceptions of the computer, for they enable it to carry out tasks that, if performed by humans, we would certain call "thinking" and "learning."

Discovering the proof of a theorem of Euclid—a task we all remember from our high-school geometry course—requires thinking and usually insight and imagination. A computer is now being programmed to perform this task (in a manner closely simulating the human geometer), and another computer has been successfully performing a highly similar task in symbolic

[1] A non-technical description of such a program will be found in [33].

logic for the past two years.[1] The latter computer is programmed to learn—that is to improve its performance on the basis of successful problem-solving experience—to use something akin to imagery or metaphor in planning its proofs, and to transfer some of its skills to other tasks—for example, solving trigonometric identities—involving completely distinct subject matter. These programs, it should be observed, do not involve the computer in rapid arithmetic—or any arithmetic for that matter. They are basically non-numerical, involving the manipulation of all kinds of symbolic material, including words.

Still other computer programs have been written to enable a computer to play chess.[2] Not all of these programs, or those previously mentioned, are close simulations of the processes humans use. However, in some direct attempts to investigate the human processes by thinking-aloud techniques and to reproduce in computer programs the processes observed in human subjects, several striking simulations have been achieved.[3] These experiments have been described elsewhere and cannot be reviewed here in detail.

4. *Business Games*. Business games, like those developed by the American Management Association, International Business Machines Corporation and several universities, represent a parallel development.[4] In the business game the decisions of the business firms are still made by the human players, but the economic environment of these firms, including their markets, are represented by computer programs that calculate the environment's responses to the actions of the players. As the games develop in detail and realism, their programs will represent more and more concrete descriptions of the decision processes of various economic actors—for example, consumers. The games that have been developed so far are restricted to numerical magnitudes like prices and quantities of goods, and hence resemble the management science and engineering design programs more closely than they do those we have described under the heading of human problem solving. There is no reason, however, to expect this restriction to remain very long.

Implications for Economics

Apart from normative applications (*e.g.*, substituting computers for humans in certain decision-making tasks) we are not interested so much in the detailed descriptions of roles as in broader questions: (1) What general characteristics do the roles of economic actors have? (2) How do roles come to be structured in the particular ways they do? (3) What bearing

[1] The program for proving theorems in logic is discussed in [51] and [52], Gelernter and Rochester's geometry program in [31].

[2] A survey of computer chess programs can be found in [54].

[3] Much of this work is still unpublished, but see [53] and [54].

[4] Two business games are described by Andlinger [1].

does this version of role theory have for macroeconomics and other large-scale social phenomena?

Characterising Role Structure. Here we are concerned with generalisations about thought processes, particularly those generalisations that are relatively independent of the substantive content of the role. A classical example is Dewey's description of stages in the problem-solving process. Another example, of particular interest to economics, is the hypothesis we have already discussed at length: that economic man is a *satisficing* animal whose problem solving is based on search activity to meet certain aspiration levels rather than a *maximising* animal whose problem solving involves finding the best alternatives in terms of specified criteria [64]. A third hypothesis is that operative goals (those associated with an observable criterion of success, and relatively definite means of attainment) play a much larger part in governing choice than non-operative goals (those lacking a concrete measure of success or a program for attainment) [45, p. 156].

Understanding How Roles Emerge. Within almost any single business firm, certain characteristic types of roles will be represented: selling roles, production roles, accounting roles and so on [22]. Partly, this consistency may be explained in functional terms—that a model that views the firm as producing a product, selling it and accounting for its assets and liabilities is an effective simplification of the real world, and provides the members of the organisation with a workable frame of reference. Imitation within the culture provides an alternative explanation. It is exceedingly difficult to test hypotheses as to the origins and causal conditions for roles as universal in the society as these, but the underlying mechanisms could probably be explored effectively by the study of less common roles—safety director, quality control inspector or the like—that are to be found in some firms, but not in all.

With our present definition of role, we can also speak meaningfully of the role of an entire business firm—of decision premises that underlie its basic policies. In a particular industry we find some firms that specialise in adapting the product to individual customer's specifications; others that specialise in product innovation. The common interest of economics and psychology includes not only the study of individual roles but also the explanation of organisational roles of these sorts.

Tracing the Implications for Macroeconomics. If basic professional goals remain as they were, the interest of the psychologist and the economist in role theory will stem from somewhat different ultimate aims. The former will use various economic and organisational phenomena as data for the study of the structure and determinants of roles; the latter will be primarily interested in the implications of role theory for the model of economic man, and indirectly, for macroeconomics.

The first applications will be to those topics in economics where the assumption of static equilibrium is least tenable. Innovation, technological change and economic development are examples of areas to which a good empirically tested theory of the processes of human adaptation and problem solving could make a major contribution. For instance, we know very little at present about how the rate of innovation depends on the amounts of resources allocated to various kinds of research and development activity [34]. Nor do we understand very well the nature of "know how," the costs of transferring technology from one firm or economy to another, or the effects of various kinds and amounts of education upon national product. These are difficult questions to answer from aggregative data and gross observation, with the result that our views have been formed more by arm-chair theorising than by testing hypotheses with solid facts.

VII. Conclusion

In exploring the areas in which economics has common interests with the other behavioural sciences, we have been guided by the metaphor we elaborated in Section I. In simple, slow-moving situations, where the actor has a single, operational goal, the assumption of maximisation relieves us of any need to construct a detailed picture of economic man or his processes of adaptation. As the complexity of the environment increases, or its speed of change, we need to know more and more about the mechanisms and processes that economic man uses to relate himself to that environment and achieve his goals.

How closely we wish to interweave economics with psychology depends, then, both on the range of questions we wish to answer and on our assessment of how far we may trust the assumptions of static equilibrium as approximations. In considerable part, the demand for a fuller picture of economic man has been coming from the profession of economics itself, as new areas of theory and application have emerged in which complexity and change are central facts. The revived interest in the theory of utility, and its application to choice under uncertainty, and to consumer saving and spending is one such area. The needs of normative macroeconomics and management science for a fuller theory of the firm have led to a number of attempts to understand the actual processes of making business decisions. In both these areas notions of adaptive and satisficing behaviour, drawn largely from psychology, are challenging sharply the classical picture of the maximising entrepreneur.

The area of imperfect competition and oligopoly has been equally active, although the activity has thus far perhaps raised more problems than it has solved. On the positive side, it has revealed a community of interest among a variety of social scientists concerned with bargaining as a part of political and economic processes. Prediction of the future is another element common to many decision processes, and particularly important to explaining business-cycle phenomena. Psychologists and economists have been applying a wide variety of approaches, empirical and theoretical, to the study of the formation of expectations. Surveys of consumer and business behaviour, theories of statistical induction, stochastic learning theories and theories of concept formation have all been converging on this problem area.

The very complexity that has made a theory of the decision-making process essential has made its construction exceedingly difficult. Most approaches have been piecemeal—now focused on the criteria of choice, now on conflict of interest, now on the formation of expectations. It seemed almost utopian to suppose that we could put together a model of adaptive man that would compare in completeness with the simple model of classical economic man. The sketchiness and incompleteness of the newer proposals has been urged as a compelling reason for clinging to the older theories, however inadequate they are admitted to be.

The modern digital computer has changed the situation radically. It provides us with a tool of research—for formulating and testing theories—whose power is commensurate with the complexity of the phenomena we seek to understand. Although the use of computers to build theories of human behaviour is very recent, it has already led to concrete results in the simulation of higher mental processes. As economics finds it more and more necessary to understand and explain disequilibrium as well as equilibrium, it will find an increasing use for this new tool and for communication with its sister sciences of psychology and sociology.

REFERENCES

1. G. R. Andlinger, "Business Games—Play One," *Harvard Bus. Rev.*, Apr. 1958, **36**, 115–25.
2. K. J. Arrow, "Alternative Approaches to the Theory of Choice in Risk-Taking Situations," *Econometrica*, Oct. 1951, **19**, 404–37.
3. K. J. Arrow, T. E. Harris and J. Marschak, "Optimal Inventory Policy," *Econometrica*, July 1951, **19**, 250–72.
4. K. J. Arrow and M. Nerlove, "A Note on Expectations and Stability," *Econometrica*, Apr. 1958, **26**, 297–305.
5. K. J. Arrow, "Utilities, Attitudes, Choices," *Econometrica*, Jan. 1958, **26**, 1–23.
6. D. Bakan, "Learning and the Principle of Inverse Probability," *Psych. Rev.*, Sept. 1953, **60**, 360–70.
7. A. Bavelas, "A Mathematical Model for Group Structures," *Applied Anthropology*, Summer 1948, **7**, 16–30.
8. M. Beckmann, "Decision and Team Problems in Airline Reservations," *Econometrica*, Jan. 1958, **26**, 134–45.
9. R. Bellman, *Dynamic Programming*. Princeton 1957.
10. H. R. Bowen, *The Business Enterprise as a Subject for Research*. New York 1955.
11. E. H. Bowman and R. B. Fetter, *Analysis for Production Management*. Homewood, Ill., 1957.
12. M. J. Bowman, ed., *Expectations, Uncertainty, and Business Behavior*. New York, 1958.
13. H. Brems, "Response Lags and Nonprice Competition," in Bowman [12], Ch. 10, pp. 134–43.

14. J. Bruner, J. J. Goodnow and G. A. Austin, *A Study of Thinking*. New York 1956.
15. R. R. Bush and F. Mosteller, *Stochastic Models for Learning*. New York 1955.
16. C. W. Churchman, R. L. Ackoff and E. L. Arnoff, *Introduction to Operations Research*. New York 1957.
17. W. G. Cochran, *Sampling Techniques*. New York 1953.
18. R. M. Cyert and J. G. March, "Organizational Structure and Pricing Behavior in an Oligopolistic Market," *Am. Econ. Rev.*, Mar. 1955, **45**, 129–39.
19. ——— and ———, "Organizational Factors in the Theory of Oligopoly," *Quart. Jour. Econ.*, Feb. 1956, **70**, 44–64.
20. W. Darcovich, "Evaluation of Some Naive Expectations Models for Agricultural Yields and Prices," in Bowman [12], Ch. 14, pp. 199–202.
21. D. Davidson and P. Suppes, *Decision Making: An Experimental Approach*. Stanford 1957.
22. D. C. Dearborn and H. A. Simon, "Selective Perception: A Note on the Departmental Identification of Executives," *Sociometry*, June 1958, **21**, 140–44.
22a. J. S. Earley, "Marginal Policies of 'Excellently Managed' Companies," *Am. Econ. Rev.*, Mar. 1956, **66**, 44–70.
23. W. Edwards, "The Theory of Decision Making," *Psych. Bull.*, Sept. 1954, **51**, 380–417.
24. R. Eisner, "Expectations, Plans, and Capital Expenditures," in Bowman [12], Ch. 12, 165–88.
25. J. Feldman, "A Theory of Binary Choice Behavior," Carnegie Inst. of Tech., Grad. Sch. Indus. Admin., Complex Information Processing Working Paper No. 12, rev., May 5, 1958. Unpublished ditto.
26. B. de Finetti "La prevision: ses lois logiques, ses sources subjectives," *Annales Inst. Henri Poincare*, 1937, **7**, 1–68.
27. M. Friedman, *Essays in Positive Economics*. Chicago 1953.
28. ———, *A Theory of the Consumption Function*. New York 1956.
29. I. Friend, "Critical Evaluation of Surveys of Expectations, Plans, and Investment Behavior," in Bowman [12], Ch. 13, pp. 189–98.
30. J. K. Galbraith, *American Capitalism: The Concept of Countervailing Power*. Boston 1952.
31. H. L. Gelernter and N. Rochester, "Intelligent Behavior in Problem-Solving Machines," *IBM Jour. Research and Develop.*, Oct. 1958, **2**, 336–45.
32. N. Georgescu-Roegen, "The Nature of Expectation and Uncertainty" in Bowman [12], Ch. 1, pp. 11–29.
33. G. L. Godwin, "Digital Computers Tap Out Designs for Large Motors—Fast," *Power*, Apr. 1958.
34. Z. Griliches, "Hybrid Corn: An Exploration in the Economics of Technological Change," *Econometrica*, Oct. 1957, **25**, 501–22.
35. H. Guetzkow and H. A. Simon, "The Impact of Certain Communication Nets in Task Oriented Groups," *Management Sci.*, July 1955, **1**, 233–50.
36. B. F. Haley, ed., *A Survey of Contemporary Economics*, Vol. II. Homewood, Ill. 1952.
37. S. P. Hayes, "Some Psychological Problems of Economics," *Psych. Bull.*, July 1950, **47**, 289–330.
38. C. C. Holt, F. Modigliani and H. A. Simon, "A Linear Decision Rule for Production and Employment Scheduling," *Management Sci.*, Oct. 1955, **2**, 1–30.
39. G. Katona, *Psychological Analysis of Economic Behavior*. New York 1951.
40. ———, "Rational Behavior and Economic Behavior," *Psych. Rev.*, July 1953, **60**, 307–18.
41. H. J. Leavitt, "Some Effects of Certain Communication Patterns on Group Performance," *Jour. Abnormal and Soc. Psych.*, Feb. 1951, **46**, 38–50.

42. K. Lewin and others, " Level of Aspiration," in J. McV. Hunt, *Personality and the Behavior Disorders*, New York 1944, pp. 333–78.
43. R. D. Luce and H. Raiffa, *Games and Decisions*. New York 1957.
44. R. Mack, " Business Expectations and the Buying of Materials," in Bowman [12], Ch. 8, pp. 106–18.
45. J. G. March and H. A. Simon, *Organizations*. New York 1958.
46. J. Marschak, " Elements for a Theory of Teams," *Management Sci.*, Jan. 1955, **1**, 127–37.
47. K. O. May, " Intransitivity, Utility, and the Aggregation of Preference Patterns," *Econometrica*, Jan. 1954, **22**, 1–13.
48. F. Modigliani and R. E. Brumberg, " Utility Analysis and the Consumption Function," in K. K. Kurihara, *Post Keynesian Economics*, New Brunswick, N.J., 1954, pp. 388–436.
49. F. Mosteller and P. Nogee, " An Experimental Measurement of Utility," *Jour. Pol Econ.*, Oct. 1951, **59**, 371–404.
50. J. von Neumann and O. Morgenstern, *Theory of Games and Economic Behavior*. Princeton 1947.
51. A. Newell and H. A. Simon, " The Logic Theory Machine," *IRE Transactions of Information Theory*, Sept. 1956, IT-2, 61–79.
52. A. Newell, J. C. Shaw and H. A. Simon, " Empirical Explorations of the Logic Theory Machine," *Proceedings of the Western Joint Computer Conference, Feb.* 26–28, 1957, pp. 218–30.
53. ———, ———, ———, " Elements of a Theory of Human Problem Solving," *Psych. Rev.*, May 1958, **65**, 151–66.
54. ———, ———, ———, " Chess-Playing Programs and the Problem of Complcxity," *IBM Jour. Research and Develop.*, Oct. 1958, **2**, 320–35.
55. A. G. Papandreou, " Some Basic Problems in the Theory of the Firm," in Haley [36], Ch. 5, pp. 183–222.
56. M. J. Peck, " Marginal Analysis and the Explanation of Business Behavior Under Uncertainty," in Bowman [12], Ch. 9, pp. 119–33.
57. F. P. Ramsey, " Truth and Probability," in the *Foundations of Mathematics and Other Logical Essays*, London 1931, pp. 156–98.
57a. A. M. Rose, " A Study of Irrational Judgments," *Jour. Pol. Econ.*, Oct. 1957, **65**, 394–402.
58. L. J. Savage, *The Foundations of Statistics*. New York 1954.
59. T. C. Schelling, " Bargaining, Communication, and Limited War," *Jour. Conflict Resolution*, Mar. 1957, **1**, 19–36.
60. ———, " An Essay on Bargaining," *Am. Econ. Rev.*, June 1956, **46**, 281–306.
61. S. Siegel, " Level of Aspiration and Decision Making," *Psych. Rev.*, July 1957, **64**, 253–62.
62. H. A. Simon, " Dynamic Programming Under Uncertainty with a Quadratic Criterion Function," *Econometrica*, Jan. 1956, **24**, 74–81.
63. ———, *Administrative Behavior*. New York 1957.
64. ———, *Models of Man*. New York 1957.
65. ———, " The Role of Expectations in an Adaptive or Behavioristic Model," in Bowman [12], Ch. 3, pp. 49–58.
66. H. A. Simon and C. P. Bonini, " The Size Distribution of Business Firms," *Am. Econ. Rev.*, Sept. 1958, **48**, 607–17.
67. H. Theil, *Economic Forecasts and Policy*. Amsterdam 1958.
68. L. L. Thurstone, " The Indifference Function," *Jour. Soc. Psych.*, May 1931, **2**, 139–67.
69. A. Vazsonyi, *Scientific Programming in Business and Industry*. New York 1958.
70. A. Wald, *Statistical Decision Functions*. New York 1950.
71. T. Wilson and P. W. S. Andrews, *Oxford Studies in the Price Mechanism*. Oxford 1951.

X

OPERATIONS RESEARCH

By

ROBERT DORFMAN[1]

Once upon a time, within the memories of men who think they are still young, there was no such thing as operations research, or at least no such phrase. To-day the Operations Research Society of America has more than 2,300 members, the Institute of Management Science has more than 2,600 members (there is considerable overlap, of course) and at a recent international conference on operations research no less than sixteen countries from four continents were represented. It is a flourishing movement.

The proper way to begin an inquiry into this movement would be to define it. But this is difficult; for operations research is not a subject-matter field but an approach or method. And, even after a study of hundreds of examples of work classified as operations research, it is by no means clear just what the method is other than that it is scientific (like all respectable methods), because operations analysts are typically resourceful and ingenious men who tackle their problems with no holds barred. I propose, nevertheless, to advance a definition; but it will help to prepare the way for that hazardous attempt if I try to convey the flavour of operations research by sketching a pair of contrasting caricatures, one of a conventional business consultant and one of an operations analyst.

Suppose that a soap company seeks advice as to whether its advertising budget next year should be larger than, the same as or smaller than this year. They might engage a business consultant who, in this case, would be a specialist in either advertising or marketing. He would have had substantial experience with advertising the same or similar products and would have at his finger-tips a good many relevant data and, besides, would be familiar with all the standard sources of such data. In addition, he would be aware of the maxim that it takes five cents' worth of advertising to sell a dollar's worth of soap, though he would not necessarily take it very seriously. With this background at his disposal he would marshal the pertinent facts. He would examine the experience of his client and would correlate sales with advertising expenditures for past years, doing it by eye if his research budget were stringent or by least-squares if he anticipated a fee that justified a more imposing report. He might well consider data by states or marketing areas, for both his client and competing firms, and might also analyse sales and advertising exposure broken down by city size. If the project were at

[1] The author is Professor of Economics, Harvard University.

*

all large he would almost certainly have a field survey made, finding out from a random sample of housewives what soaps they bought and what advertisements they were aware of. Finally, with this information all carefully organised, he would determine the level of advertising expenditure appropriate to the budgeted level of sales. In all likelihood this figure would turn out to be fairly close to 5% of anticipated gross sales, partly because you can't go far wrong by sticking close to an established norm, and partly because nearly all his data will be in this range, with the exception of a few observations relating to attempts to launch brands that, for one reason or another, did not catch on, or relating to advertising campaigns that had been successful beyond reasonable hope of duplication. In short, he would arrive at a recommendation based on a reasoned scrutiny of past experience.

But now suppose that the soap company turned to an operations analyst for advice. Typically, this man or firm would have no particular experience with either soap or advertising, and would feel the need of none. More likely than not, the analyst would be a graduate physicist or mathematician. With this background at his disposal he would formulate the problem. The first words he would say to himself might be: "Let p_{xt} be the probability that the xth household will buy my client's soap during the tth week.[1] Then p_{xt} is the product of two factors: p'_{xt}, the probability that they will buy any soap during the week, and a_{xt}, the probability that if they buy any soap it will be my client's brand. Assume that p'_{xt} cannot be influenced by my client's advertising but that a_{xt} can be. In fact, suppose that the Weber–Fechner law applies so that the rate of increase of a_{xt} with respect to advertising expenditure is inversely proportional to the level of advertising expenditure already attained, *i.e.*,

$$\frac{da_{xt}}{dE} = \frac{c}{E}$$

where E is the level of advertising expenditure and c is a constant of proportionality. Then, integrating this differential equation, $a_{xt} = \log kE^c$, where k is a constant of integration to be determined from the data. Then $p_{xt} = p'_{xt} \log KE^c$ and total expected sales can be estimated by integrating this expression over the entire population (*i.e.*, all values of x). Thus, assuming p'_{xt} and k to be given data, total sales can be estimated as:

$$s_t = \log kE^c \int p'_{xt} dx$$

and

$$\frac{ds_t}{dE} = \frac{c}{E} \int p'_{xt} dx$$

[1] In this and most later examples the mathematical details are not essential to the general discussion and may be skimmed.

Thus the optimal level of advertising can be found by finding the value of E at which the profit per dollar's worth of sales multiplied by this derivative equals 1, the cost of an additional dollar's worth of advertising."[1] In short, he would arrive at a recommendation based on logical deduction from simple first premises which are a plausible approximation to the laws underlying the phenomenon being studied.

Each of these approaches is " scientific " according to its own canons, but they are quite different. We can characterise this difference by saying that the operations analyst, in contrast with the conventional business analyst, has a strong predilection for formulating his problems by means of formal mathematical models. By a model I mean a symbolic description of a phenomenon in which its observable characteristics are deduced from simple explanatory first principles (*i.e.*, assumptions) by manipulating symbols in accordance with the laws of some formal logic (usually ordinary mathematics).

Argument *ad hominem* is generally regarded as unscholarly, but in trying to characterise operations research it seems important to note who the operations analysts are. According to a survey conducted by the American Management Association [2], more than 40% of operations analysts are engineers by training, another 45% are mathematicians, statisticians or natural scientists.[2] It is only natural that the point of view in which these men are schooled should permeate operations research. The essence of this point of view is that a phenomenon is understood when, and only when, it has been expressed as a formal, really mechanistic, quantitative model, and that, furthermore, all phenomena within the purview of science (which is probably all the phenomena there are) can be so expressed with sufficient persistence and ingenuity. A second characteristic of men of science, amounting to a corollary of the first, is their preference for symbolic, as opposed to verbal, modes of expression and reasoning. These characteristics I take to be the style of operations research, and I define operations research to be all research in this spirit intended to help solve practical, immediate problems in the fields of business, governmental or military administration or the like.

There is an important corollary to the tendency of operations analysts to cast their thinking in terms of formal mathematical models. Operations research is not a descriptive science but a prescriptive one. Therefore the deduction of adequate descriptive models is only part of the task of the operations analyst. In the end he must come up with a recommendation for action, and this requires that he know what the operation in question is intended to accomplish. We rather side-stepped this issue, in the fable at the beginning of this essay, by assuming that the objective of the

[1] In constructing this fable I have followed the spirit of the only operations research study of advertising with which I am acquainted, but have carefully diverged from that study in all details.

[2] For bibliographical references see pp. 73–74.

advertising was to attain the maximum possible excess of gross sales over the sum of production costs and advertising expenditure. But the conscientious operations analyst does not so glibly assume the objective of the operation he studies; and the extensive literature devoted to studying the objectives of business enterprise shows that he is wise to be circumspect about this point. In the soap example it may well be highly important to maintain total sales at a level that makes it worth while for retailers to stock the brand in question, even if the marginal net return is negative. The long run may have to be considered, if the brand has to establish or maintain a market position in the face of vigorous competition. In short, the objectives of an operation are likely to be complicated, obscure and composed of several incommensurable aspects. A major part of the task of the operations analyst is to construct a " measure of merit " for the operation he studies to accompany his formal description of it. The logical precision of the model enforces corresponding precision in expressing the objectives that the operation is intended to attain. The orthodox business consultant, on the other hand, is under no such pressure to formulate precisely the goals of the enterprise he studies.

When the operations analyst has formulated the model of his undertaking and the goals it serves he is still nearer the beginning of his analysis than the end. He must still particularise his model by estimating the values of the various " given " parameters that enter into it. For this purpose he employs, usually, more or less advanced statistical methods. Then he must solve the model, that is, find explicit relationships between the parameters under the control of his client, on the one hand, and the measure of merit, on the other. When this has been done he is in a position to determine the optimal values of the decision parameters, to make his recommendations and to try to persuade the management to adopt them.

In the next two sections we shall discuss a number of aspects of the problem of model formulation. Then we shall examine some of the problems and pitfalls of determining measures of merit or objective functions. The concluding section is devoted to the conditions for successful operations research and to some general conclusions and remarks.

I. Some Standard Models

There are three aspects to model building, closely related to each other but requiring different skills. The first is straightforward description; expressing the situation under study in terms of the symbolism adopted. This involves inventing symbols for the various components of the system and writing down the relationships connecting them. Usually the symbolism adopted is algebraic and the basic relationships take the form of equations and inequalities. Frequently, though, block diagrams are used. Then the components are represented by labelled boxes and the relationships by lines connecting the boxes. Less frequently, a logical symbolism is employed, with the elements of the problem conceived of as classes or members of classes and the relationships being those of class inclusion, overlapping and the like. In any event, the process is one of translating the real world situation into a set of abstract and simplified symbols. The result is an essentially tautological and sterile description of the problem, for it yields almost nothing more than definitions and identities.

The second stage we can call creative hypothesising. This is the stage at which the motivational, behavioural and technological assumptions are introduced. It entered the soap example in two ways. First in the selection of relevant variables, as when we decided that the price of the soap, competitors' advertising expenditures, the level of national income, the season of the year and many other conceivable variables could all be omitted. Our fictitious operations analyst made the same kind of conjectural judgment when he decided that the probability that a household's total purchases of soap of all brands was uninfluenced by his client's advertising. But the most vigorous exercise of creative hypothesising occurred when he conjectured the form of the relationship between advertising and the conditional probability that any soap purchased would be his client's brand. The first aspect of model formulation is a craft, but the second is an art and introduces the crucial assumptions of the model.

The final aspect of model formulation is quantification: the assignment of numerical values to the parameters of the model. In the soap example these parameters are c and p'_{xt}, the latter being a different number, presumably, for each class of household. This last aspect is clearly a more or less involved problem in statistical estimation.

It is clear that the operations analyst works, basically, as an applied mathematician with some statistics and numerical analysis thrown in. His principal tools, aside from his own judgment and imagination, are algebra, the calculus, differential equations, probability theory and statistics. In addition, he has some special-purpose tools of his own.

In principle, each time a problem is referred to an operations analyst he could construct a tailor-made model to fit the case, and in practice he does so a large proportion of the time. But fortunately problems of essentially similar form arise repeatedly in widely differing contexts. Consider, for example, the problems of providing facilities for checking customers out of a supermarket, accommodating aircraft arriving at an airport, servicing locomotives at a repair depot and meeting the needs of telephone subscribers. In each case the problem is to provide tolerably prompt service to a demand whose timing cannot be predicted exactly, by means of expensive facilities. This problem, in all its variants, is the problem of queuing theory. Similarly the problem of allocating limited resources among a number of uses pervades businesses and administrative organisations of all kinds. This family of problems is the concern of programming, linear and otherwise. And in like manner, game theory, inventory theory, servo-mechanism theory all study types of problems that are likely to occur throughout a wide variety of business and administrative circumstances. The operations analyst has at his disposal a large and growing kit of such tools, and is thus provided with an efficient apparatus whenever he recognises that a particular problem fits into one of these tidy categories. Naturally these ready-made models are the most communicable, teachable and talked about aspects of the craft and tend to receive a disproportionate emphasis both in the public image of operations research and in professional instruction. They will also receive disproportionate emphasis here.

1. *The Linear Programming Model*[1]

Essentially linear programming is a mode of expressing the problem allocating scarce resources that has the peculiar virtue of lending itself to statistical estimation and numerical solution. It applies when the activities of an enterprise are limited by a number of resources in limited supply and when these resources are to be allocated to a number of activities, each of which absorbs them in proportion to its level of utilisation. Each of the activities also contributes to the attainment of the objectives of the enterprise in proportion to its utilisation. The problem is to discover a set of activity levels attainable within the resource limitations which leads to the maximum possible attainment of the objectives.

One of the most frequent and successful practical applications of linear programming is to the scheduling of oil-refinery operations.[2] We can convey the flavour of the method by laying out a highly simplified example of this application. Suppose a refinery has 1,000 units of blending capacity which it uses to produce regular and premium motor fuel (to be denoted by subscripts 3 and 4 respectively) from two grades of blending stocks (to be indicated by subscripts 1 and 2). Introduce four decision variables x_{13}, x_{14}, x_{23}, x_{24}, where x_{ij} denotes the number of barrels of blending stock i devoted to the production of motor fuel j. Now consider the consequences of decisions regarding these four variables. The total input of blending stock 1 is $x_{13} + x_{14}$ and that of blending stock 2 is $x_{23} + x_{24}$. If the two stocks cost $1.26 and $1.68 per barrel respectively the total cost of fuel inputs is:

$$1{\cdot}26(x_{13} + x_{14}) + 1{\cdot}68(x_{23} + x_{24})$$

The total output of regular-grade gasoline is $x_{13} + x_{23}$, that of premium-grade is $x_{14} + x_{24}$. If the regular grade is woth $4.20 per barrel at the refinery and premium grade is worth $5.04 per barrel the value of product is:

$$4{\cdot}20(x_{13} + x_{23}) + 5{\cdot}04(x_{14} + x_{24})$$

[1] For a more complete discussion of linear programming from an economist's point of view see Baumol [6] or Dorfman [14].

[2] See Charnes, Cooper and Mellon [12] and Manne [28] for more realistic examples.

By subtraction we find the excess of the value of outputs over the value of inputs to be:

$$2{\cdot}94x_{13} + 3{\cdot}78x_{14} + 2{\cdot}52x_{23} + 3{\cdot}36x_{24}$$

We suppose that the objective of the plan is to make this number as large as possible.

Now turn to restrictions on choice. Suppose that the only quality specification to be considered is octane rating. The octane rating of any blend is a weighted average of the ratings of its components. Thus suppose that the octane rating of blending stock 1 is 75 and that of blending stock 2 is 93. Since regular-grade motor fuel is a blend of x_{13} barrels of stock 1 with x_{23} barrels of stock 2, its octane rating is:

$$\frac{75x_{13} + 93x_{23}}{x_{13} + x_{23}}$$

Similarly, the octane rating of the premium fuel is:

$$\frac{75x_{14} + 93x_{24}}{x_{14} + x_{24}}$$

Now suppose that regular fuel must have an octane rating of at least 82 and premium fuel a rating of at least 88. Then we have the constraints on the decision variables:

$$\frac{75x_{13} + 93x_{23}}{x_{13} + x_{23}} \geq 82$$

$$\frac{75x_{14} + 93x_{24}}{x_{14} + x_{24}} \geq 88$$

which are equivalent to:

$$-7x_{13} + 11x_{23} \geq 0$$

$$-13x_{14} + 5x_{24} \geq 0$$

respectively.

Finally, suppose that each barrel of regular fuel produced requires 1 unit of blending capacity, and each barrel of premium fuel requires 1·2 units. Then, since, 1,000 units are available in all, we have the capacity constraint:

$$(x_{13} + x_{23}) + 1{\cdot}2(x_{14} + x_{24}) \leq 1{,}000$$

Gathering all these formulae we have the purely formal problem: Find x_{13}, x_{23}, x_{14}, x_{24} so as to make:

$$2{\cdot}94x_{13} + 3{\cdot}78x_{14} + 2{\cdot}52x_{23} + 3{\cdot}36x_{24}$$

as large as possible, subject to the restrictions:

$$7x_{13} - 11x_{23} \leq 0$$

$$13x_{14} - 5x_{24} \leq 0$$

$$(x_{13} + x_{23}) + 1{\cdot}2(x_{14} + x_{24}) \leq 1{,}000$$

The rest is arithmetic calculation.

Besides being of substantial practical importance, this example has a number of pedagogical virtues. In the first place it illustrates the flexibility of linear programming. Note that the numbers we had to choose, x_{13}, x_{14}, x_{23}, x_{24} were " activities " in only a very strained sense. In this context what we would ordinarily think of as an activity would be blending one of the grades of motor fuel by a specified chemical formula (*e.g.*, blending a barrel of regular fuel by using 0·6 barrel of blending stock 1 and 0·4 barrel of blending stock 2). Linear programming cannot take account of more than a finite and fairly small number of activities (say 200) when defined in the ordinary way, but with our particular choice of variables we have admitted to consideration an infinite number of activities, viz., all physically possible blends. The resource scarcities also represent resource scarcities in only a very extended sense. The " 1,000 " is the quantity of a genuine limiting resource, but the two zeros of the right-hand side of the restricting inequalities are artifacts resulting from the manipulation of the quality specifications. This flexibility—the fact that the words " activity " and " resource limitation " do not have to be taken at all literally in setting up a linear programming problem—is largely responsible for the widespread applicability of the method. Any problem that can be expressed by means of linear equations and inequalities is amenable to linear programming, whatever the physical interpretation of the variables and relationships. Indeed, there are methods for incorporating non-linear relationships at the cost of substantially increased difficulty in computation.

One important limitation of linear programming has always been that the variables whose values are to be determined must be continuously variable, but recently methods have been developed for solving problems where the decision variables must be integers (*e.g.*, the number of aircraft flights per day between two points).[1] Another important limitation, on which less progress has been made, is that linear programming formulations do not allow for uncertainty.

Let us return to the blending example for another remark. A key theorem of linear programming states that there always exists an optimal solution in which the number of decision variables with positive values does not exceed the number of constraints, in this case three. Now suppose, for example, that the positive variables turn out to be x_{13}, x_{23}, x_{24}. This indicates that the premium fuel would be 100% pure blending stock 2. But this cannot be optimal, since the quality specification for premium fuel would be overfulfilled and money could be saved by adding in some of the cheaper blending stock. Clearly, no admissible combination of three positive values can be optimal in this problem, so there must be a solution with only two of the decision variables at positive value. This means that only one of the two products is made, *i.e.*, the refinery produces either regular or premium fuel, but not both. Which product should be made can

[1] See Gomory and Baumol [19] and Markowitz and Manne [30].

be ascertained readily by computing which of the two yields a greater gross revenue per unit of blending capacity absorbed. Thus the arithmetic turns out to be even more trivial than it promised to be at first glance.

An even more common application of linear programming than the refinery blending problem is the so-called transportation problem, which arises whenever a standardised commodity is to be shipped from a variety of sources to a variety of destinations.[1] Newsprint companies use it to decide which of their customers should be supplied from each of their mills, oil companies use it in assigning bulk distribution plants to refineries, the National Coal Board in England uses it to allocate markets among mines, Henderson applied it to an appraisal of the economic efficiency of the coal industry in this country [20]. There has accumulated a large literature which deals with such complications as differences in production costs at different supply points, limitations on the capacity of shipping routes, fixed charges for opening or constructing shipping routes and a cascading of problems such as where distribution involves a chain of factory to warehouse (of limited capacity) to retail store.

All the problems in this wide family are surprisingly easy to solve (though I wouldn't recommend that you try a large one with pencil and paper) for a number of technical reasons, among them the fact that all the restraints take the form of simple sums, like for any factory the sum of shipments to all its customers cannot exceed its capacity. As a result, transportation problems involving literally thousands of origins and destinations can be solved readily. It seems that even more efficient methods of solution result when the linear programming point of view is abandoned and the problem is conceived of as routing a flow through a network so that shipments of commodities are analysed as if they were currents in electric circuits or flows of liquids through systems of pipes.[2] To use electrical terminology, transportation costs are analogous to resistances, and differences in the value of the commodity at different points are the voltages.

2. *Information Theory*

Information theory rests on the discovery of a quantitative measure of information, originally by R. V. L. Hartley and put into its current form by C. E. Shannon [36]. The unit of information is the " bit," which is the amount of information in a message that tells which of two equally likely possibilities is the case. Thus, the telegram " It's a boy " conveys (approximately) one bit of information to a receiver who knew previously that a birth had occurred. Or consider a kind of message that is more common in industry: a requisition sent by a production department to a store-room. It contains at least three kinds of information: (1) which item is desired.

[1] For a typical small-scale example see Vazsonyi [39, p. 26 ff.].

[2] The network approach to transportation problems is due mostly to Ford and Fulkerson. See [17] [18].

This selects one of a large number of not-equally-likely possibilities, but its information content is measurable in bits by a formula that we do not have space to explain. (2) The quantity desired—again a selection from a large number of not-equally-likely possibilities. (3) Which department desires the items—again quantifiable in the same way. The formulae for information quantity are constructed in such a way that the information content of the message is the sum of these three components (and any others, such as the date desired, that may be present). Of course, there are many messages whose information content cannot be measured. For example, I do not suppose that the information-content of this essay can be quantified.[1] But equally obviously, the smooth running of any organisation depends on the flow of messages that are sufficiently standardised so that their information content can be estimated numerically.

The metric for information content is accompanied by measures of the information-carrying capacity of channels and the information-processing capacity of centres. A centre is any person or group who originates messages or receives and acts on them. A channel is any group of devices or persons that transmits messages between centres. *E.g.*, a channel might be typist–messenger boy–receptionist–secretary; or microphone–transmitter–radio waves–receiver–loud-speaker.

The capacity of a centre depends on the kinds of messages it processes, the kind of action or decision required and the technical characteristics of the centre. The capacity of a channel depends on the amount of interference present in it (*i.e.*, irrelevant signals, technically called " noise "), the forms of the messages it handles, the rate at which it can transmit the elementary symbols of which messages are composed, its susceptibility to error, etc. The capacities of the physical components of a channel (*e.g.*, electronic amplifiers) can often be estimated from engineering considerations, the capacities of the human components have to be derived from statistical studies.

The relevance of the form of message to the capacity of a channel is particularly significant. It is contained in the notion of " redundancy," *i.e.*, the ratio of the actual information content of the message to the maximum amount that could be packed into a message of the same length (subtracted from unity, of course). Thus, the information content of the vital statistic telegram mentioned above is entirely contained in the zero-redundancy message " B " or the somewhat more redundant " Boy." Redundancy of form is expensive, but it is also useful, up to a point. Thus, if a channel is subject to error (as all are) redundancy often saves the day. The message " F " conveys no information, but " Foy" is practically as good as the correct message. Mail-order companies recognise the virtue of redundancy when they require that an order include the name of the item

[1] But an upper limit can be placed on it by using the estimate that text written in English contains about 1·5 bits per letter.

desired along with the catalogue number. The optimal amount of redundancy in a system, *i.e.*, the optimal form of message, is an important field of application of information theory. For example, the ordinary method of transmitting television signals is more than 99% redundant (because it is practically certain that the spot following a bright spot will also be bright; the only information needed after a few bright spots is when the first dark spot occurs). One of the more important advances that made colour television feasible, since colour TV requires much more information per second, was a less redundant scheme for encoding the signals for transmission.

The relevance of information theory to communications engineering is evident, but would not qualify it as a model for operations research. Its contribution to operations research derives from its bearing on the structures of organisations. Here the essential principle is that an organisation will not function smoothly if the amount of information to be sent on any channel or processed at any centre exceeds the capacity of that channel or centre. Thus the information structure of an organisation can be depicted by representing it as a kind of network with the centres shown by capacitated nodes and the channels by capacitated links. Then the required flow of information between any pair of centres can be compared with the maximal attainable flow.[1] Bottlenecks as well as underutilised channels can then be detected and corrective actions indicated. Possible ameliorative measures are: (*a*) increasing physical channel capacity (*e.g.*, increasing the number of trunk lines), (*b*) reducing the redundancy of messages (which is always unduly high in organisations that have not given conscious attention to this problem), (*c*) routing messages indirectly via underutilised channels, (*d*) increasing the capacities of centres (*e.g.*, installing more counters in the store-room) and (*e*) reassigning functions away from overloaded centres.

3. *General Systems Analysis*

General systems analysis or cybernetics is fairly closely related to information theory and indeed incorporates it. Like information theory, it visualises an organisation in terms of a block diagram with centres connected by lines of communication. The separation of centres entails that no centre will have all the information available to the organisation (contrast with the ideal entrepreneur or firm of economic theory), and that there will be delays (lags) in transmitting information to centres where decisions are made and in transmitting and executing instructions from executive centres. This circumstances gives rise to the problem of systems

[1] From this point of view Paul Revere's communication system (two lanterns, one if by land, two if by sea) was just adequate. There was one bit of information to be transmitted and his channel had a capacity of one bit per night. It was insufficiently redundant, however, and if there had been much noise (mist, gusty winds) the course of the Battle of Lexington might have been other than it was.

analysis: to deduce from the structure of information flows in an organisation and the decision rules employed by its various centres how the organisation will respond to changes in its environment and conditions. As a corollary, systems analysis is concerned with methods of ascertaining the information flows and decision rules in organisations—which often differ from those in the official organisation chart—and with finding optimal information flows and decision rules.

The fundamental assumption of systems analysis is that all decision rules can be thought of as responses to discrepancies between the actual state or performance of the organisation and some " standard " or desired state, and are intended to reduce those discrepancies. Now it has been noted that many mechanisms behave in just this way (the conventional examples are gyro-pilots on ships and thermostats attached to home heating systems) and, indeed, so do the nervous systems of most organisms. Thus, automatic control devices, neuromuscular responses and organizations are all recognised as instances of control by feedback, *i.e.*, by comparison of actual state with desired state. The mathematics and concepts developed for the study and design of electronic control devices thus become applicable to the study of nervous systems and organisations; indeed, the " servomechanism " becomes the model employed in all such studies.

Consider a very simple example which evades all the interesting but complicated mathematical concepts that dominate this area of operations research. Suppose a firm has the policy of keeping 100 units of some item in inventory. Each Monday the stock-room reports to the purchasing department its actual stock as of the close of business the previous Friday. If the stock is less than 100 units the purchasing department orders an amount equal to three-quarters of the discrepancy, which is delivered eight to ten days later. Sacrificing realism to simplicity, we also assume that if the stock exceeds 100 units the purchasing department disposes of three-quarters of the excess, say by sale to a subsidiary at a sacrifice price. This disposal (or negative delivery) also takes place in the week following the report of the discrepancy. This very bad inventory policy can be portrayed as in Fig. 1. This diagram is interpreted as follows.

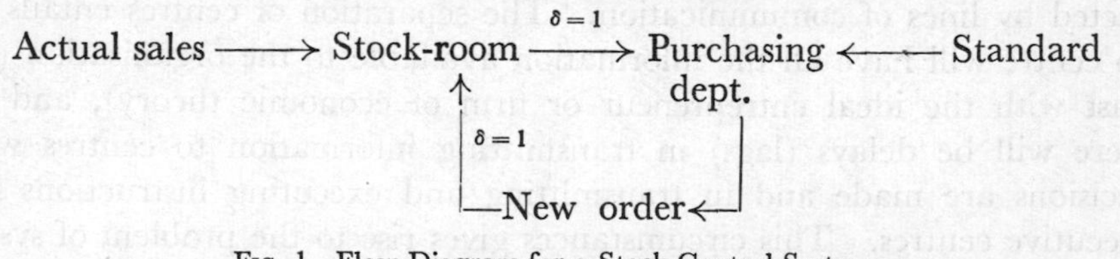

Actual sales ⟶ Stock-room $\xrightarrow{\delta=1}$ Purchasing dept. ⟵ Standard

Purchasing dept. ⟶ New order $\xrightarrow{\delta=1}$ Stock-room

Fig. 1 Flow Diagram for a Stock Control System.

The condition of the stock room is influenced by sales and new orders, the formula being:

$$I_{t+1} = I_t + R_t - S_t$$

where I_t = inventory at the beginning of the tth week;
R_t = replenishment stocks received during the tth week (which may be negative);
S_t = sales during the tth week.

The condition of the stock-room is reported to the purchasing department with a delay to the following week, symbolised by $\delta = 1$. The purchasing department compares this report with the standard (100 units) and issues a replenishment order according to the formula:

$$\text{Order} = {}^3/_4\,(100 - I_t)$$

This order reaches the stock-room the following week and influences the terminal stock according to the inventory balance equation. Now:

$$R_t = \text{Orders in week } t - 1 = {}^3/_4\,(100 - I_{t-1})$$

so we can write the difference equation for inventories as:

$$I_{t+1} = I_t + {}^3/_4\,(100 - I_{t-1}) - S_t$$

or:

$$I_{t+1} - I_t + {}^3/_4\,I_{t-1} = 75 - S_t$$

This is a familiar kind of difference equation from which we calculate how the level of actual inventories will respond to any pattern of sales. The solution, skipping over the tedious details, is:

$$I_t = k(0{\cdot}866)^t \cos\,(55t + \phi)^\circ + 1{\cdot}06 \sum_{r=0}^{t-1} (0{\cdot}866)^r \sin 55r^\circ(100 - {}^4/_3 S_{t-r})$$

where k and ϕ are disposable constants to be assigned in accordance with the initial conditions. As would be expected from a second-order difference equation, this solution displays a combination of exponential and trigonometric behaviour. It consists of two terms. The first term is a damped cycle, but the notable aspect of it is that it does not depend at all on the sales or the desired level of inventories. It is a damped oscillation caused by the lags and decision processes in the system itself. One of the virtues of systems analysis is that it calls attention to such built-in tendencies of organisations to oscillate. Though this firm allows a bad inventory policy, it is not as bad as it might be; for at least the inherent oscillations it generates do tend to die out.

The second term in the formula is a peculiar weighted average. To interpret it imagine first that sales were equal to zero for a long enough sequence of weeks so that the transient died out and inventories no longer changed. Then we should have:

$$I_{t+1} = I_t = I_{t-1}$$

and, substituting in the difference equation we should find $I_t = 100$, as desired. But if sales were steady at any non-zero level, the steady-state level of inventories would be:

$$I_t = 100 - {}^4/_3\,S_t$$

Thus, each of the terms in parentheses in the weighted average is the steady-state level of inventories corresponding to the level of sales τ weeks previous to the date for which the calculation is made. The whole term averages these historical steady-states with weights that decline generally as we recede into the past. This term, also, is characteristic of the responses of a feed-back system—their current behaviour is a weighted average of responses to past stimuli. The scheme of weights, in this case $(0{\cdot}866)^t \sin 55t°$, is one of the important traits characterising an organisation or mechanism.

Our example was so simple that we determined the inherent oscillations and the weighting function by straightforward, elementary means. In this respect the example was atypical of systems analyses. More generally, fairly advanced mathematics (in particular, Laplace transform methods) are required; and still more generally an explicit general solution cannot be obtained at all, though the formulation without solution may be illuminating. We shall return below to the treatment of problems that defy explicit solution.

4. *Inventory Models*

Churchman, Ackoff and Arnoff state, " More O. R. has been directed towards inventory control than towards any other problem area in business and industry " [13, p. 195], and this may be true. The literature devoted to inventory problems is enormous, and even the early work in the field, contributions published thirty years ago and more, displays the mathematical-engineering approach characteristic of operations research. The purpose of all this work, of course, is to determine most-profitable inventory policies. It takes it for granted that inventories are held to facilitate production operations (including within " production " the activities of purely trading firms). Though holding inventories is costly, it is generally essential to the economical conduct of other operations. The methods we are now concerned with seek to determine the efficient levels of these buffer stocks.[1]

Because of the enormous variety of inventory problems—style goods *vs.* standardised goods, goods purchased from outside supplies *vs.* goods manufactured within the firm, goods obtained under conditions of increasing, decreasing or constant costs, seasonal goods *vs.* non-seasonal ones, predictable *vs.* unpredictable demand, situations where stock-out penalties are severe *vs.* those where they are negligible, etc.—there can be no simple, generally applicable body of sound inventory doctrine. Instead, " inventory theory " consists of a battery of techniques for deducing efficient inventory policies adapted to specific circumstances. These techniques can

[1] Quite clearly these studies of inventory problems have only slight connection with the aspects of inventory behaviour that typically attract the attention of economists. Economists typified by Abramovitz, Hawtrey and Metzler concentrated on the aggregative consequences of inventory fluctuations and on the speculative motives for changes in stocks, with relatively light attention to the more work-a-day motives. Whitin, however, has tried to bridge the gap [40].

be divided into three classes that I shall call static analyses, stationary-state analyses and dynamic analyses, in order of increasing sophistication.

Static analyses concentrate on average behaviour in a single period considered in isolation. A typical and important result is the "square root law," which can be deduced, in a very simple context, as follows. Suppose that the average weekly requirement for some inventoried item is n units, that it costs $\$k$ to place an order for this item over and above the cost of the goods ordered and that the carrying costs are $\$c$ per unit per week. Suppose that re-orders are placed in time so that the new stock arrives just when the old stock is exhausted. (The reader can see the difficulties hidden in this assumption when delivery lags are at all appreciable.) Then the only decision to be made is the quantity to order when an order is placed. Call it x. On these assumptions, n/x orders will be placed per week, on the average, giving rise to an average weekly order cost of $\$kn/x$. The size of the inventory will range from x units, just after new stock has been received, down to zero units, just before replenishment, averaging at $\frac{1}{2}x$ units. The associated carrying cost is then $\$\frac{1}{2}cx$ per week and the total weekly cost of maintaining the item in inventory is $\$kn/x + \$\frac{1}{2}cx$. The optimal value of x is the one that minimises this cost, and is easily found to be

$$x = \sqrt{2\frac{kn}{c}}$$

Thus, the optimal size of order and of average inventory, in these circumstances, varies in proportion to the square root of (i) the rate of consumption or sales, and (ii) the ratio of ordering cost to carrying cost.

The reader is surely unpleasantly aware of how many simplifying assumptions were made, implicitly and explicitly, in the course of this derivation. Most of them can be dispensed with, at the cost of increasing the complexity of both the argument and the result. Schlaifer [34, Ch. 15], for example, presents a full discussion of a case in which demand during the interval between placement and receipt of an order is a random variable, so that there is substantial danger of being out of stock before the replenishments are received. The general approach, the calculation of average results, is the same, but the technical difficulty of the analysis is magnified manyfold.

An essential prerequisite for using static analysis is that it be possible to divide up time into a sequence of independent periods. These periods need not all be of the same length or even of predictable length, but they must be independent in the sense that no decision or event in any period affects the situation in any subsequent period. In the preceding analysis, for example, we can define a period as extending from one date at which the stock is precisely x, the order quantity, to the next date at which this is the stock. Then periods will be of varying length, depending on fluctuations in rate of consumption, but at the outset of each period the position of the firm will be precisely the same as at the outset of any other period and the consequences of any inventory policy can be synopsised by taking the average results of that policy in a single period. That is just what we did.

Unfortunately it is not always possible to divide time up into such independent periods. For this there are several reasons. It may not be possible to order new stock just when the level of the inventory makes it desirable. Thus, canneries must contract for produce once a year, ships can replenish only when in port, etc. Sometimes even when irregular ordering is technically possible-it may be undesirable. It may be administratively necessary to establish a periodic ordering routine, or it may be economical to consolidate orders for a variety of items into a single requisition. In such cases a schedule of ordering dates has to be established, and they become the natural points of division between time periods because they are the dates on which decisions have to be made. When a regular ordering cycle is established the periods cannot be independent because each period's initial stock is influenced by what went on before.

But independence may fail even when irregular ordering is permitted.[1] For example, if stock is exhausted orders may be backlogged. Then when new stock is received its utilisation does not begin *ab initio*, but is influenced by the extent of the backlog. Thus in many actual situations inventory policies have to be devised without making the assumption that time can be sliced into a sequence of independent periods. Then it is invalid to appraise an inventory policy by its average results in a single period; more complicated techniques have to be used.

Stationary-state analyses comprise one family of such techniques. If we contemplate a long sequence of periods extending into the future we can consider the probability distribution of the state of the firm (*e.g.*, the size of inventories and backlogs) at the outset of each period. In the first period, of course, the initial state is known. The probability distribution of the initial state of the second period depends on the initial state of the first period, the inventory policy followed, the probability distribution of demand (which we shall for simplicity assume to be the same in all periods), etc. The third-period probability distribution depends on the second-period probability distribution, the inventory policy, the probability distribution of demand, etc.[2] If we continue in this manner it fortunately happens that the influence of the initial conditions of the first period gradually dies out and the probability distribution of initial states generally ceases to change from period to period. In other words, a stationary state is attained.

Once the stationary state has been reached we can apply the averaging

[1] Howard Raiffa taught me this.

[2] It may also depend directly on events in the first period, as when delivery lags are longer than a period or when usage in any period affects the probability distribution of demand in several subsequent periods. We have ample precedent for neglecting this kind of complication.

procedure in two steps. First we consider each possible initial state in turn and compute the average results of the inventory policy in a period that begins with that inital state. Then we average those results over all possible initial states, giving each a weight equal to its probability. The result is an over-all average profit (or cost, if that is desired) per period in the long run.

All of this sounds very complicated, and is, but a simple example may clarify it. Consider the problem of a machine shop that stocks a part

TABLE I

Probability Distribution of Monthly Demand for a Part

Number of times demanded	0	1	2	3
Probability . . .	0·5	0·3	0·1	0·1

that is expensive to store and is infrequently demanded. When it is demanded the shop gets a job if the item is in stock and nets, let us say, $15; but if it is out of stock the sale is lost. The carrying cost for the part we take as $3.00 a month. Inventory is taken on the first month, and if an order is placed the new stock is received on the first of the following month in time to be included in that month's inventory. The probability distribution of demand is given in Table I.

With these data the consequences of any inventory policy, in the stationary state, can be computed. Three possible inventory policies are listed in Table II. We shall consider policy I in detail, it being the least tedious.

TABLE II

Three Possible Inventory Policies; Number of Parts to Order When Current Inventory is Given

Current inventory.	Number of parts to order under.		
	Policy I.	Policy II.	Policy III.
0	1	1	2
1	0	1	1
2	0	0	0
3 or more	0	0	0

First note that if this policy is followed there can never be more than one part in stock. Next write down a table of "transition probabilities." These give the probabilities of either possible inventory level, 0 or 1, at an inventory date when the inventory level at the previous date is given. These are displayed in Table III.

This table states that if inventory is zero on one inventory date it will surely be one on the next (since one part will be ordered and none will be sold), and that if inventory is one on any date, then the chances are 50–50 that it will be zero or one on the next date. Now let P_0 and P_1 denote the probabilities of the two inventory levels and assume that the stationary state has been reached, so these probabilities are constant over time. Then, from the first column of Table III, the probability of having no items in stock on any date is half the probability of having one in stock on the previous date, or $P_0 = 0{\cdot}5P_1$. From column 2, the probability of having one item in stock is the sum of two contingencies: none in stock on the previous date plus one in stock on the previous date and still unsold. Thus, $P_1 = P_0 + 0{\cdot}5P_1$. This, of course, is the same equation as before. But the two probabilities have to add up to unity. Thus, $P_0 = {}^1/_3$, $P_1 = {}^2/_3$ are the steady-state probabilities of the two possible inventory levels.

TABLE III

Transition Probabilities for Policy I

Previous inventory.	Current inventory.	
	0	1
0	0	1
1	0·5	0·5

If inventory is zero there are neither sales nor inventory costs. If inventory is one inventory costs of \$3 are incurred and there is a 50% chance of making a sale, so that average profit is $\frac{1}{2}$\$15 − \$3 = \$4.50. The long-run average profit per period resulting from this policy is then ${}^1/_3\,(0) + {}^2/_3$\$4.50 = \$3.00. The other two policies in Table II can be assessed similarly. For policy II the steady state probabilities are 1/11, 5/11, 5/11 for stocks of 0, 1, 2 respectively, with an average profit per period of \$4·09. For policy III the probabilities are 1/9, 3/9, 5/9 and the average profit is \$4.00. Thus, policy II is the best of the three.

This brings up three comments. First, the policy is a bit peculiar. It tells us that when stocks are down to zero we should order one part and then, whether or not it is still unsold at the end of the month, order another. Why not order the two together? Because inventory carrying costs are too high to justify carrying a second item in stock when there is sure to be a first item, but are not too high to risk carrying a second item when there is only a 50% chance of having a first. Second, there is no unique optimal stock level in this example. If the part is out of stock we should order up to a stock level of one; if the stock level is one we should order up to a stock level of two. Now, much of inventory theory presumes that there is an optimal stock level and attempts to find it. In this case such a search would not discover the optimal available inventory policy.[1] Third, we have considered three policies and have found the best of the three, but how do we know that there is not a still better policy? Stationary-state analysis will not tell us, because the computations require the table of transition probabilities, and

[1] Dvoretzky, Keifer and Wolfowitz [16] present a full discussion of the conditions in which an optimal stock level exists.

these, in turn, require that the inventory policy be given. This mode of analysis is convenient for assessing the consequences of any given policy; it is inconvenient for discovering an optimal policy except in some special cases.[1] Thus we must advance to full-fledged dynamic analysis, which meets this need.

Dynamic inventory analysis rests on two ideas, both most thoroughly expounded by Bellman [7]. The first is a recurrence relationship connecting optimal inventory policies for different planning horizons. Suppose that on a given inventory date the stock is N and it is desired to take into account the consequences of any decision for H periods into the future. (H may be infinite, but it will do no harm to talk as if it were finite.) Since we plan to take account of consequences that may extend over a considerable length of time, time preference becomes relevant. Therefore, assume that the current valuation placed on a dollar t periods in the future is $\$a^t$, *i.e.*, assume a rate of discount of $(1\text{-}a)/a$ per period.

Suppose it is decided to order x units. The consequences of this decision can be divided into two parts: its effects on the present period and its effects on the $H - 1$ subsequent periods. The effects on the current period are the average level of profits in a period with initial inventory N if x units are ordered. This value can be ascertained by the kind of calculation we have already illustrated. Denote it by $r(N, x)$. The effect on later periods is a bit more complicated. One cause of complication is that we do not know what the initial inventory of the second period will be. We can, however, calculate its probability distribution from the probability distributions of demand and deliveries in the first period. Accordingly, let $p_M(x)$ be the probability that the inventory inherited from the first period will be M if x units are ordered in the first period. We now assume, and this assumption will be justified later, that we already know the optimal inventory policy for an $H - 1$ period horizon. That is, we know the maximum discounted profit that can be obtained in $H - 1$ periods beginning with an inventory of M. Denote this number by $f^*_{H-1}(M)$. Then, taking the discount factor into account, the total present value of profit in H periods beginning with an inventory of N and ordering x units is $r(N, x)$ plus the average $H - 1$ period profit taken over all values of M, or:

$$f_H(N, x) = r(N, x) + a \sum_M p_M(x) f^*_{H-1}(M)$$

Let x^* be the value of x that maximises this expression. Then the maximum value of $f_H(N, x)$ is $f_H(N, x^*)$, and this is $f^*_H(N)$ in the notation previously introduced. We thus have the recurrence formula:

$$f^*_H(N) = \max_x \left\{ r(N, x) + a \sum_M p_M(x) f^*_{H-1}(M) \right\}$$

[1] Situations in which an optimal stock level exists are among such special cases. Morse [31, Ch. 10] discusses the use of stationary-state analysis for finding optimal stock levels.

where all the numbers inside the braces are known. Thus we can find the value of $f^*(N)$, and the corresponding optimal order quantity, simply by trying all permissible values of x and noting the one that maximises the value in the braces. This may be laborious, but it is a practicable undertaking by hand for small problems and by electronic computer for large ones.

The second basic idea of dynamic inventory analysis is that if we determine optimal inventory policies successively for planning horizons of 1, 2, 3, . . . , periods, the sequence of policies will converge to the long-run optimum.

TABLE IV

$f_1^*(N)$ or $r(N, O)$ for the Machine-shop Example

N.	$f^1*(N)$.	*N.*	$f_1^*(N)$.
	$		$
0	0	4	0
1	4·50	5	−3·00
2	4·50	6	−6·00
3	3·00	etc.	

To see how this approach works let us return to the machine-shop example. For a planning horizon of one period $f_1(N, x) = r(N, x)$. But in this example the placement of an order does not affect the current period, *i.e.*, $r(N, x)$ is a constant in x. Let us then take the optimal value of x to be zero, whatever N may be. Thus $f_1^*(N) = r(N, 0)$. Table IV is a table of this function computed from the previous data on costs and the probability distribution of demand.

Next consider a planning horizon of two periods, using a discount factor of $a = 0{\cdot}99$. Applying the basic formula for the consequences of ordering x units when N are on hand,

$$f_2(N, x) = r(N, x) + 0{\cdot}99 \sum_M p_M(x) f_1^*(M)$$

For every possible value of N we now require the value of x that makes this expression as large as possible. The ensemble of these values of x will be the optimal inventory policy for the two-period case. The calculation is protracted, so we illustrate it for a single value, $N = 1$. In this case there is a probability of 0·5 that the part on hand will be sold. Thus $r(N, x) = \$4.50$ for all values of x and $M = x$ with probability 0·5 and $M = x + 1$ with probability 0·5. Substituting these results in the formula:

$$f_1(1, x) = \$4.50 + 0{\cdot}99[\tfrac{1}{2} f_1^*(x) + \tfrac{1}{2} f_1^*(x + 1)]$$

The values of $f_1^*(x)$ and $f_1(x + 1)$ for all values of x can be read off from Table IV. Thus we find that $f_2(1, x)$ assumes its maximum value when $x = 1$, so that

$$f_2^*(1) = f_2(1, 1) = \$4.50 + 0{\cdot}99(\tfrac{1}{2}\ \$4.50 + \tfrac{1}{2}\ \$4.50) = \$8.955$$

The calculation for other values of N is similar. Then, having found an optimal inventory policy and its results for $H = 2$, we advance to $H = 3$, which can be analysed using the results for $H = 2$ and the fundamental recurrence formula. After that we go on to $H = 4$, 5, etc. Table V summarises the results of a number of these computations which, remember, are readily mechanised. The entries in this table, of which we computed the one for $N = 1$, $H = 2$, are the optimal size of order for the given initial stock and planning horizon. Note that in this instance the optimal policy is the same for all horizons of three months and greater. The convergence

TABLE V

Optional Inventory Policies for a Number of Initial Inventories and Planning Horizons

(Number of parts to order with given initial stock)

Initial inventory.	Planning horizon in months.				
	1.	2.	3.	4.	5.
0	0	1 or 2	1	1	1
1	0	0	1	1	1
2	0	1	0	0	0
3	0	0	0	0	0
4	0	0	0	0	0
5	0	0	0	0	0

of the short-horizon optimal policies to the long-run optimum is not always this fast, of course.

As this illustration shows, dynamic inventory analysis leads straightforwardly to the discovery of the optimal inventory policy for given data. Its major drawback, aside from its laboriousness, is that it does not lend itself to analysis. It just gives the answer without disclosing how the optimal policy would change in response to changes in any of the data. If any of the data (such as prices, probability distribution of demand, delivery lag, etc.) should change there is nothing to do but to perform the whole computation over.[1]

II. *Ad Hoc* Models, Simulation

1. *Two More Models: Queuing and Sequencing*

Limitations of space and time fortunately prevent me from extending this catalogue of methods used in operations research. There are, however, two more important families of models that must at least be mentioned: queuing theory models and combinatorial models.

[1] Exceptions to this dictum occur when the probability distribution of demand and other data are sufficiently tractable. A few instances are given in Arrow, Karlin and Scarf [4].

Queuing problems occur very widely: the unanswered letters in your desk are a queue, so are the aircraft waiting to land at a busy airport and the machines standing idle waiting for the repairman. In general, any backlog of tasks waiting to be performed is a queue. (The tasks may be very simple, like admitting passengers through a bank of turnstiles, or they may be complicated, like treating casualties after a battle.) Queues are generally unpleasant to the people who are waiting for the service, and frequently expensive. On the other hand, the provision of additional or improved serving facilities to reduce or eliminate the queue is also expensive. The task of queuing theory is to determine the optimal quantity and characteristics of the facilities that serve a queue, having regard to both of these costs. It performs this task by studying the way in which the serving facilities influence the probability distribution of the length of the queue, the probability distribution of waiting times, etc., treating the arrivals to the queue as a given datum.

Queuing problems are closely related to inventory problems. Both models are concerned with accumulations (of tasks or of stocks as the case may be), with accretions to them and with subtractions from them. In inventory problems the accretions are subject to at least partial control, through reordering policy, but the subtractions are governed by a random process that is largely beyond the control of the firm or organisation that maintains the inventories. In queuing problems the reverse is true: the accretions are random and beyond direct influence, while the subtractions can be controlled through control of the serving facilities. Thus, it is not surprising that the analysis of queues depends on the same general principles and methods as the analysis of inventories, though, of course, there are substantial differences in detail.

The most interesting general conclusion yielded by queuing theory is the following: Consider a queue attended by a single server. Suppose that tasks arrive, on the average, one in every a minutes and require, on the average, b minutes to perform. Then in a fairly long interval, of length T, say, approximately T/a tasks will arrive, the server will be busy Tb/a minutes, and the average proportion of the time that the server will be busy will be b/a. This ratio, known as the utilisation factor, is the key to the behaviour of the queue. If it exceeds one, and the system doesn't break down, then obviously the length of the queue will grow towards infinity and so will the average waiting time. It is a little shocking to learn that this same result holds if the utilisation factor equals unity, but this fact seems more reasonable when we recall that the queue is caused by the fact that the number of arrivals in any time interval is a random variable and the variance of this variable increases indefinitely as the length of the interval increases. Finally, if the utilisation factor is close to unity the average waiting time will be finite but large. It follows that if the queue is to be kept short the utilisation factor must be substantially less than unity, *i.e.*, the server must be idle a large proportion of the time. Thus, ostensibly idle capacity is essential to prompt service. Old-fashioned efficiency experts will please take notice.

Combinatorial or sequencing models are used most frequently to describe production problems in which the decision to be made concerns the order in which certain operations are to be performed. Typical applications are decisions as to the order in which the parts of a complicated product are to be assembled (*e.g.*, it is obvious that you should put on your socks before your shoes, but less obvious whether the socks should precede the trousers) and, in a job-shop, the order in which jobs should be performed (*e.g.*, if black and white paint are to be mixed on the same machine it is usually better to mix the white paint first). Another group of combinatorial problems concerns the assignment of tasks. Thus, on a moving production line the various operations should be assigned to the various stations so that (*a*) operations are not performed in an awkward order, and (*b*) the operations assigned to all stations should require, as nearly as possible, the same length of time. The hallmark of a combinatorial problem is that it cannot be formulated as the choice of a value of a quantitative variable. Thus, the most powerful tools of mathematical analysis, algebra and the calculus, do not apply and problems that appear quite innocent on the surface are likely to prove very intractable. Nevertheless, combinatorial problems can frequently be solved, sometimes, surprisingly, by an adaptation of linear programming.

2. Ad hoc *Models*

I am fighting against giving the impression that this list of ready-made models, or any similar list, can include the bulk of the conceptual frameworks used in operations research. On the contrary, most operations research work employs *ad hoc* models, exemplified by the one in the soap advertising fable. In order to redress somewhat the balance of emphasis I must therefore sketch, very cursorily, two illustrations of *ad hoc* approaches, both taken from the very valuable compendia, *Operations Research for Management* [26] [27].[1]

The first illustration concerns the efficient utilisation of the vehicular tunnels operated by the Port of New York Authority, one of the prominent users of operations research [33]. The problem was to determine the traffic conditions conducive to the largest feasible flow of traffic through the tunnels, in vehicles per hour. The volume of traffic, V, in vehicles per hour, is the product of traffic density, D (vehicles per mile), and speed, S, in miles per hour, as can be seen by noting that if traffic moves at S miles per hour all the vehicles within S miles of a given point will pass that point in an hour. Speed and density are closely related. It was assumed on the basis of previous empirical observations that the relationship was linear and, indeed, traffic counts in the fast lane of the Lincoln Tunnel led to the regression

[1] Summarised with the kind permission of the publishers, The Johns Hopkins Press.

equation $S = 42{\cdot}1 - 0{\cdot}324D$ with a correlation coefficient of $r = 0{\cdot}97$. Multiplying both sides of this equation by D therefore yields $V = DS = 42{\cdot}1D - 0{\cdot}324D^2$. Differentiating this expression with respect to D and settling the derivative equal to zero produces an optimal density of $D = 65$ vehicles per mile, corresponding to a speed of 21 miles an hour and a vehicular spacing of 81 feet. How to persuade drivers to adopt that speed and spacing is another problem, not dealt with in this report. A minimum speed of 20 miles an hour was posted and had a discernible effect in increasing the flow of traffic.

This project, of course, employed a very simple model, invoking only the empirical functional relationship between speed and density and the definitional relationship of those two variables to volume. The bulk of the work in this case was observational and statistical: observing and analysing traffic conditions in the different tunnels and lanes. But the model, primitive though it was, was at the centre of the project, dictating what was to be observed and how the results were to be used.

My second example is inherently more tedious to describe because I have selected it in order to illustrate the kind of elaborate technical and technological analysis that is a part of the work of operations research. I shall therefore, in the interest of brevity, do considerable violence to the actual facts of life. The reader who wishes a more accurate description of the project is referred to the original report by Dunlap and Jacobs [15].

The project dealt with strip mining of phosphate rock. This is accomplished by enormous power shovels called draglines, costing over $7 million each, with buckets of as large as 30 cubic yards capacity and earth-moving capabilities of as much as 1,500 tons an hour. In operation they excavate a linear strip of ore that can be several hundred feet wide by taking a certain stand, excavating the ore that can be reached conveniently from that stand, then backing up a distance along the strip, excavating again and so on. The shape of the hole dug at each stand may be visualised as a piece of pie with the point cut off or as a segment of a doughnut. But, and now we come to the problem, both the geometrical shape and the dimensions of the excavation made at each stand are variable within very wide ranges. The problem was to ascertain the optimal shapes and dimensions to employ, depending on the width of the ore vein, the thickness of the ore vein and its depth below the surface. More specifically, the problem was to find the mode of operation of the dragline that would maximise the tonnage excavated per hour.

The opposing considerations, severely simplified, were as follows. On the one hand, a dragline is an unwieldy vehicle, to say the least. It moves slowly, cannot dig while it is being moved, and what is more to the point, the time required to prepare it for moving and to unlimber it after each move is considerable. Thus, it is desirable to move it as infrequently as possible. On the other hand, as we shall soon see, the rate of excavation per hour is adversely affected if the area excavated at each stand is too large. The analysis of this second effect was the heart of the problem. To introduce the quantitative concepts let V denote the volume excavated at a single stand. Then, as you may recall from elementary calculus, if the shape of the excavation is a segment of a doughnut

$$V = \int_{r_1}^{r_2} \int_{\theta_1}^{\theta_2} \int_{z_1}^{z_2} r.dz.d\theta.dr$$

In this formula r denotes the distance from the dragline cab to an elementary volume of ore and varies from r_1, the radius of the inner rim of the doughnut, to r_2, the radius of the outer rim. θ indicates the angle from the cab to the elementary volume of ore, measured from the centre line of the strip being excavated. It varies from θ_1, the maximum angle of swing to the right, to θ_2, the maximum swing to the left. Finally, z is the depth below ground level of the elementary volume of ore, varying from z_1, the depth of the top of the vein, to z_2, the depth of its bottom. Of these variables, z_1, z_2 and the width of the vein are determined by geological happenstance, while r_1, r_2, θ_1, θ_2 are subject to decision within wide ranges. The problem is thus to determine optimal values of the last four variables and, moreover, since it is not necessary to cut in doughnut shape, the entire geometric configuration of the excavation. This last, non-quantifiable, range of possibilities helps make the problem really fascinating, but we shall for simplicity continue to pretend that the excavation will be doughnut-shaped.

We now introduce the considerations that determine the time required to excavate a volume V from a given stand. The elementary cycle of operation begins when a load has just been discharged at the dumping point on the rim of the excavation. It consists in swinging the bucket back to the elementary volume of ore to be excavated, filling the bucket, swinging back to the dumping point and emptying the bucket. The time required for the filling and emptying operations does not depend on the location of the unit volume of ore being excavated; we denote it by t_d. The time required for swinging to and from the point of excavation does depend on where the point is. We denote it by the function $t(r, z, \beta - \theta)$, where β is the angle from the dragline to the dumping point and all other variables have been defined. Finally, the number of times that the bucket must be returned to the point (r, z, θ) is the ratio of the elementary volume at that point, $r.dz.d\theta.dr$ to the bucket capacity, denoted by D. Assembling these expressions, the total time required to excavate volume V is:

$$T = \frac{1}{D} \int_{r_1}^{r_2} \int_{\theta_1}^{\theta_2} \int_{z_1}^{z_2} [t_d + 2t(r, z, \beta - \theta)] r.dr.d\theta.dz.$$

This formula gives the time actually spent in excavating the volume V. In addition, in order to obtain this volume the dragline must be moved into position, which means that it must be shut down after finishing at its previous stand, moved and unlimbered. The time required for actual moving is irrelevant, since the dragline will have to travel the entire length of the strip no matter what the mode of operation, but the time consumed in shutting down and setting up has to be charged against the V cubic feet excavated at the stand. Denoting this time by t_p, the total time required to obtain the V cubic feet at a stand is $t_p + T$ and the volume excavated per hour is $V/(t_p + T)$. This is the figure of merit, the quantity to be maximised by proper choice of operating parameters. If V and T are small the critical ratio will be small because of t_p in the denominator. If V and T are large the ratio is approximately V/T, and may be small because of the time consumed in swinging the bucket back and forth over large angles. It appears that there is likely to be some intermediate optimum.

Clearly this formulation of the problem, the identification of relevant variables, the rejection of minor variables and the determination of how the relevant variables affected the results, was attained only after careful observation of the actual operation and hard, careful thinking. There was additional empirical labour also. The formula, it will be remembered, involved the swinging-time function, $t(r, z, \beta - \theta)$. This function had to be determined statistically by observing a great many excavations with different operators and working conditions. Other relationships, not mentioned in my summary, also had to be estimated empirically.

Even after the formula relating cubic yards per hour to the operating parameters had been established, substantial difficulties remained. As I set it up, there were 4 parameters to be decided; in the actual problem there were 10. Now, finding the maximum of a complicated function with respect to 8 or 10 decision parameters is a formidable undertaking. (This contrasts with the vehicular tunnel example, where the maximising step was trivial.) The report does not state how the optimal decision parameters for different geological conditions were determined, other than that " it was necessary to carry out the total set of solutions on a high-speed computer "[1] [15, p. 191].

And still, when the optimal modes of operation had been determined, the task was not completed. The recommendations had to be applied by foremen who are not skilled in substituting in mathematical equations or even in using ten-dimensional tables. Thus, the recommendations had to be translated into a number of usable guide-charts and nomograms together with an extensive manual of instructions. One of the analysts spent three months with the operation after the conclusion of the study, training the personnel in the application of the results. All this effort seems to have been worth while, since it led to an increase of some 40% in output per hour.

[1] This kind of vagueness, enforced by the proprietary nature of many of the data, mars much of the literature of operations research.

3. *Simulation and Gaming*

This extended example may suggest the extreme mathematical, statistical and technical difficulties that confront the operations analyst. They occur whether special-purpose or general-purpose models are employed. I have already mentioned that in the area of general systems analysis the equations describing the performance of an organisation defy solution more often than not. The same is true of inventory problems and queuing problems. Even linear programming, whose salient virtue is the ease with which it lends itself to solution, is constantly pressing against the limitations of the most modern and powerful computing machines.

As a result, the operations analyst, like every other research worker, lives nearly always near the end of his tether. He simplifies his problems as much as he dares (sometimes more than he should dare), applies the most powerful analytic tools at his command and, with luck, just squeaks through. But what if all established methods fail, either because the problem cannot be forced into one of the standard types or because, after all acceptable simplifications, it is still so large or complicated that the equations describing it cannot be solved? When he finds himself in this fix the operations analyst falls back on "simulation" or "gaming."

Simulation is to the operations analyst what a pilot model or experiment is to a natural scientist. If you can't predict how a machine will behave the only thing to do is to try it out and see. The operations analyst cannot usually try out an enterprise of the characteristics he is considering, but he can frequently duplicate it, at least approximately, on paper. To see how this works, pretend that we had failed to solve the machine-shop inventory problem of the last section. Then we should have to analyse it by simulation.

The most popular methods of simulation use high-speed computing machines. To simulate our inventory problem we should select a starting inventory at random, read the data of the problem into the machine and instruct the machine to follow some specific inventory policy. The machine would then look at the given starting inventory and decide in accordance with the assigned inventory policy whether to place an order for replenishment and if so how large. Then it would draw a random number from the range 0–9 inclusive. If the number were in the range 0–4 it would interpret this to mean that no parts were demanded in the first month, if it were in the range 5–7 it would assume that one part was demanded, an 8 would mean that two parts were demanded and a 9 would represent a demand for three parts. Whatever the result, the machine would satisfy the demand as far as possible, subtract those sales from the initial inventory, increase the inventory by the replenishment stocks received in response to orders placed, if any, print out the results of interest and go on to perform the same calculations for the second month.

All this would take about a thousandth of a second.[1] In this way the machine would generate a thousand months of synthetic experience with the assigned policy, equivalent to nearly a century, in a second. When a sufficient amount of experience with a given inventory policy had been accumulated the machine would calculate the average inventory, average number of sales per month, average number of refusals, average re-order and inventory carrying cost, etc. Then it would turn to a new inventory policy and perform the same calculations.

In this way very large samples of synthetic experience can be obtained quickly and estimates can be obtained of all desired characteristics of probability distributions that are too complicated to be calculated mathematically. Analyses by simulation can do even more than that. The machine can be programmed so that after it has tried a few inventory policies assigned by the analyst it will then review the results and decide which would be the most promising inventory policy to try next. Then it could try the policy it has selected, again review the results, concoct a new promising policy, try it and continue this process of trial and revision until it could not find any avenue that promised improvement within the range of inventory policies that it was permitted to explore. All this a calculating machine can do quickly, accurately and without human intervention. What more could be desired?

Well, unfortunately, a great deal more. The result of a simulation is always the answer to a specific numerical problem without any insight into why that is the answer or how the answer would be influenced by a change in any of the data. In our inventory example a change in the probability distribution of demand, in the length of the delivery lag, in the re-order cost or in net profit per sale would presumably change the solution, but a simulation with given data gives no hint of size or direction of changes in inventory policy resulting from such changes in data. Thus, each variant of a problem analysed by simulation has to be solved by a separate computation; and computation is expensive. In practical affairs, of course, it is usually more important to know how to respond to changes in conditions than how to behave optimally in any single set of circumstances. This is so because, first, circumstances do change, and second, because we never do know precisely what circumstances are but have to base decisions on estimates and, therefore, have to know how consequential errors in these estimates are.

There is a second serious limitation, also. Above I said that a computing machine could be programmed to search iteratively through a family of possible inventory policies and, through a guided process of trial and error, pick out the best. This is an oversimplification if the problem is at all complicated, say complicated enough to warrant simulation. Most

[1] So much celerity is, unfortunately, extremely rare. Half a minute to a minute of machine time (costing $5 to $10) per cycle would be more typical.

decision problems tackled by operations research involve a number of interrelated variables. In the inventory example the variables are the numbers of parts to be ordered when the inventory is at each of its possible levels. In transportation problems the variables are the quantities to be delivered by each supply point to each consumer. A review of the other models we have discussed will show that typically they are multi-dimensional and that much of their difficulty stems from the wide variety of possible solutions to be contemplated. When explicit methods of solution cannot be found, therefore, we find ourselves in an area known as " analysis of response surfaces," about which a few words have to be said.

Suppose that we are interested in maximising profit or minimising cost, or something else of the sort, where the profit or cost in question depends on a number of variables under our control but where the manner of dependence is so complicated that we cannot actually write it down in the form of an equation. Then we can select any set of values of the variables under our control and, say, by simulation, estimate the value of the profit corresponding to that selection. This profit, together with the values of the variables that gave rise to it, is "a point on the response surface," and, subject only to limitations of patience and expense, we can calculate any number of such points that we please. What we now need is some procedure for finding the set of values of the decidable variables that gives rise to the highest possible profit, by means of a practicable number of simulations or similar computations. All that simulation provides is a method for finding single points on the response surface, and the best that can be said about finding optimal points is that research on this problem is being prosecuted vigorously [9] [10]. As things stand at present no fully satisfactory general-purpose method is known.

Be that as it may, simulation comes nearer to solving the unsolvable than any other device known, a fact that justifies fully its importance as a tool of operations research. Except in problems as trivial as our inventory example it is, however, a difficult tool to use well. It entails two main kinds of technical difficulties, those relating to the exploration of the response surface, which we have already discussed, and statistical problems such as deciding how large a sample to take of each set of circumstances and policies. *E.g.*, in our inventory example the statistical problem is how many months of synthetic experience should be accumulated with each inventory policy examined. With a given research appropriation, more policies can be examined if each examination employs a smaller sample, but the disadvantages of using unduly small samples is evident. These are formidable problems in technical mathematical analysis and statistics, and have an important bearing on the cost and precision of the analysis, but do not have much influence on the result, or, at least, should not.

A device quite similar to simulation in form but entirely different in objective is " gaming " or " operational gaming." Formally, gaming is simulation with human intervention. To "game" our inventory example we should omit the inventory policy from the machine program and replace it by the following routine. Each time that a new initial inventory is computed the machine would print out the results of the previous period's operations, including the terminal inventory, and wait. Then the subject, which might be either an individual or a team, would decide on the basis of his best judgment how many parts to order. This would be read into the machine, which would then compute the results of the period's operations, print them out and wait for the next decision. In working through an operational game of this sort, the subject might or might not be informed of the basic data, for example the probability distribution of demand. If he is not informed of some of the relevant data he would be expected to deduce them as experience accumulates.

This device will not, of course, disclose the optimal policy to be followed, but it can serve any of several other purposes. It can be used to investigate how close an experienced subject can come to the mathematical optimum in given circumstances and how long it takes him to do so. It can be used to test how changes in the circumstances and in the data available change the performance of subjects, and in this way to throw light on the practical value of additional information in the real-life situation being simulated. Thus, in the inventory example, if the probability distribution of demand is not known such an experiment could reveal how much should be spent on market research or other methods for ascertaining it.

Gaming can also be used as a psychological-experimental device for studying executive behaviour. Thus, in one set of such experiments it was found that executives started by basing their decisions on rough rules of thumb and revised them, in the light of experience, much too slowly in the sense that when they changed their policies they usually moved them only a small fraction of the distance between the current policy and the optimum, and only very rarely overcorrected. Further, it was found that this conservative bias tended to be more marked in proportion to the importance of random and unpredictable elements in the game.

Gaming can also be used to study the optimum of some decisions when other decisions are too complicated or are based on considerations too vague to be formalised. In this application various policies for making the decisions to be optimised are programmed into the machines, while the unmanageable decisions are made by a team as required. Finally, gaming can be used as a pedagogical device.

Gaming is fun, but, if a skilled team is required, very expensive. The expense frequently precludes sufficient replication to generate reliable probability distributions of consequences; and even where expense is not prohibitive, the memories, learning processes and tendencies to habit formation on the part of the teams make much replication impracticable. Even if the replication problem can be surmounted, there is a more fundamental difficulty in using gaming as a research tool. In any series of repetitions of a game the teams will either base their decisions on some well-defined policy or, more usually, will "play it by ear," using their best judgment as experience accumulates. In the former instance the results of the experiment will be an assessment of the consequences of the policy used, but, as we have seen above, any well-defined policy can be assessed more cheaply and conveniently by programming a computing machine to follow that policy and conducting a simulation experiment. In the latter instance it is hard to say what the results mean, since no expressible or reproducible policy was followed. The results will reflect an amalgam of the potentialities of the situation, the approximations used in constructing the game, the abilities of the teams under somewhat unnatural conditions and the vagaries of chance. If a large number of teams is used the gaming may produce an evaluation of how well an "average" team will perform under the conditions of the game, but still another dimension of sampling variability crops up in this application [38].

As a result of these problems, the literature does not indicate that gaming has played a significant role in solving operations research problems. It seems to hold more promise as a device for executive training, for investigating the psychology of decision making and for stimulating effective planning by confronting managers vividly with various contingencies they should be prepared to meet. Even in these last applications, however, it does not seem feasible to impose rewards and penalties cruel enough to approximate the pressures of real-life decision problems.

III. The Objective Function

A review of the models we have considered will show that each can be divided into two parts: a part describing the structure of the operation and the relationships among the variables (both controllable and uncontrollable), and a part that evaluates the consequences of any choice of variables in terms of profit, cost or some other measure of desirability. We shall refer to the first part as the constraints and to the second as the objective function or criterion. Most operations research problems take the form of searching for the values of the decidable variables that maximise or minimise the value of the objective function while satisfying the constraints.

An economist can sympathise readily with this habit of formulating problems as if the purpose were to maximise this or minimise that, but he is also aware of the pitfalls in this approach. In the first place, it is by no means axiomatic that the purpose of an operation can be expressed as maximising anything less vacuous than desirability, all things considered. The objectives of business enterprise are obscure. Among recent economic writers, Baumol [5] has argued that businessmen typically seek to maximise sales volume subject to a constraint on the rate of profit, Lanzillotti [24] found that predominantly they seek to attain some target rate of profit, Simon [37] maintains that they are "satisficers" attempting to reach some aspiration-level but not trying to maximise anything in particular. It seems clear that short-run profit maximising is neither a sensible nor a prevalent business objective, but, beyond that, what objectives are prevalent is a matter for conjecture.

In any specific context, then, the operations analyst has the task of ascertaining his client's objectives, and this task is complicated by the fact that his client is not likely to be very clear on the matter himself nor, since the client is generally not a single person, entirely of one mind. An appealing way out is to ask the client what his objectives are. B. O. Koopman, in a thoughtful presidential address to the Operations Research Society of America [23], stigmatised this practice as "authorititis" and included it in his catalogue of prevalent fallacies in operations research. His point was that no businessman, still less a second vice-president in charge of planning and research, can be expected to answer such questions with enough prevision or authority to provide a sound basis for research.

The question is far from academic because typically a business firm watches manifold consequences of its operations, including rate of profit, value of its shares, sales volume, share of market, public image, reputation of product, *et hoc genus omne*, and is not willing to increase its performance in any of these respects at unlimited sacrifice in the others. What is needed for operations research is a reasonably precise idea of how the varied goals trade off against each other, but in fact the interrelations are extremely complex. It is a frequent experience in operations research, when the job is done and the recommendations are presented, to have them greeted with, "Oh, but I guess we forgot to tell you that in this company we are very anxious to keep our reputation for prompt deliveries by having a separate warehouse in every major market area, even if some of them run at a loss." This sends the analyst back to his drawing board. Even though it does endanger the analyst's rapport with his client, it might not be so bad if it caused only a revision or two in each project, but the number of controlling policies that amount to collateral objectives can be very large and so well understood within the organisation that no one bothers to mention them until they are elicited by deep probing or a final report that violates them. A case in point is our example applying linear programming to the scheduling of petroleum blending operations. Our conclusion was that the refinery should produce either regular or premium fuel, but not both. This recommendation would almost certainly be unacceptable, since refineries are generally committed to producing a full line of products. Linear programming, which tends to yield extreme (all or nothing) solutions, is especially likely to recommend insufficient variety of products or action.

Typically where there are manifold objectives, as there nearly always are, some of them are treated within the company as constraints, or limits on the concentration of effort on the attainment of some of the others. In Baumol's experiences, for example, the rate of profit, which economists traditionally regard as a primary objective, tended to play the role of a constraint on efforts to maximise sales volume. How does one tell the difference between a constraint and an objective? In principle, I suppose, it cannot be done. John Dewey taught us long ago that means and ends, constraints and objectives, might roughly be separated for purposes of discussion but were so intimately intertwined that they were fundamentally indistinguishable.

Conceding this, a practicable distinction between constraints and objectives might go as follows: A requirement is a constraint if (*a*) it must not be violated at any cost, however high, or with any probability, however low, and (*b*) there is no gain or advantage in overfulfilling it. On the other hand, a requirement is one of the objectives of the firm if it can be violated, though at a cost or penalty, or if there is an advantage in overfulfilling it. Mixed cases can occur. Thus, if deliveries must be made within two weeks at all cost, and if there is an advantage in quicker deliveries, the maximum delivery time is a constraint while, say, the average delivery time enters into the objective function. If this distinction be accepted it will be seen that only technological requirements will qualify as constraints (*e.g.*, the output of a refinery cannot exceed the volume of crude oil inputs); the attainment of all other requirements is part of the objective. In other words, every practicable design of an operation is subject to failure in sufficiently adverse circumstances; one designs so as to balance the risk of failure against the cost of decreasing that risk. Thus, the use of policy contraints, though prevalent and perhaps inevitable, must entail some loss in attainment of the " real " (alas, inexpressible) purpose of the enterprise.

To get on with the discussion, suppose that it is possible to decide which of the consequences of an operation are constraints and which are objectives. The problem remains of combining the various objectives into a single objective function to be maximised. The difficulties encountered here are familiar to economists for most part, but worth summarising. There is, first of all, the problem of comparing consequences that occur at different times. The comparison of a number of courses of action whose consequences extend over time requires either the comparison of a number of detailed time paths, which is too difficult for most human minds, or some discounting procedure that accords relative values to costs, revenues, etc., at different dates.

The fact that the consequences of decisions are uncertain gives rise to a similar difficulty. The result of a decision or action is not, strictly, a predictable cost or income but a probability distribution of costs or incomes. Hence the comparison of the desirability of consequences presumes that we are able to compare the desirability of probability distributions. Still a third difficulty of the same general type arises from the conundrum that we have already discussed at some length, namely that not all of the consequences of a decision are commensurable in any convenient unit. A more

*

specific example of this difficulty arises in inventory theory. If inventories are adequate or overadequate to meet demand the consequences take the form of sales, carrying charges and the like, all of which are easily measured in dollars. But if inventories are inadequate to meet demand the consequences will lie in a different realm: there will be disruption of production processes, loss of customer's good-will and so on. Ultimately these consequences too may be reflected in dollars and cents, but the measurement of such indirect monetary effects is a research project of forbidding difficulty. In queuing problems, again, the different consequences flowing from the same action tend to be incommensurable.

I have grouped together these three difficulties—time discounting, risk preference and incommensurability of consequences—because they all have to be handled in about the same way. One conceptual approach is to try to construct preference maps. Fisher's theory of interest, for example, applies this construction to the time discount problem. A number of treatments of the risk problem, for instance Shackle's [35] and Markowitz's [29] are based upon it, and its relevance to the incommensurability problem is obvious. This device, however, is little more than a way of formulating the issue, because preference maps are almost impossible to ascertain empirically.

Another approach is to take the position that these complicated, multidimensional consequences are not the ultimate objectives served by the operation but are only intermediate ends to some ultimate, uni-dimensional goal such as maximising the current net worth of the enterprise. This approach requires that we be able to measure the influence of each aspect of the intermediate consequences on the ultimate goal and, as suggested above, this task is generally prohibitively difficult. It amounts, of course, to attempting to construct the overall utility measure that lies behind the preference map utilised in the first approach, and presumes that there is such a measure.

Still another approach is to apply a Paretian criterion as far as it goes and then to turn the task of further evaluation and choice back to the client. The analyst who follows this approach limits himself to seeking efficient decisions, *i.e.*, decisions that cannot be improved in any dimension without an offsetting sacrifice in some other, and leaves it to the client to decide which of all efficient decisions he prefers. Of course, there are other devices, too, familiar to economists, since the problems are familiar ones, which are more effective in eliminating grossly inappropriate decisions than in optimising anything to a very fine degree. A typical one would be to work through the consequences of a decision, find that it would be optimal if the rate of time preference were, say, at least 15% per annum, and then put it up to the client to decide whether his rate of time discounting is in fact that high.

The problem of evaluating risk preferences has received more attention lately than the other two problems because it lies at the heart of statistical decision theory. A number of principles for choosing among policies whose consequences are uncertain have been proposed, all plausible, none free of serious defects; but to discuss them would take us far afield. Illuminating surveys of thinking about decision-making under uncertainty can be found, for example, in Arrow [3] and Luce and Raiffa [25, Ch. 13].

Fortunately, this galaxy of unsolvable problems is less obtrusive in narrow operational contexts than in broad strategic ones. It is easier to ascertain the objectives of a department than of a firm, of a section than of a department, of a particular phase of the work than of a section. There are several reasons for this. First, the narrower the scope of an operation, the narrower is the range of consequences and the greater is the likelihood that all of them will be commensurable, usually in terms of dollars. Linear programming models are cases in point, though queuing and inventory models are contrary instances. Second, departmental and subdepartmental decisions frequently concern matters that have short time horizons; often all the consequences are practically immediate. Nearly all the models discussed above except the inventory models illustrate this assertion. Finally, the range of uncertainty associated with detailed operating decisions is generally smaller than that surrounding more comprehensive choices and, besides, the range of uncertainty engendered by each operating decision is small enough in relation to the size of the enterprise, and such decisions are numerous enough so that they can be treated appropriately from an actuarial point of view.

For all these reasons the objectives of operations conducted at the middling and lower levels of an enterprise are likely to be fairly well defined. There is, however, one special danger that arises when an objective function is devised for a part of an organisation or a specific operation. This is the danger that economies and diseconomies external to the department in question will be neglected. When an objective function is adopted for, say, a department, that department and the operations analysts who advise it will be induced to make the choices that seem optimal in the light of that function. Therefore it is important that such partial objective functions conduce to decisions that are consistent with the overall goals of the enterprise. Unfortunately, it is just about impossible to find performance criteria that meet this requirement in all circumstances. A lurid example of this difficulty arose in war-time operations research in the air force, where the efficiency of bombing groups was judged in large part by the percentage of their bombs that fell within a thousand feet of the targets they aimed at. This standard encouraged bombing commanders to refrain from releasing bombs when visibility was poor. The effectiveness of the bombing groups went down while their paper scores went up.

The same conflict between real and paper performance occurs in business operations. Suppose, for example, that a manufacturing department is given the objective of producing its assigned output at minimum average cost. Then the manager being judged by this criterion has a strong incentive: (*a*) to avoid overtime work even though other departments or customers may urgently require his output, and (*b*) to shave his specifications in a way that will increase the proportion of rejects at a later stage of fabrication. Any simple criterion of departmental performance must therefore be hedged by some artificial standards or constraints—like the subsidiary objectives discussed above—for example, quality standards and regulations about permissible delays in delivery. The shortcomings of such standards have already been mentioned.

This is probably as good a place as any to call attention to another pitfall in the selection of objective functions or performance criteria. This is the seductive simplicity of critical ratios like cost per unit, output per man-hour, or the one I used in the dragline example, cubic yards per operating hour.[1] Such ratios are invariably dangerous, as Hitch and McKean, particularly, emphasise [21]. Consider the dragline case. The criterion I suggested would discourage excavating to the very edge or bottom of the vein, even though it would be profitable to do so, since doing so would reduce the time-rate of excavation. There are two fallacies tucked away in my criterion. First, it assumes that dragline time is the only scarce resource, and encourages economising it at the expense of all other resources, such as excavated ore. Second, it is a ratio and, as economists are well aware, the objectives of an operation are almost invariably to maximise some difference (some measure of benefit minus some measure of cost) rather than any ratio. Profit maximisation is not the same thing as unit cost minimisation.

Thus, there are dangers in assigning objectives to parts of an enterprise, but they are far more tractable than the problems encountered in trying to establish objectives for an enterprise as a whole. Because of the relative concreteness of the purposes of parts of an enterprise, suboptimisation is a valuable concept and applicable even when overall goals must remain vague. Suboptimisation will be treated briefly in the final section.

IV. The Role of Operations Research

Such is the nature of operations research. I hope that I have made an adequate case for the assertion that its essence lies in a strong tendency to tackle administrative problems via formal models constructed in the spirit of the natural sciences. We turn now, and finally, to the role of operations research in business and economic administration.

If an experienced operations analyst were asked to describe the problem he would most like to meet, I suspect that he would mention four characteristics: first, the objective of the operation should be clearly defined, second, the operation should be describable by a reasonably manageable model, third, the data required for estimating the parameters of the model should

[1] In fairness to Dunlap and his associates I must point out that a somewhat more sophisticated objective function was used in the actual study, though the published report did not define it precisely [15, p. 182].

be readily obtainable, and fourth, current operating practice should leave plenty of room for improvement. These are the characteristics of the ideal problem, from the analyst's point of view, and sometimes he encounters it, but more often he must be content with projects that fall short of perfection in one respect or another. Each of these characteristics deserves a little discussion.

For an operation to have a clearly defined objective it is not necessary, of course, that the businessman or other client be able to write down its objective function at a moment's notice. It does require that the analyst be able to obtain a consensus on the purpose of the operation specific enough so that he can judge how conflicts in goals are to be resolved. With a little care to assure that the objective function does not conflict with higher-level goals and that the measure of cost is appropriate, the definition of objectives should present little difficulty at the operating levels. More trouble is likely to occur at the executive levels, where decisions are likely to have widespread and incommensurable ramifications. Glen Camp, in fact, warns against undertaking such problems: ". . . best results will be obtained if the scientist meticulously avoids the evaluation of intangibles" [11, p. 630]. The narrower and more specific the problem, then the more likely it is to possess this characteristic.

The second characteristic of a promising project was that it be possible to formulate a manageable model to describe the impact of various possible decisions on the objective function. Again we may cite Glen Camp: "The function of the operations research team is to assist the responsible authority of an organization by clarifying those uncertainties in the factors on which action is based, and *only* those, which can be clarified by scientific study" [11, p. 629]. Now, how is one to tell, in a preliminary survey of a problem, whether its essence can be caught in a manageable model or whether, in Camp's words, it can be clarified by scientific study?

Model building is the analyst's primary skill and contribution, and he cannot expect when he approaches a problem to find that his work has already been done for him. Thus, the question is not whether a model exists ready-to-hand, but whether one can be built in reasonable time. The answer depends basically on whether or not the problem involves kinds of relationships that have not been established by previous scientific study or, as I shall say, whether or not it involves gaps in fundamental scientific knowledge. Consider, for example, the advertising fable that we used to characterise the operations analytic approach. In that fable the analyst boldly extemporised a model of the relationship of advertising expenditure to sales. It was, of course, a shot in the dark. No one really knows what the relationship in question is. The problem involved a gap in scientific knowledge.

When he encounters such a gap the operations analyst has a choice of three options: he can proceed on the basis of a bold conjecture, he can undertake the substantive research necessary to fill the gap or he can abandon the problem as unsolvable at the current state of knowledge. Much of the analyst's skill lies in determining which option to choose in given circumstances. A bold conjecture is refreshing, but an insubstantial foundation for an important decision. Abandoning the project is manifestly distasteful. Undertaking fundamental research entails the usual hazard that it may not be successful, plus an unwelcome delay in arriving at a useful recommendation.

In practice, this third option is frequently chosen and frequently well advised. Much of the work of the practising analyst is the work of filling gaps in substantive knowledge, just as much of the value of the model-building approach resides in disclosing and defining those gaps. There is much testimony to indicate that the most valuable results of operations research are by-products. Again and again businessmen have stated gratefully that they learned more about their business by answering an analyst's questions, supplying data for his model and checking over the model with him than they did from his final report. (Is the analogy with psycho-analysis a coincidence?) Similarly, the substantive research undertaken as part of an operations research project is often of great value, quite apart from the value of the final recommendations.[1] Thus, the attempt to construct a model may be worthwhile, even in unpromising circumstances.

But not always. Frequently the gaps in knowledge that prevent constructing a reliable model are already perfectly well known to the client, and not of a kind to be filled by short-term research. The advertising fable is, very likely, a case in point. Such gaps in knowledge are frequently what induce the client to call in the operations analyst. If he could fill them he could solve the problem himself, and his hope is that the magic of operations research will help him to reach a well-founded decision in spite of certain areas of ignorance. Such hopes are doomed to disappointment. Operations research is not a substitute for substantive knowledge but a way of employing it, nor can the operations analyst be expected to complete scientific knowledge to order as required by his clients.

If gaps in substantive knowledge prevent the formulation of a complete model clearly the analyst cannot hope to ascertain the optimal decision. He may then address himself to a more modest, but still useful goal, as pointed out by P. M. S. Blackett in one of the earliest and most important papers on operations-research methodology [8]. He can seek to discover a policy that is better than the current one, though not necessarily best. This approach is one that economists are schooled in. Blackett recommended that instead of attempting to ascertain the objective function as a function of the various decision variables, the analyst undertake the much easier task of estimating its partial derivatives with respect to each decision variable

[1] For a famous and fascinating illustration see Thornthwaite, " Operations Research in Agriculture " [27, pp. 368–80].

(essentially the net marginal productivities of the decision variables) in the neighbourhood of the currently used values of those variables. If any of those partial derivatives is substantially different from zero (*i.e.*, if any marginal productivity is substantially different from the corresponding marginal cost), then a direction in which current policies can be improved is apparent.

Just as the operations-research approach is not peculiarly adapted to solving fresh scientific questions, so it is not well adapted to discovering fresh lines of action or technological innovations (with an exception to be noted below). A range of possible actions or decisions is built into the model from the outset; the solution of the model yields the best solution within that range. For example, linear programming yields the optimal combination of the activities listed in the matrix; it will not disclose the existence of some still better activity not foreseen in advance. In short, the technique of operations research is designed to uncover better ways of organising the use of given resources by means of given techniques; it does not extend the range of technical possibilities.

This is not to say that operations analysts have not been instrumental in technical innovations. They are typically imaginative and resourceful men, unfettered by traditions of which they are frequently unaware, and often do suggest courses of action that would never occur to men schooled in the habits of an enterprise or branch of technology. But the methods of operations research are of little help in the field of substantive invention, though the practitioners often do have patents to their credit.

There is, however, one field of operations research that does bear directly on the process of technical invention, namely "requirements studies." In a requirements study an operation is surveyed in order to determine the characteristics of desirable technical innovations. Models are built which incorporate as yet non-existent hardware, and the performance characteristics of the hardware are varied (on paper) in order to ascertain their influence on the overall operation. Thus, a set of specifications for new equipment can be established and the gain flowing from meeting those specifications can be estimate. This type of analysis has been most prevalent in establishing military requirements—the RAND Corporation was studying the usefulness of artificial satellites as early as 1946—and has also been used by commercial airlines in planning for new equipment. Thus, studies are now in progress on the usefulness of supersonic passenger aircraft.

The third characteristic of a promising operations-research project was that an adequate fund of experience be available to permit statistical estimation of the parameters required by the model. This requirement will be satisfied most adequately by repetitious, even routine, types of operation. Morse and Kimball, for example, state, "Patrol or search is an operation which is peculiarly amenable to operations research. The action is simple, and repeated often enough under conditions sufficiently similar to enable satisfactory data to be accumulated" [32, p. 38]. Nearly all our examples, indeed, have been of this sort. They concerned scheduling a refinery, which is done at least once a month, re-ordering inventories, similarly periodic, and so on. In all such repetitive decisions the necessary statistics are accumulated over time as an administrative by-product if not as part of a formal reporting system. If the requisite statistics are not available the situation is analogous to that which occurs when there is a gap in scientific knowledge, discussed above, except that gathering statistics is less of a gamble than undertaking to establish a new scientific relationship.

If the problem being studied is non-repetitive even the statistical outlook is more doubtful, since, after all, statistics require a population from which a sample can be drawn. The statistical characteristic also, therefore, is more likely to be fulfilled at the operating levels of an enterprise than at the highest executive levels, since operating decisions are much less likely than broad policy and strategy decisions to be *sui generis*.

The final characteristic of a promising operations-research study was that current operations admit of substantial improvement by means of the kinds of decisions discoverable by studying the operation of a model. This last characteristic, unfortunately, works somewhat in opposition to the first three. If an operation is repetitive, well recorded, intended to serve a well-defined goal and of a kind in which the influences of decisions on the attainment of the goal do not transcend available technical knowledge, then it is not likely that current practice will fall far short of the most efficient practice attainable. And, indeed, the usual upshot of a linear programming analysis or a transportation problem study is to find a plan that will reduce costs by 2 or 3 or 5%. To be sure, in a large operation, 5% is not contemptible. But neither is it dramatic; and in view of the approximations used in reaching such solutions and the possible errors in the statistical estimates it cannot even be certain that such small savings are genuine rather than paper results. This finding stands in unhappy contrast to the state of affairs during the Second World War, on the basis of which Morse and Kimball wrote, ". . . successful application of operations research usually results in improvements by factors of 3 or 10 or more" [32, p. 38]. This is as if a successful operations-research project can be expected to treble the capacity of a factory or divide its unit costs by three.

The contrast between the peace-time and war-time yields of operations research is explained by the fact that the Second World War was largely a race of technological improvements. Efficient submarines led to the development of airborne search-radar; airborne search-radar induced the invention of snorkel-equipped submarines. Technological innovations followed each other so quickly that a new device was in the field before trial-and-error methods could discover efficient means for employing its predecessor. Operations research proved to be a very effective means for accelerating the discovery of effective ways of using novel equipment. In more stable circumstances, however, the situation is otherwise. Blackett, also relying on war-time experience, wrote, ". . . in the course of repeated operations by many different participants, most of the possible variations of tactics will be effectively explored, so that any large derivatives will eventually be discovered, and given intelligent control, improved tactics will become generally adopted" [8, p. 33]. On the other hand, considerable room for improvement may remain even under fairly stable technological conditions, as the dragline example showed. The explanation in that instance probably lay in the numerousness and the complexity of the decision variables, which precluded efficient exploration of possibilities by unsystematic means.

These considerations suggest that in just those kinds of business operation in which the first three requirements for productive operations research are likely to be met, the requirements for the discovery of efficient methods by more traditional means are also likely to be met, and there may not be very much improvement left for the operations analyst to discover. The major exception to this conclusion is problems of adapting to new circumstances or of employing novel techniques or instruments. In those cases operations research can often speed up the process of adaptation. An optimal situation for operations research is one in which conditions are changing too rapidly for experience to be assimilated by informal, unsystematic methods, but slowly enough to permit the formulation of a model applicable to both the recent past and relevant future, and to permit the accumulation of the data needed for estimating the parameters of the model.

All in all, conditions auspicious for operations research are more likely to be met at the middling and lower levels of an organisation than at the topmost ones: the clarity of objectives, the simplicity of relationships and the availability of technical knowledge and statistical data all point in this direction. Thus, the device of "suboptimisation" recommends itself. Suboptimisation is defined by Hitch and McKean, its principal expositors, as the ". . . process of choosing among a relatively small number of alternatives by an administrative level other than the highest" [21, p. 172]. More explicitly it is the organisational policy in which the higher echelons of an organisation assign tasks to the lower echelons and establish performance criteria for them, and then leave the lower echelons free to perform the tasks in the best way they can as judged by the criteria established. That, after all, is how a market economy works. Suboptimisation is a new word for decentralisation, and its advantages are the familiar advantages of decentralisation. From the point of view of operations research, its major advantage is that it enables the relatively manageable problems of detailed operation to be solved separately from each other and from the more intractable problems that arise on the higher executive levels.

The foregoing summarises the circumstances in which operations research is likely to be successful in the sense of disclosing significantly improved policies and practices. But operations research can be successful in other senses also. We have already noted the educative value of collaborating with an analyst and looking at problems from his viewpoint. We have seen that operations research often suggests and sometimes accomplishes valuable substantive research. In many instances the contribution of operations research is to improve the planning process itself, without improving the quality of the plans.

Consider planning petroleum refinery operations, which now is quite prevalently accomplished with the use of programming models. Before programming was introduced, monthly refinery schedules were developed by a planning section in the refinery engineer's department and required about two weeks of computation by highly trained engineering personnel. After a programming system is introduced the same plans are developed in three or four hours by clerical personnel and computing machine operators under the general supervision of an engineer. The new planning system has at least three advantages over the old one, even though the resultant plans are not appreciably superior to those developed by tedious hand calculations using the same data. First, it is vastly cheaper in terms of both monetary cost and drain on scarce, highly trained man-power. Second, because of its speed, more timely data can be employed. Before the mechanised planning made possible by operations research, the forecasts for, say, the March plan had to be based on data available on February 14; after mechanisation the closing date for forecast data becomes February 26. Thus, even where programming does not produce superior plans given the same data, the speed with which it can be performed permits the use of improved data. Third, the probabilities of errors in both arithmetic and judgment are greatly reduced when formalised, mechanised planning supersedes informal, skilled-judgment methods. The programming procedure includes a built-in guarantee that the resulting plan is optimal, avoiding the hankering worry that a misjudgment was made somewhere in a protracted computation.

In more general terms, where plans or decisions are based on large masses of data and complicated inter-relationships—where, for example, a large number of operations have to be co-ordinated—the model developed by an operations-research study provides a framework within which the data can be assembled, analysed and digested in a swift, mechanical, error-free and inexpensive way. Such a model makes the planning process itself more efficient and reliable.

Finally, consider the really tough and important problems where there is no objective basis for making a usefully precise evaluation of the consequences of possible actions or policies. Contending with such imponderables is the primary responsibility of the high executive, a responsibility that cannot be delegated, not even to an operations analyst. Nevertheless, an operations-research study of such a problem can help the executive by organising the data, focusing the issues, bringing out the implications of possible assumptions and hunches, delimiting the range of the inevitable uncertainty. Any detached, analytic, sceptical viewpoint can help clarify such problems, and the analyst has such a viewpoint to contribute.

There is much room for folly, though, when an operations analyst participates in conjecturing answers to unanswerable questions. The executive is under a strong temptation to pass the buck to the analyst, and the analyst is tempted just as strongly to accept it. When there is no "right" decision there is a tendency to adopt one that can be justified—for who can be blamed for following a recommendation supported by an imposing dossier? And what dossier is more imposing, these days, than an operations-research report? Thus, the analyst may find that his simplifying assumptions, perhaps made for exploratory purposes, have become the basis for weighty decisions, even decisions important to the safety of the nation.

It is all very well to inveigh against the executive who permits his judgment to be overborne by elaborate calculations that he does not understand. Though the executive must retain the responsibility, he must also accept much on faith, and when his analyst assures him that the recommendations are well-founded, what is he to do? The businessman cannot audit the technical reasoning. Though the analyst can remain detached and impartial as regards the affairs of his client, he is as liable as any man to fall under the spell of his own handiwork. I see no satisfying way to resolve this difficulty. Glen Camp, as we saw, advised analysts to abstain from such dangerous enterprises but also, as we remarked, the analyst can serve usefully in smoothing the way for a decision. The accumulation of experience in the use of operations research will probably help some, particularly by reducing the pressure on the analyst to produce clear-cut recommendations.

It appears, in summary, that operations research is best adapted to dealing with routine, semi-technical, quantifiable problems, and that it can also contribute in a larger realm by showing businessmen how to view their problems from a sophisticated scientific standpoint. It has developed powerful methods for solving the day-to-day problems of middle management and, I think, can fairly claim to be an indispensable tool at that level. Operations analysts aspire higher, of course.[1] But when they will attain a special competence in dealing with larger, more conjectural problems is itself a very conjectural question.

We noted at the outset that operations research is dominated by, and takes its style from, men trained in the natural sciences. There is, however, a large handful of practising operations analysts who were trained as economists and, permitting myself a parochial evaluation, these men have contributed to the development of the science far out of proportion to their numbers. The economist comes to operations research with a number of important ideas already instilled, among them an appreciation of the importance of substitution, a sophistication about the objectives of enterprises,

[1] See, for example, Ellis A. Johnson [22] and Russel Ackoff [1].

an awareness of the importance of marginal trade-offs and, most important, a realisation that physical quantities are subsidiary to " values " in a decision process. He also inherits from his training a number of disabilities, including ignorance of the technical side of business and industry and a belief in the existence of production functions. On balance, it appears that the older science has more to contribute to the younger than the other way round, as is right and proper. But still we can learn from our juniors, and we fail to do so at our own risk.

The most important lessons operations research has to teach is how much we are asking of businessmen when we ask them to behave " rationally." Even when businessmen would dearly like to do so, it turns out that the most powerful tools of mathematics cannot, for example, help them discover a " rational " inventory policy; and that is only one small part of the businessman's problem. Since the profit-maximising or risk-minimising course of action is undiscoverable, he must perforce rely on hunches and rules of thumb. It is by no means clear what rational behaviour consists of in such circumstances. On the other hand, it turns out that business performance is frequently quite close to the rational optimum for problems of the sort that operations research is able to solve.

Thus, the lesson of operations research appears to be a heavy score against the belief that firms maximise anything, either in the short run or the long. Instead we must conceive of actual firms as operating according to certain rules of thumb that would be rational if life were much simpler than it is and that are not disastrous under actual circumstances. It makes one tolerant of such practices as pricing by conventional mark-ups, costing with conventional overhead burdens and investing in accordance with tried and proven pay-off periods. These practices are what businessmen must follow until operations research provides them with better standards. The success of operations research testifies to the willingness of businessmen to abandon operation by rule-of-thumb when a better alternative becomes available. The best we can say is that businessmen would like to behave " rationally " and are eager to be taught how.

For many purposes of economic analysis the current crude image of the firm, as a responsive extension of the personality of a fully informed, aggressive entrepreneur, is probably adequate. But for some other purposes —the understanding of inventory and investment behaviour, for example— we must recognise the firm for what operations research has disclosed it to be: often fumbling, sluggish, timid, uncertain and perplexed by unsolvable problems. Since its discriminating power is low, it responds only to gross stimuli; since its decision processes are uncertain the timing and vigour of its responses are unpredictable. It reacts in familiar ways to the familiar and avoids the novel as long as it dares. We need economic theories that incorporate these ingredients. They will remain valid until operations research has made much more progress against businessmen's problems.

REFERENCES

1. R. L. Ackoff, "Operations Research and National Planning," *Op. Res.*, Aug. 1957, **5**, 457–68.
2. American Management Association, "Progress in Industrial Operations Research, Results of a Survey," *Management News*, Dec. 1957.
3. K. J. Arrow, "Alternative Approaches to the Theory of Choice in Risk-Taking Situations," *Econometrica*, Oct. 1951, **19**, 404–37.
4. K. J. Arrow, S. Karlin and H. Scarf, *Studies in the Mathematical Theory of Inventory and Production.* Stanford 1958.
5. W. J. Baumol, "On the Theory of Oligopoly," *Economica*, Aug. 1958, N. S. **25**, 187–98.
6. ——, "Activity Analysis in One Lesson," *Am. Econ. Rev.*, Dec. 1958, **48**, 837–73.
7. R. Bellman, *Dynamic Programming.* Princeton 1957.
8. P. M. S. Blackett, "Operational Research," *Advancement of Sci.*, Apr. 1948, **5**, 26–38.
9. G. E. P. Box, "The Exploration and Exploitation of Response Surfaces," *Biometrics*, Mar. 1954, **10**, 16–60.
10. S. H. Brooks, "A Comparison of Maximum-seeking Methods," *Op. Res.*, July–Aug. 1959, **7**, 430–57.
11. G. D. Camp, "Operations Research: The Science of Generalized Strategies and Tactics," *Textile Res. Jour.*, July 1955, **25**, 629–34.
12. A. Charnes, W. W. Cooper and B. Mellon, "Blending Aviation Gasolines —A Study in Programming Interdependent Activities in an Integrated Oil Company," *Econometrica*, Apr. 1952, **20**, 135–59.
13. C. W. Churchman, R. L. Ackoff and E. L. Arnoff, *Introduction to Operations Research.* New York 1957.
14. R. Dorfman, "Mathematical or Linear Programming: A Non-Mathematical Exposition," *Am. Econ. Rev.*, Dec. 1953, **43**, 797–825.
15. J. W. Dunlap and H. H. Jacobs, "Strip Mining Phosphate Rock with Large Walking Draglines" [26, Ch. 9].
16. A. Dvoretzky, J. Kiefer and J. Wolfowitz, "On the Optimal Character of the (s,S) Policy in Inventory Theory," *Econometrica*, Oct. 1953, **21**, 586–96.
17. L. R. Ford, Jr. and D. R. Fulkerson, "Solving the Transportation Problem," *Mgt. Sci.*, Oct. 1956, **3**, 24–32.
18. ——, "A Primal Dual Algorithm for the Capacitated Hitchcock Problem," *Nav. Res. Log. Quart.*, Mar. 1957, **4**, 47–54.
19. R. E. Gomory and W. J. Baumol, "Integer Programming and Pricing." *Econometrica*, forthcoming.
20. J. M. Henderson, *The Efficiency of the Coal Industry.* Cambridge, Mass. 1958.
21. C. Hitch and R. C. McKean, "Suboptimization in Operations Problems" [27, 168–86].
22. E. A. Johnson, "The Long-range Future of Operations Research," *Op. Res.*, Jan.–Feb. 1960, **8**, 1–23.
23. B. O. Koopman, "Fallacies in Operations Research," *Op. Res.*, Aug. 1956, **4**, 422–26.
24. R. F. Lanzillotti, "Pricing Objectives in Large Companies," *Am. Econ. Rev.*, Dec. 1958, **48**, 921–40.
25. R. D. Luce and H. Raiffa, *Games and Decisions.* New York 1957.
26. J. F. McCloskey and J. M. Coppinger, ed., *Operations Research for Management*, Vol. II. Baltimore 1956.
27. J. F. McCloskey and F. N. Trefethen, ed., *Operations Research for Management*, Vol. I. Baltimore 1954.

28. A. S. Manne, *Scheduling of Petroleum Refinery Operations*. Cambridge, Mass. 1956.
29. H. M. Markowitz, *Portfolio Selection*. New York 1959.
30. H. M. Markowitz and A. S. Manne, " On the Solution of Discrete Programming Problems," *Econometrica*, Jan. 1957, **25**, 84–110.
31. P. M. Morse, *Queues, Inventories and Maintenance*. New York 1958.
32. P. M. Morse and G. E. Kimball, *Methods of Operations Research*. New York 1951.
33. E. S. Olcott, " The Influence of Vehicular Speed and Spacing on Tunnel Capacity " [26, Ch. 3].
34. R. Schlaifer, *Probability and Statistics for Business Decisions*. New York 1959.
35. G. L. S. Shackle, *Expectation in Economics*. Cambridge 1949.
36. C. E. Shannon and W. Weaver, *The Mathematical Theory of Communication*. Urbana 1949.
37. H. A. Simon, " Theories of Decision-Making in Economics," *Am. Econ. Rev.*, June 1959, **49**, 253–83.
38. C. J. Thomas and W. L. Deemer, Jr., " The Role of Operational Gaming in Operations Research," *Op. Res.*, Feb. 1957, **5**, 1–27.
39. A. Vazsonyi, *Scientific Programming in Business and Industry*. New York 1958.
40. T. M. Whitin, *The Theory of Inventory Management*. Princeton 1953.

XI
LINEAR THEORY

By

J. R. HICKS[1]

THE subject which I shall be discussing in this survey concerns the group of techniques—Linear Programming, Activity Analysis, Input–Output and Theory of Games[2]—which have come to us, chiefly from America, during the last fifteen years. It is apparent, from the most casual inspection of these topics, that they are very closely related. Further examination shows that they can be set around a recognisable core, which may be regarded as a restatement of a central part of conventional economic theory. It will be my object, in what follows, to isolate this core; and to consider what there is that the economist, who has no intention of becoming a practitioner of the techniques, may yet have to learn from it.[3]

This being the intention, it will obviously be proper to put what I have to say into a form in which the mathematics are kept down as much as possible; but it is useless to conceal from the reader that we are dealing with a mathematical subject. The phenomenon which we are to examine is the application to economics of a new kind of mathematics. The most obvious difference between this new mathematical economics and the older variety (which goes back to Cournot) lies in the kind of mathematics that is being used.

All through the " neo-classical " period—in the age of Marshall, of Pareto, of Wicksell, even in that of Pigou and Keynes—the economist's

[1] The author is Fellow of All Souls College, Oxford; when he wrote this Survey, he was Drummond Professor of Political Economy in the University of Oxford.

[2] I shall have much less to say about game theory than about the others.

[3] My purpose is therefore quite different from that of the numerous text-books which seek to teach the techniques to the practitioners. It is, however, not far from that which might have been expected from the authors of *Linear Programming and Economic Analysis* (Dorfman, Samuelson and Solow); it is certainly true that without their work the present paper could not have been written. My main criticism of their performance is that they did not sufficiently differentiate their task from that of the text-books. I accordingly propose to begin in quite a different way from that in which they begin, though in the latter stages of my work I shall draw on them very heavily. (It would then be a great nuisance not to have a single name for this composite author; I shall make bold to christen him, when I need to do so, DOSSO.)

Reference must also be made to the excellent survey by W. J. Baumol ("Activity Analysis in one Lesson," *A.E.R.*, December 1958). His purpose has been nearer to mine, but I think he would be the first to admit that there is room for both of us.

The text-books from which I have derived most benefit are those of S. Vajda (*Theory of Games and Linear Programming*) and S. I. Gass (*Linear Programming*). Both of these are highly mathematical; but they have helped me to grasp the structure of the theory (with which I shall be largely concerned) more clearly than I could get it elsewhere.

main mathematical tool was the differential calculus, expressed (when necessary) in the form of symbols, reduced (when possible) to the form of curves. This, of course, was perfectly natural; most economic problems were problems of maxima and minima, and (since the days of Newton and Leibniz) the differential calculus has been the standard method by which such problems had been approached. It has, however, long been known that there are some quite elementary maximum problems (such, for instance, as those concerned with perimeters of triangles) for which the calculus method is not at all well suited; they may, however, give no trouble if they are tackled on an *ad hoc* basis, usually in Euclidean terms. The development of systematic methods for the study of such cases as these has been an object to which, in our time, quite formidable mathematical ability has been devoted. And the new methods, once found, have often proved to be more satisfactory than the old, even in fields where it is possible for both to be applied.[1] The linear theory, which we are to examine, derives much of its character from the fact that it is an application of some of these newer mathematical methods to economics.[2]

So much must be said, even at the start; though it is inevitable that by saying it one raises the suspicion that economics is being used as a mere opportunity for mathematical exercise, valuable enough to the mathematicians who disport themselves upon this parade-ground, but with a marginal product (in terms of the things in which economists are interested) that is, after all, infinitesimal. I would not myself deny that there is something in this. It is easy to find pieces of "activity analysis" that do no more than re-state a fairly obvious point in esoteric terms. Nevertheless, after all discounting, there are substantial things that remain. Most obviously, there are the contributions which have been made by the associated techniques to the solution of certain kinds of business (or other practical economic) problems; but these, though their importance is unquestionable, will not be our main concern in what follows. The contributions which have been made by the new methods to economic theory look, at first sight, much slighter. One cannot claim much more for most of them than that they are improvements in the statements we can now make of familiar points: things of which

[1] Thus Hardy, Littlewood and Polya (*Inequalities*, p. 108), writing (in 1934) of a distinct but related field: "The (calculus) method is attractive theoretically, and always opens a first line of attack on the problem; but is apt to lead to serious complications in detail (usually connected with the boundary values of the variables) and it will be found that, however suggestive, it rarely leads to the simplest solution." As we shall see, it is much the same story here.

[2] Since my own formal mathematical education (such as it was) ended in 1923, I do not pretend that I myself feel at all at home with these newer methods. I can, however, feel fairly confident about the use which I have had to make of them, because of the advice which I have received from a number of experts. My greatest debt is to Dr. H. W. Kuhn (of Princeton), who was spending the year of 1958–59 in London, and who was kind enough to criticise a first draft in considerable detail. Afterwards, in California and in Japan, I had the benefit of consultations with Michio Morishima, with Kenneth Arrow and with George Dantzig himself. To each of these (and also to the Assistant Editor of this Journal, who called my attention to a qualification not easy to disentangle from the literature) I offer my thanks.

we were (more or less) aware, but which one can now realise that we were putting rather badly. I shall consider such matters in some detail. I would, however, maintain that they are chiefly worth considering because they do carry with them a deepening in our understanding of something that is rather central—nothing less than the ends–means relationship which is what so much of economics is about. Something of that will, I hope, emerge before I have finished.

I. Origins

It is convenient to let the story begin from a simple pedagogic point.

Anyone who has attempted to put the Walrasian theory of general equilibrium (with fixed coefficients of production) on to a classroom diagram will have had something like the following experience. One cuts it down to the simplest possible case—two goods and two factors. Measuring quantities of the two goods along two axes, one gets a diagram such as that shown in Fig. 1. The quantities of the two goods that can be produced with a

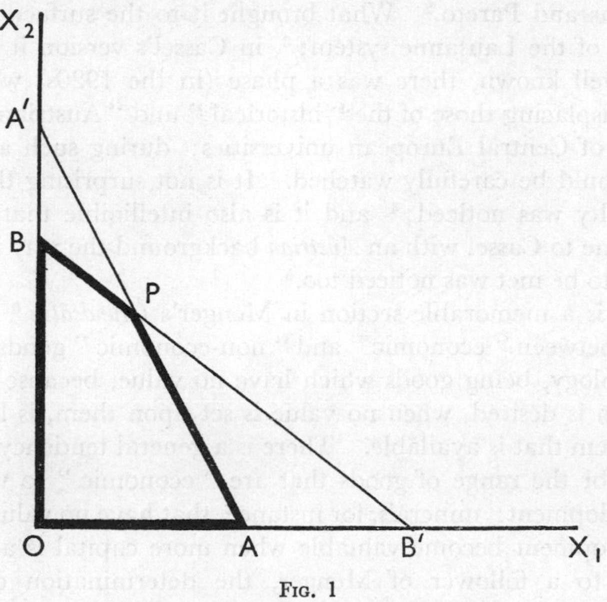

Fig. 1

given supply of factor *A* are shown by the straight line *AA′*; the quantities that can be produced with a given supply of factor *B* are shown by the line *BB′*; thus it is *only* the set of quantities represented by *P*, the point of intersection, that *can* be produced, so long as one assumes (as Walras assumed) that both factors are to be kept fully employed. The quantities of products, and the quantities of factors employed in the production of each, seem therefore to be determined, before anything has been said about prices, or about demands. The general equilibrium system, which is supposed to show the way in which output adjusts itself to demand through the price-mechanism, has the serious defect, when it is regarded as a means of teaching economics: that in the simplest example, the example which it is most natural to take as an illustration, it does not work.

Now, it is, of course, true that as soon as we introduce another product (or, more generally, so long as we keep the number of products greater than the number of factors) the difficulty disappears, or at any rate becomes less acute. The quantities of products cease to be technologically determined, so that the price-mechanism can begin to function. For many Walrasians [1] that has been enough. The case of fixed coefficients, with fixed supplies of factors, has been for them no more than a stepping-stone on the way to something more general; the rigidities which appear in the elementary case have not therefore seemed to be so very interesting. Yet it must be admitted to be a defect in a theory that it does not clear up its own elementary cases. Mere consideration of the elementary case is enough to show that the Walras theory cannot be quite right.

It does not appear that much attention was paid to this weakness in the days of Walras and Pareto.[2] What brought it to the surface was Cassel's simplification of the Lausanne system; [3] in Cassel's version it rather stood out. As is well known, there was a phase (in the 1920s) when Cassel's treatise was displacing those of the " historical " and " Austrian " schools in the curricula of Central European universities; during such a struggle its weaknesses would be carefully watched. It is not surprising that this particular difficulty was noticed; [4] and it is also intelligible that by some of those who came to Cassel with an *Austrian* background the way in which the difficulty has to be met was noticed too.[5]

For there is a memorable section in Menger's *Grundsätze* [6] in which he distinguishes between " economic " and " non-economic " goods—the latter, in his terminology, being goods which have no value, because the amount of them which is desired, when no value is set upon them, is less than the quantity of them that is available. There is a general tendency (so Menger maintained) for the range of goods that are " economic " to widen in the course of development; minerals, for instance, that have no value at an early stage of development become valuable when more capital is accumulated. Accordingly, to a follower of Menger, the determination of economic equilibrium would not merely involve the determination of the prices of those goods that have prices (as in Walras); it should also involve the

[1] Including the present author, when he wrote *Value and Capital* (1939).

[2] It should be noticed that Walras' basic fixed-coefficient model did not assume fixed factor-supplies.

[3] *Theory of Social Economy*, Part II.

[4] See the discussion of W. L. Valk's *Principles of Wages* (1928) in D. H. Robertson " Wage Grumbles " (*Economic Fragments*, p. 52).

[5] Articles by Neisser (*Weltwirtschaftsliches Archiv*, 1932), Stackelberg (*Zeitschrift für Nationalökonomie*, 1933) and Zeuthen (also in *Zeitschrift für Nationalökonomie*, 1933) are widely quoted.

[6] Chapter 2.

determination of which goods are to have prices, and which are to be free. The weakness of the Walras–Cassel construction lies in the implied assumption that the whole amount of each available factor is utilised; once that assumption is dropped, the awkwardness of the construction (even in the two-good, two-factor case) can be shown to disappear.

It is at once apparent, if we drop the assumption that both factors must be fully utilised, that the possible combinations of products that can be produced from available resources are not confined (in Fig. 1) to the point P; they comprise all those combinations that are represented by the whole area $OAPB$. Nor is P the only *efficient* combination; for if product X_2 were not *wanted*, OA would be the maximum amount of X_1 that could be produced; there would be a sense in which production would be maximised all along the broken line APB. The only peculiarity of the point P is that it is the only point at which both factors are scarce. If we do not assume that, the whole of APB becomes a *frontier*. As demand varies, the equilibrium point can move from one end of this frontier to the other. Throughout the whole of this process the price-mechanism is working.

It is easy for the " intuition " of the " literary " economist to get that far; but there would have been little progress beyond that point if it had not been for the mathematicians. It was the fact that mathematical methods were being prepared, which were capable of dealing with the equilibrium of a system which is restricted by inequalities, that made it possible to go on. The next events to be recorded are therefore the appearance of two mathematical papers, which I shall make no attempt to discuss in detail, but which must be mentioned, since from them everything subsequent has sprung. An attempt will be made later to describe the substance of their contributions in different terms.

The first of these papers, in order of publication, was the "proof," by Abraham Wald, of the existence of an equilibrium of the Walras–Cassel system, extended (as just explained) so as to allow for the possibility of free, as well as scarce, factors. This was not in fact a satisfactory proof, since it assumed that the demands for products would not fall to zero, however high prices rose—an assumption that can hardly be admitted. It did nevertheless establish that the " extended " system is capable of mathematical manipulation; it may therefore be said to mark the first stage in the process by which the "Austrians" had their mathematical revenge on the followers of Walras.[1]

[1] Wald's paper was presented (with an introduction by Karl Schlesinger) to a seminar in Vienna presided over by Karl Menger (mathematician son of the economist Menger) in March 1934. It was printed in *Ergebnisse eines mathematischen Kolloquiums*, Heft 6, 1935. There is a further paper in the following issue of the same publication, and an article (which, among other things, summarises the results of these mathematical papers) in *Zeitschrift für Nationalökonomie*, 1936. The *Zeitschrift* article was translated into English (*Econometrica*, 1951).

The reasons which led Wald to make his curious assumption about demand functions have been explored by Dr. Kuhn (" On a Theorem of Wald " in *Linear Inequalities and Related Systems*, Annals of Mathematics Studies 38, Princeton, 1956). I shall be returning to this matter later. (See below, p. 103.)

Much more important, for what followed, was the other: the famous paper by John von Neumann "A Model of General Economic Equilibrium" (to give it the title by which it is known to English readers).[1] It has been the extraordinary achievement of this work that it has had a profound influence on the development of economic thinking in several different directions. As a dynamic model of an expanding economy, it has been the father of many growth models; but it also has some more static aspects (which alone concern us in this place [2]); as things have turned out so far, the influence of these has been at least as important. The dynamic model is built up as a sequence of "single-period" links; each of these links, since there is no opportunity for adjustments over time *within* it, can be regarded as a static (or timeless) system. The form in which von Neumann studies this static system is substantially that which we have been calling the "extended Walras–Cassel"; but in his hands this is already passing over into *activity analysis*. He does not content himself with allowing for the possibilities that available inputs may not be used, feasible outputs may not be produced; he allows for the possibility of joint products, and that available processes may not be employed. Besides, there is included in von Neumann's construction a first statement of what was to become known as the Duality principle (of which I shall have much more to say later). It is singularly appropriate that it was von Neumann who introduced that principle into the theory of economic optimisation, for it is the link which establishes a connection (we shall be examining later what sort of a connection) between that theory and the Theory of Games.

From this point, the later developments begin to branch out; but before discussing these later developments, it will be well to attempt a statement of the stage so far reached. There is indeed no single work which can be said to correspond at all exactly to the stage I have in mind. New ideas tumble out one after another with such rapidity in von Neumann's few pages, that he is already in the middle of the next chapter before he has finished with the first. It will be useful here to take things more slowly. The "prototype" theory which I shall describe in the next section will still run in terms of "extended Walras–Cassel"; that is to say, it is solely concerned with the allocation of given factor supplies in the production of a number of products, each of which is to be made by combining factors in proportions that are technically given. Only afterwards shall I go on to the reinterpretations, by von Neumann and others, which have not merely allowed for variable

[1] There is an awkward question of priority. The von Neumann paper was also published in the Menger *Ergebnisse* (Heft 8, for 1935–36, published 1937). (The English translation is in *Review of Economic Studies*, No. 33, 1945–46.) It is, however, understood that it was originally presented to a seminar at Princeton in 1932, which puts it before Wald, and even before such things as the Neisser article above mentioned. (I know, from personal recollection, that he had these things in mind in September 1933, when I met him with Kaldor in Budapest. Of course I did not understand what he was saying!)

[2] Although all the theories we shall be discussing have (or can have) dynamic aspects, the static side will give us quite enough to deal with.

proportions of factors, for joint supply and for intermediate products (all of which things are left out in the prototype), but have enabled the analysis to be applied to problems of business management which are at first sight of quite different kinds. One of the main difficulties with later writings is that they are (rightly) so impressed by these reinterpretations that they insist on beginning their exposition on a high plane of generality. I find it easier to take one thing at a time; though the theory which will now be described is mainly interesting because it can be generalised, it is easiest to put it, at the first round, in a rather conventional setting.

II. The Prototype

1. Given amounts of M factors of production are available; we will call these amounts $b_1, b_2, \ldots b_M$. There are N products which can be produced by the utilisation of these factors; the (as yet undetermined) amounts of these products we call $x_1, x_2, \ldots x_N$. There are fixed technical coefficients; that is to say, the amount of each factor required to make a unit of each product is given. The amount of the ith factor needed to make a unit of the jth product we call a_{ij}.

It is clearly implied, when the problem is stated in these terms, that the constants (a's and b's) must obey certain restrictions if they are to make economic sense. Though these restrictions look terribly obvious, we shall get into serious trouble if we do not put them down. (1) Every b_i must be positive; negative factor supplies are meaningless, and a product that required a factor that was in zero supply could not possibly be produced. (2) The technical coefficients a_{ij} cannot be negative; we may, however, allow some of them to be zero—not every factor need be required for every product. (3) But some amount of at least one factor must be required for every product; there can be no j for which $a_{ij} = 0$, for all i. Mathematically, these restrictions define what we are calling the prototype problem. Since they were (I believe) first set out formally by Wald, I shall call them (together with a fourth rule to be mentioned later) the *Wald rules*.

If a set of outputs $(x_1, x_2, \ldots x_N)$—or, more briefly (x_j)—is to be *feasible* it must satisfy two sets of conditions, or *restraints*. First, no x_j may be negative (though some or all may be zero); this again looks obvious, but again it is vital that such obvious matters are not overlooked. Secondly, the amount of any factor that is required to produce the set (x_j) must in no case exceed the amount of that factor that is available. The first set of restraints —that $x_j \geqslant 0$ for all j—might be called product restraints, but (with an eye on subsequent generalisation) I prefer a more general description. I shall therefore call them *sign restraints*. The second set, which imply that

$$\begin{array}{c} a_{11}x_1 + a_{12}x_2 + \ldots + a_{1N}x_N \leqslant b_1 \\ a_{21}x_1 + a_{22}x_2 + \ldots + a_{2N}x_N \leqslant b_2 \\ \cdot \quad \cdot \quad \cdot \quad \cdot \\ a_{M1}x_1 + a_{M2}x_2 + \ldots + a_{MN}x_M \leqslant b_M \end{array}$$

I shall for the same reason call *specific restraints*. There are N sign restraints and M specific restraints, $M + N$ in all. There are N x's to be determined. Thus the number of restraints is always *greater* than the number of unknowns, when all restraints are taken into consideration.

As always in such cases, it is a great help to make as much use as we can of a diagrammatic representation. The problem which has just been set out, for M factors and N products, is precisely that which was expressed, for two factors and two products, in Fig. 1. The feasible *region*,[1] as drawn, was bounded by straight lines that corresponded to the four restraints: two sign restraints (OA and OB), two specific restraints (AA' and BB'). The Wald rules have made it necessary that we should get a feasible region that is something like $OAPB$. It is clearly not excluded that one of the specific restraints might have been ineffective (if AA', BB' had failed to meet within the positive quadrant) so that the feasible region might have been reduced to a triangle. And it is clearly not excluded that one (or both) of the specific " arms " might have been parallel to an axis; what is excluded is that they should both be parallel to the same axis, for that would mean that there was a product which did not require any factor, and that is ruled out. It would therefore seem that the polygonal form (such as $OAPB$), or something like it, is going to be typical.

2. It would now be possible to pose the problem before us in the form of asking for a determination of all feasible solutions: the answer to that question, in the case illustrated, would be the definition of the whole area $OAPB$. But out of all these points, it is only those that lie upon the frontier APB which are really interesting; it is only these which, in some sense or other, " maximise output." How do we distinguish between these frontier points and the rest of those that are feasible? There are, in principle, two ways of making the distinction.

One is to say that a feasible point is a frontier point if it is a terminus of a vector from the origin; that is to say, if it is laid down that the various outputs are to be produced in fixed proportions, the quantity of any product (and hence of the composite product) that is produced must be maximised. The other is to say that if the products are valued at fixed prices ($p_1, p_2, \ldots p_N$) the value of output ($\sum p_j x_j$) must be maximised. (It must be clearly understood, if we adopt this second distinction, that the p's must be non-negative; we may allow some of them to be zero, but it will be nonsense for all to be zero. This is the fourth of the Wald rules.)

There are economic purposes for which the difference between these two approaches is very important; the whole theory of increasing returns may be said to depend upon it. It can, however, be shown [2] that under present

[1] I am aware that for mathematicians the term *region* has connotations of continuity which are not necessarily implied in the uses I shall be making of it. A more correct terminology would, however, involve explanations which for present purposes are largely irrelevant. In this, and some other cases, I must ask forgiveness for a use of terms in something looser than the strict mathematical sense.

[2] See below, p. 93.

assumptions they come to the same thing, so it does not matter which we use. It has proved to be more convenient to work with the test by value of output, according to which a position on the frontier is found by maximising $\sum px$ for given (p). A set of outputs which does this, subject to the restraints, is called an *optimum*.

It is at once apparent that for the case which is shown in our diagram there are two sorts of optima. (1) The optimum may be *at a vertex*, such as A, P or B. (2) The optimum may be, as we shall say, *on a flat*—on AP or PB. There will be several values of the price-ratio (p_1/p_2) which will correspond to each vertex optimum; but it is only particular values of the price-ratio which will give a flat optimum—but for those values any point on the flat can be optimum. It will now be shown that the distinction between vertex optima and flat optima is quite generally valid; but for that purpose we need some more general definitions.

3. Let us begin by looking at the vertices on our diagram more closely. At P the two products are both being produced, and the two factors are both scarce; thus we have two positive products (as we may call them) and two scarce factors. At A (and at B) there is only one positive product, and one scarce factor. At O (which must be reckoned as a vertex, though—so long as the Wald rules hold—it cannot be an optimum) we have no positive product and no scarce factor. Thus at all the vertices the number of positive products is equal to the number of scarce factors.

When a factor is scarce the corresponding specific restraint becomes an equation; we may then say that the restraint is *operative*. Thus the vertex P is determined by two specific restraints which are operative. At A there is only one specific restraint which is operative; but the place of the other is taken by a sign restraint, which now becomes operative $(x_2 = 0)$. At O it is only the sign restraints which are operative. Thus each of the vertices is determined by two operative restraints—two equations to determine the two unknowns. A general rule for the determination of a vertex is accordingly suggested: a vertex is a set of N outputs (x_j) which is determined by N operative restraints, to be selected from the total number of restraints $(M + N)$. But this is not quite the whole story.

For (as is again apparent from the diagram) the list of points which would be calculated by this rule is longer than the list of vertices. When the above procedure is applied to that elementary case it would not only throw up the true vertices (A, P, B and O); it will also throw up the pseudo-vertices (A' and B'). These must clearly be excluded; what excludes them? They are excluded by their failure to satisfy some of the restraints which in their determination have been taken as non-operative. A true vertex is a set of outputs which is determined by selecting N of the $M + N$ restraints to be operative, and which also satisfies (as inequalities) the remaining non-operative restraints. Thus, when the optimum is at a vertex, the number of positive outputs should be equal to the number of scarce factors; and the non-scarce factors should be in excess supply.

4. So much for the vertices; now for the optima which lie *on the flat* between the vertices. It is clear that the number of scarce factors cannot ordinarily [1] be greater than the number of positive products; for if it was, we should have more equations than unknowns, and the system would be over-determined. But it is perfectly possible that the number of scarce factors may be *less* than the number of positive products. (Thus for an optimum between A and P, on Fig. 1, we have two positive products, and only one scarce factor.) It will later be shown that this is a general characteristic of flat optima; but it will be more convenient, for the moment, to define them, and to get out their properties, in another way.

It is a well-known rule that if α, β are two points on a line, with co-ordinates (x_α, y_α) (x_β, y_β), the co-ordinates of any other point on the line can be expressed as $(k_\alpha x_\alpha + k_\beta x_\beta, k_\alpha y_\alpha + k_\beta y_\beta)$ where $k_\alpha + k_\beta = 1$. In terms of these *weights*, the point α is (1, 0); the point β is (0, 1); any point on the line *between* α and β will have both weights positive; any point outside $\alpha\beta$ will have one weight negative. There is therefore a sense in which we can regard any point on the line between α and β (including α and β) as being a *weighted average* of α and β; it being understood that the weights are non-negative, and add up to 1.

The points on the flat between A and P (on Fig. 1) can thus be regarded as weighted averages of A and P—two vertices which, in the case where the optimum is on the flat, must be such that at them the value of output $V (=\sum px)$ is the same. It is accordingly suggested that we might define the flat optimum as a condition in which two (or more) vertices give the same value of output; any weighted average of these vertices may then be an optimum. It is evident that if V takes the same value at each of the points $(\alpha, \beta, \ldots \lambda)$, it will also take the same value at any weighted average of $(\alpha, \beta, \ldots \lambda)$. But before we can accept this definition there is a further matter to be cleared up.

If a point is to be an optimum it must be feasible; how do we know that these points, defined as weighted averages of vertices, are feasible? It can in fact be shown that they must be; this is a special case of a general, and very important property—*any weighted average of a set of feasible points must be feasible*. The mathematical name for this property is *convexity*; [2] what we have to show is that the feasible region is convex. The proof is as follows.

Let $(\alpha, \beta, \ldots \lambda)$ be feasible points. Take the point which is expressible as the weighted average $(k_\alpha, k_\beta, \ldots k_\lambda)$. Substitute its co-ordinates (written in full) into any one of the specific restraints, say the ith. Then

$$a_{i1}x_1 + a_{i2}x_2 + \ldots a_{iN}x_N = k_\alpha(a_{i1}x_{1\alpha} + a_{i2}x_{2\alpha} + \ldots + a_{iN}x_{N\alpha}) + \ldots + k_\lambda(a_{i1}x_{1\lambda} + a_{i2}x_{2\lambda} + \ldots a_{iN}x_{N\lambda}) \leqslant k_\alpha b_i + k_\beta b_i + \ldots + k_\lambda b_i$$

[1] It will later appear that there is a qualification to this statement which is of some importance.

[2] For a further discussion of this concept, see below, p. 91.

since (α, β, . . .) satisfy the restraints, and the k's are non-negative. Then, since the k's add up to 1, the last sum is b_i. Thus any weighted average satisfies the specific restraints, and can be shown to satisfy the sign restraints in the same way. Thus it is feasible.

It is accordingly safe to lay down that when there is a " tie " between vertex optima any weighted average of these vertex optima is itself an optimum. That is what the *flat optimum* means.

5. So far we have (basically) been arguing from analogy; the method described in the last paragraph can, however, be used to give something which is a bit nearer to a proof of the properties in question.

It is not only the points *on the flat* which can be regarded as weighted averages of vertices; if we bring all the vertices into account, any point within the feasible region (inside the region, or on its boundary) can similarly be expressed as a weighted average of vertices. (This can often be done in several ways, but that does not matter.) Further, in view of the convexity of the region, it is *only* points that are within the region that can be thus expressed. Suppose that we now take (α, β, . . . λ) to be the vertices, and consider a point which can be expressed by (k_α, k_β, . . . k_λ). Substituting its co-ordinates into the value of output, as we have previously substituted into the restraints, we get

$$V = \sum px = k_\alpha V_\alpha + k_\beta V_\beta + \ . \ . \ . + k_\lambda V_\lambda$$

where V_α, V_β, . . . V_λ are the values of output at the vertices. Then, since the weights are non-negative and add up to 1, it is obvious that in the case where there is one of the V's which is larger than any of the others, the optimum is reached if the whole weight is placed at that vertex; while in the case where there is a " tie," an optimum will be reached by dividing the weight between the tying vertices *in any manner*. That is all that there is to be said.

6. So far as the determination of the optimum is concerned, that completes the prototype theory; the most remarkable development of the theory is nevertheless still to come. This is concerned with the determination of factor prices.

Let us go back, for a moment, to the " Walras " model, of the two factors and two products, with which we began. It is not merely the case that if we analyse it in Walras' manner, outputs appear to be established independently of demands; it is also the case that (if product prices are assumed to be given),[1] factor prices appear to be determined independently of the supplies of the factors. Corresponding to the *equations*

$$a_{11}x_1 + a_{12}x_2 = b_1, \quad a_{21}x_1 + a_{22}x_2 = b_2$$

(which make outputs seem to depend upon technical coefficients and factor

[1] Walras, of course, did not assume that they were given. That this is an important assumption has nevertheless been brought to the attention of economists by Samuelson (see his Factor Price Equalisation Theorem).

D

supplies only), there are the equations of prices and costs (that there is no profit that cannot be imputed to some factor); these will read

$$w_1a_{11} + w_2a_{21} = p_1, \quad w_1a_{12} + w_2a_{22} = p_2$$

Taken by themselves, they seem to make the factor prices w_1, w_2 depend upon product prices and technical coefficients only.

As we have seen, the first set of equations is not universally valid. It needs to be completed so as to allow for the possibility of a factor being in excess supply; when that is done, demands come back into the picture. An exactly analogous argument, applied to the second set, uncovers the assumption that the outputs of both products are positive. If that is not so, if (say) $x_2 = 0$, there is no reason why the cost of the second product should equal its price. A possible combination of factor prices would be such that price equalled cost for the first product, but fell short of cost for the second. The second would not then be produced; it would not pay to produce it.

This simple example is sufficient to show that the theory of imputation (derivation of factor prices from product prices) needs to be completed by an inclusion of "inequality" cases, just as has been done for the theory of quantity optimisation. It also suggests (what proves to be true) that there is a sense in which the one theory is a mirror image of the other. Let us look at this more generally.

7. Suppose that at a particular optimum, n of the N possible products are positive products, the remaining $N - n$ having zero outputs. And suppose that m of the M factors are scarce factors, the remaining $M - m$ having zero factor prices.[1] Then it would appear from our preceding discussion (though there is qualification to this to be made in a moment) that at a vertex optimum $m = n$, while at a flat optimum $m < n$. We must again look at these two cases separately.

At the vertex optimum we have $m = n$ equations of the form $\sum a_{ij}x_j = b_i$ to determine the n positive outputs; and (since price equals cost for each of these n products) we have an equal number of equations, of the form $\sum w_i a_{ij} = p_j$, to determine the $m = n$ prices of the scarce factors. Corresponding to the other factors, where $w_i = 0$, we have the inequalities $\sum a_{ij}x_j < b_i$. Corresponding to the other products, where $x_j = 0$, we have the inequalities $\sum w_i a_{ij} > p_j$. Apart from the difference in sign of the two sets of inequalities, there is complete symmetry.

The flat optimum is at first sight more perplexing. Here we have $m < n$; there are only m equations to determine the n positive outputs; these outputs are therefore under-determined, but that (it will be remembered) is what they should be. On the other hand, we have n equations $\sum w_i a_{ij} = p_j$ to determine the m prices of the scarce factors; these seem therefore to be over-determined. The explanation is that it is not possible for a flat optimum to occur at any arbitrary set of prices (p); it can only

[1] I take it for granted that the factor prices of the non-scarce factors are zero.

occur at particular sets of (p), which are related in such a manner that the n equations of prices and costs can be simultaneously satisfied. (The *labour theory of value*, regarded as a statement that the prices of positive products must be proportional to their labour costs, when labour is the only scarce factor, may be regarded as a particular case of this proposition.) If we have begun with an appropriate (p), we can get a flat optimum, with a corresponding (w). The restraints on the (x) will be operative, for all factors where w_i is not zero; and the restraints on the (w), as we may begin to call them, will be operative, for all products where x_j is not zero. Where w_i is zero, and where x_j is zero, we have the same inequalities as before.

But now, having found a way of overcoming the obstacle of over-determinateness in the case where $m < n$, we should look back to see whether we have not been too precipitate in the other case. Would it not have been possible to have found a way round, in a similar manner, which would have salvaged the possibility that $m > n$? The factor prices would then have been under-determined, so that there would have been " flatness " on that side—there is no difficulty about that; but the only way in which m operative equations on n positive products can all be satisfied, when $m > n$, is for there to be some special relations between the factor supplies (b), just as there had to be suitable relations between the (p) in the opposite case. There is no doubt that this way out is mathematically valid, and it is useful as showing how we may complete the symmetry; but I have refrained from bringing it in until now, since I think that the economist is justified in feeling a little shy of it, at least in the present application. He is undoubtedly interested in the optima that will be reached at various (p), some of which will certainly be inter-related, so that the case where $m < n$ is important to him; but he had begun by thinking of the factor supplies as *given*, so that inter-relations between them, which would enable more than n factors to be scarce simultaneously, would be rather a fluke. Still, it is a possibility, and it is a possibility which, at this stage, has important consequences.

For what we now come to is the Principle of Duality. The conditions which govern the outputs (x) and the factor prices (w), in an optimum position, correspond exactly. We had, however, determined the (x) in a way which could be completely described without introducing the (w); since the restraints on the (w) are so remarkably similar, it is strongly suggested that the (w) might themselves have been *independently* determined in a similar way. That this is in fact so can be shown as follows.

8. We started with the condition that the (x) should be *feasible*: in the sense that they are non-negative, and that their factor requirements do not exceed the available factor supplies—that is to say, that $\sum a_{ij}x_j \leqslant b_i$ for all i from 1 to M (the specific restraints). We found ourselves imposing a parallel set of restraints on the (w): that they should be non-negative, and that the costs of the products, at these factor prices, should equal or exceed the given product prices—that is to say, the $\sum w_i a_{ij} \geqslant p_j$, for all j from 1 to N (which

we may now regard as specific restraints on the (w)). Evidently we may say that the (w) are *feasible* if they satisfy the restraints just laid down.

Now take the specific restraints on the (x), multiply each of them by the corresponding w, and add. Since if the (w) are feasible, they must be non-negative, the resulting inequality will hold, whenever both (x) and (w) are feasible. What it states is that the cost of the set of outputs (x_j), valued at the factor prices (w_i), cannot exceed the aggregate value of the factors, at those same factor prices. If this cost is C, and this factor value B, we have $C \leqslant B$, whenever (x) and (w) are both feasible.

Then take the specific restraints on the (w), multiply each by the corresponding (x), and add. If both (x) and (w) are feasible, the inequality which results from this operation must also hold. What it states is that the aggregate value of the products, at prices (p), cannot exceed the aggregate cost of those products, at factor prices (w). $V \leqslant C$, when (x) and (w) are both feasible.

So far we have made no use of the optimum conditions. But it is easy to show that when (x) is optimum, $C = B$; for when w_i is positive the corresponding restraint is then an equation, and when it is not an equation, the corresponding $w_i = 0$. Similarly, when (w) is optimum—or such as to correspond to an optimum (x)—we have $V = C$. Thus, when (x) and (w) are both optimum, we have $V = C = B$. (The social accounts come out right!)

For any feasible (x) and (w), $V \leqslant B$; no feasible V can exceed any feasible B. The feasible B's lie above the feasible V's, except for the possibility that some feasible V's and some feasible B's may be equal. At the optimum, $V = B$, so that at the optimum this equality is realised. It follows that no feasible V can exceed the optimum V, so that at the optimum V is maximised; that, of course, does no more than confirm the definition with which we started. But it also follows that no feasible B can be less than the optimum B, so that at the optimum B is minimised. We could have determined the " equilibrium " factor prices as an *independent* optimum problem: by seeking those factor prices which minimise factor value, subject to the condition that the unit cost of no product shall fall below its given (product) price.

9. That, I think, is the easiest way of demonstrating, or at least of explaining, the Duality Principle; but there is perhaps a little more to be said in order that the significance of the principle should be fully brought out. It is rather a defect of the foregoing treatment that it has had to introduce the factor prices, in Walras' manner, as elements in a model of competitive capitalism, in which the factor prices govern *distribution*; in the other part of the theory, in which the optimum *quantities* had been determined, no such assumption as this had been required. It would in fact have been possible to have introduced the factor prices, without reference to distributive shares, as instruments of quantity optimisation; though it would not have been so

easy to carry through the argument in detail, we might have proceeded on something like the following lines.

Suppose that arbitrary (non-negative) prices are set upon the factors, and that an entrepreneur (or planner) is provided with a fund which is just sufficient to enable him to employ the whole of the available supplies of the factors at those given factor prices. Suppose that he seeks to maximise the value of output, under the single (specific) restraint that the cost of output is not to exceed the value of his fund; that is to say, that $C \leqslant B$. The outputs which he will select will, very likely, not be feasible; they will infringe some or other of the *separate* specific restraints, which (we are of course supposing) do still in fact hold. It does, however, follow from our previous analysis (it would be nice if there were some simple *direct* proof, but I do not see one) that there will be some set of factor prices, our optimum (w), at which the optimum that he selects will in fact be feasible, and will indeed be an optimum of the whole system. The optimum factor prices are the *right* factor prices in this sense.

On this approach, distribution only comes in, if at all, in a secondary manner. If all the factor prices are changed in the same proportion the restraint $C \leqslant B$ is unaffected *in real terms*; just the same combinations of outputs are open, or appear to be open, as before. Thus, by the preceding test, the optimum (w) remains indeterminate, to the extent of a multiplier; in order to determine its level, we have to impose some additional condition, and the condition that the value of output, at the optimum, should be equal to its cost is one that will obviously be convenient to impose. Then it all falls out as explained.

This is more the way in which economists have thought of the determination of factor prices belonging in with that of product quantities; the discovery that factor-price determination is an optimum problem in its own right, so that we can begin at either end, is distinctly harder to place. One can see that it makes sense in economic terms (when the possibility of zero outputs is allowed for); but it is hardly a formulation which would have occurred to the economist if it had not been suggested to him by the mathematician. The nearest thing which might have occurred to him would have been to say that the maximisation of output is a minimisation of the scarcity of the resources applied. That is a way in which an economist might want to talk, but he would hardly have believed that he was quite correct in doing so. What he is now to learn is that there is a way in which he is justified in doing so, after all.

III. Beyond the Prototype

The summary which has just been given has been confined to a statement of the Linear Theory in Walras–Cassel terms; it should, however, be emphasised that none of the standard works do put it in those terms, and the reason why is fairly evident. The reactions which we have appeared to be analysing so minutely—the changes in the sorts of factors that are scarce, and of producible products that are actually produced—are hardly so important in the real world, as to be deserving of such elaborate attention. Certainly it seems odd to deal with them in such detail before we deal with more important matters. The Walrasian habit of taking these things as settled, *before* the equilibrium system is set up, is not (in direct application) so very unreasonable. The chief reason why the prototype theory is very well worth having is that, once we have it, it can so easily be interpreted in other ways.

On the way to these economic reinterpretations there are, however, some mathematical reinterpretations and extensions which need to be noticed. To the mathematician these are rather obvious; they are the reason why no mathematician would ever stop at the prototype theory. But since they have been excluded from the prototype theory, they must be set down before going further.

1. It will be remembered that in our formulation of the prototype we began by imposing certain "economic" restrictions on the constants—the Wald rules. The *a*'s were to be non-negative (with the qualification that some factor must be required for every product); the *b*'s were to be positive; and then there was the supplementary rule that the *p*'s were to be non-negative (but not all zero). Useful as these restrictions were to begin with, it may have been noticed that by the end of our discussion they were wearing rather thin. The minimisation problem, which emerged as the dual, could itself have been stated as a maximisation problem, in the same form as the original (or "primal," as it is coming to be called); but in that case the signs of *all* the constants would have had to be reversed. We took it for granted that a problem of that kind could be dealt with in much the same way. But this raises the broader question: do we need to put any restrictions on the constants?

Mathematically, the answer is no. Almost the whole of the foregoing can be re-worked without the Wald rules; so that any *a*, *b* or *p* can be allowed to be positive, zero or negative. The chief trouble which arises if this is done (it is the reason why it seemed best to begin with the Wald rules) is that we have to allow for some side possibilities, which are obviously excluded in many economic interpretations, so that it was rather a convenience to be able to ignore them at a first round. I shall not attempt, even here, to work them in properly; some brief description must, however, be given.

It is possible, in the first place, if no restrictions are set upon the constants, that there may be no feasible solution, no "feasible region." The specific restraints may be mutually contradictory, or they may contradict the sign restraints. (For example, $x_1 \leqslant -6$ is a possible specific restraint if we allow any constants; but it contradicts the sign restraint $x_1 \geqslant 0$.)

Secondly, even if there is a feasible region, it is not necessary that it should be optimisable for a given (p). Clearly, if there were no specific restraints (only sign restraints), while the p's were positive, there would be no optimum, since V could be indefinitely increased. The same thing may happen if there are specific restraints, when they fail to confine the feasible region in some direction.

Neither of these things can happen under the Wald rules; they cannot happen with the primal,[1] nor (it is important to notice) can they happen with the prototype dual.[2] This is a particular case of a general theorem, the general *Duality Theorem*, which states that if an optimum exists for the primal, it exists also for the dual. I shall make no attempt to prove this theorem, which is true for any values of the constants. There is also an extension of the theorem, which connects the two exceptions: it states that if the primal, though feasible, is unoptimisable, the dual will not be feasible.[3] Since (of course) either problem may be regarded as primal, the correspondence holds (in a sense) both ways. It is, however, worth noticing that the possibility remains open that both primal and dual may not be feasible.[4] This is a rare case, but it can arise.

2. *Convexity*. If a feasible region exists it must be convex; for the proof of convexity (which was given above [5]) is independent of the Wald rules; it will hold for any values of the constants.[6] We are still dealing with convexity properties, and shall continue to do so in all the forms of the linear theory. Since this has the effect of setting a sharp limitation on the range of economic problems to which the theory is applicable, it will be well to consider the concept a little more deeply before going further.

What is the relation (we may begin by asking) between this convexity concept and that which has hitherto been more familiar to economists, in the works, for instance, of Pareto or Joan Robinson? We are accustomed to say that a curve such as AB (Fig. 2) is " convex outwards " if its steepness continually increases as one moves downwards along it. This definition is clearly different from that to which we have here come, since the one is a property of a region, the other of a curve; but since the region OAB is

[1] Under the Wald rules the origin (all outputs zero) is always feasible. That is enough to show that a feasible region must exist. Increasing (x) along any vector will always encounter a restraint; V must therefore have a maximum value.

[2] Under the Wald rules a zero value for all w is *never* feasible; but a feasible solution can always be found by giving the w's sufficiently large *positive* values. Between the corresponding value of B and the zero value (which is not feasible) a minimum value must exist.

[3] This can easily be illustrated by a slight variation of our Prototype case.

If we maintain the other rules, but allow the existence of one product which does not require any factor to make it, the primal will be unoptimisable, if that product has a positive price. But the cost of that product must be zero, at any factor prices; so it must fall short of the positive product price; the dual cannot be feasible.

[4] An example is given in Vajda, p. 78.

[5] See above, p. 84.

[6] Other parts of the " prototype " argument would require more modification; but I shall not go into that here.

convex on the new definition,[1] while $O'A'B'$ is not, it does look as if there would be some sense in saying that a convex region is one that is bounded by something like a " convex outward " curve.

It is indeed true that a convex region can be defined in something like this manner. The convexity of the curve AB (Fig. 2) could have been indicated by the fact that the tangent, at any point of the curve, lies outside the region OAB except at the point of contact. We can get rid of the exception about the point of contact (rather awkward in the case of linear boundaries) if we put the same property a little differently. We can define a convex region as one which is such that through any point *outside* the region

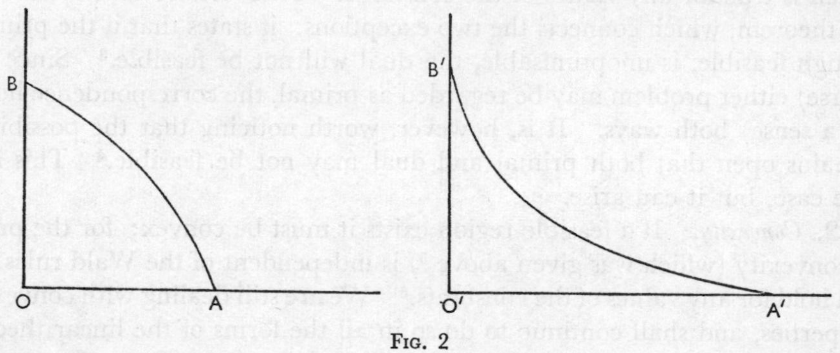

FIG. 2

a line [2] can be drawn so that the whole of the region lies on one side of the line (with no point of the region lying on the line). It is obvious that if a region is " dented " (like $O'A'B'$), this condition will not be satisfied at a point which lies within the " dent." It can be proved that this " no dent " definition amounts to the same thing as the " weighed average " definition which we used previously.

I shall not attempt to prove this equivalence; it is one of the things which economists may reasonably take over from the mathematicians.[3] It is nevertheless of much use to the economist to know that the equivalence exists. For once we have it, we can at once see that the convexity, which is so important in the linear theory, is fundamentally the same thing as that which we are accustomed, in our diagrams, to think of as a phenomenon of *diminishing returns*. Convexity, in the new sense, covers constant returns as well as diminishing returns (if AB were a straight line, the region OAB would still be convex). What it does not cover is increasing returns (as illustrated

[1] It is sufficient to observe that if α and β are two points within the region (or on its boundary) any point between them on the line joining them will be within the region in the same sense.

[2] In two dimensions; plane, or whatever corresponds, in more than two.

[3] To prove that " convexity no-dent " implies " convexity weighted-average " is not difficult; to prove it the other way (the " theorem of the supporting hyper-plane ") is distinctly more awkward. There is a proof in von Neumann and Morgenstern, *Theory of Games*, pp. 134 ff.; see also Vajda, *op. cit.*, p. 22. The neatest proof which I know is that given by Debreu in an appendix to Koopmans and Bausch, *Selected Topics in Economics involving mathematical reasoning*, Cowles Foundation Paper No. 136, p. 96.

by $O'A'B'$). We can check this by observing that, under increasing returns, an output of zero at a cost of zero may be feasible, an output of x at a cost of c may be feasible, but an output of $\frac{1}{2}x$ at a cost of $\frac{1}{2}c$ will *not* then be feasible.

Under increasing returns, also, there will be a lack of correspondence between the two senses of optimum. A position which maximises output in the quantity sense (that it is the maximum that can be produced when the output of commodities are to be combined in fixed proportions) will not necessarily be one which maximises the value of output at *any* set of product prices. It is a convexity property (a consequence of the equivalence of the two definitions of convexity) that the two senses of optimum come together.

We are accordingly in sight of a rather powerful re-statement of a distinction which has long been known to be crucial for cconomics. The reason why constant-returns assumptions, and diminishing-returns assumptions, are so much more manageable than increasing-returns assumptions, is that in the former cases we can use convexity properties, while in the latter we cannot. There is in fact not much difficulty in dealing with phenomena of diminishing returns by linear methods (a curve can always be approximated by a polygon); [1] but the linear theory, since it is based upon convexity, cannot be extended, without losing most of its virtues, into the realm of increasing returns.

3. *The Equational Form.* This is a convenient point at which to mention another complication—that the form in which we have been posing the optimisation problem is by no means the only form in which what is in substance just the same problem can be put.

The excess supplies of the factors (which are zero in the case of scarce factors, and have to be positive when the factor is not scarce) are themselves a part of the (primal) problem; they are determined, along with the outputs (x_j), when we maximise V subject to the restraints. If they had been introduced explicitly, the primal problem could have been expressed as a maximisation of V, subject to the *equations*

$$a_{i1}x_1 + a_{i2}x_2 + \ldots + a_{iN}x_N + e_i = b_i$$

(for all factors), together with the sign restraints on the outputs and on the excess supplies ($x_j \geqslant 0$, $e_i \geqslant 0$). Now, as soon as we have left the Wald rules behind us (so that we do not have to worry about the signs of the constants), this is exactly the same thing as maximising

$$\sum q_j x_j + \sum q_i' e_i$$

[1] I do not mean that we have to introduce a linear re-statement in order to make use of the "weighted-average" concept of convexity. It is indeed obvious from the diagrams of Fig. 2 that we do not. It is possible (and useful) to re-state Paretian economics (with curved frontiers and indifference curves) in terms of convexity properties. This has been done, in a manner which should become classic, in the first of Tjalling Koopmans' *Essays on the State of Economic Science* (1957). I should like to take this opportunity of expressing the debt which I owe to that admirable work, which has had more effect upon the present paper than may appear on the surface. (The companion piece, that is mentioned in the previous footnote, did not appear until after this survey had been substantially written.)

*

where q and q' are new sets of price-weights; for the e's could always be eliminated from the latter sum with the aid of the given equations. (It would then reduce to the familiar form $\sum p_j x_j$, with p's depending on the given q and q' and on the given a's.) The optimisation problem is therefore the same as the maximisation of a " weighted sum " of s variables, *all* of which are to be non-negative, and which are connected by t equations $(t < s)$.[1]

The " equational " formulation, which reduces all the restraints to sign restraints, at the expense of increasing the number of variables, is indeed that which is most commonly used in works on Linear Programming.[2] I have preferred to put the matter the other way, which (since it operates with fewer variables) offers more scope for geometrical illustration. Besides, the equational method is less obviously in touch with traditional economics. It is, however, well suited for some economic applications (as we shall see in a moment). There is much to be said for being ready to work either way.[3]

IV. Linear Programming

Our sketch of the underlying theory is now complete; we can return to the story.

In order that Linear Programming should be born, two more things were necessary.

1. It had first to be realised that there are problems, other than the straightforward " economic " maximisation of the value of output from given resources, which are formally equivalent to economic optimisation. Opportunities, that is, for the application of the generalised theory (which has been described in the preceding section of this survey) had to be discovered. It is usual to associate this stage with two examples that have become classic—the " transportation problem " posed in 1941 by F. L. Hitchcock,[4] and the " diet problem," which was posed in a (still unpublished) paper by Jerome Cornfield that was circulated in the same year.[5] But it is probably more

[1] If $t > s$, and the equations are independent, the problem would be over-determined, and could not have a solution. If $t = s$, and the equations are independent, they will themselves determine a single solution, which will be the actual solution if it satisfies the sign restraints.

[2] The reason for this is mainly computational. If a problem is presented in inequality form it is easily converted into equational form by the introduction of " slack " variables (such as our e's). The reverse process involves solving the equations, which may well be extremely laborious.

[3] If the primal variables (x) are completed by the introduction of the excess supplies of the factors, the dual variables (w) must be similarly completed by introducing the differences in the dual inequalities. These, in our prototype formulation, are the differences between cost and price—the *unprofitabilities* of the products, we may call them. When these are included the dual problem is in turn reduced to the minimisation of a weighted sum of N variables, subject to sign restraints, and connected (now) by $N - M$ equations.

[4] In the *Journal of Mathematics and Physics*, Massachusetts Institute of Technology, Vol. 20, pp. 224–30.

[5] These have been described in innumerable places. There is a simple account in G. Morton, " Notes on Linear Programming," *Economica*, 1951; and a fuller in DOSSO, Chapters 2 and 5.

correct to regard these as no more than forerunners. The true begetters of Linear Programming were those who perceived the opportunities in question in connection with war production: Tjalling Koopmans, who rediscovered the transportation problem in connection with shipping, and G. B. Dantzig, who encountered similar questions in his work for the U.S. Air Force.[1] It was when Koopmans and Dantzig got together, after the War, that things really happened.[2] Here, however, we may content ourselves with a word about the conventional examples.

The *diet* problem—to determine the cheapest diet by which a minimum intake of given nutrients can be achieved—is very near to our prototype; indeed, when set out, it fits exactly into the prototype dual. (The amounts of nutrients in each food are the *a*'s; the quantities of foods are the *w*'s; the minimum intakes are the *p*'s; and the costs of the foods are the *b*'s. Every nutrient must be contained in some food, or—as is at once apparent—the problem cannot be feasible.) The *transportation* problem—to determine the cheapest pattern by which given demands of *m* markets can be supplied from *n* sources, with given unit costs of transport from any source to any market—is in a sense more interesting, since it is a beautiful example of a problem that sets itself up in terms of *equations* between non-negative variables. (The amount to be delivered from *each* source to *each* market has to be determined; these are connected by equations, since the total supply from each source, and demand from each market, is given.) Though some of the variables can be eliminated by means of the equations, so that it may be thrown back to the determination of $(m-1)(n-1)$ variables, connected by $m+n-1$ specific restraints, the choice of variables to be eliminated is very arbitrary; and though the initial unit costs are all positive, there is no guarantee that the same will hold for the coefficients which take their places, after elimination. Thus the transportation problem already requires the more general theory, while for the diet problem the prototype is sufficient.

2. The mere posing of these problems would not have been an advance, if there had existed no method by which the problems could have been solved. The main development in that direction was to follow a little later. It should, however, be made clear that, even before the invention of the Simplex method, the problems were *in principle* solvable; as soon as it is known that the optimum (if there is an optimum) must be at a vertex, or between *tying* vertices, identification of the vertices (and there was a rule for that) and calculation of the cost (as it was in these examples) at the vertices, would always lead to a solution *in the end*. With simple classroom examples, that is often by no means an impossible undertaking. But in any practical

[1] The influence of Leontief's work in demonstrating the practical applicability of one form of allocative theory, and in turning the attention of economists to a model in which produced commodities figure as inputs (this, as we shall see, itself means going beyond the Wald rules) also requires recognition.

[2] See their (indigestible) volume, *Activity Analysis of Production and Allocation*, ed. Koopmans (1951).

instance the amount of work to be done piles up very rapidly.[1] Even with the aid of computers (the simultaneous development of which has been a most important element in the practical success of Linear Programming), the solution of most real problems would still have been out of reach without the invention of better methods.

Any detailed discussion of such methods must clearly lie outside the scope of this survey. Reference must, however, be made to the Simplex method (discovered in 1947 by Dantzig [2]), which was historically the means by which this difficulty was sufficiently overcome to make Linear Programming a usable technique. Effectively, what the Simplex method provides is a means by which we can recognise an optimum when we have reached it; and by which, once any vertex (true vertex) has been identified, we can move from it in the *direction* of the optimum. It is itself a consequence of convexity. If one was trying to climb a mountain, and one knew that it was a convex mountain (without valleys or saddles), the shortest way of getting to the top would be to go straight up, from wherever one happened to be. That is (more or less) [3] what the Simplex method does—in n dimensions!

The weakness of the Simplex method (as so far described) is that it requires the identification of some (true) vertex as a starting-point. Sometimes this can be found by inspection (for a problem which satisfied the Wald rules it would present little difficulty); but very often it cannot, save by luck. If it cannot, there is a preliminary investigation which must be carried through before the above process can start. Various methods have been suggested whereby this preliminary stage can be systematised; that which seems to be most generally useful is an adaptation of the Simplex method

[1] It may be useful to take an example from the transportation problem. If there are no more than 5 sources and 4 markets there are 20 variables to be determined; even after elimination, these cannot be reduced to less than $4 \times 3 = 12$ variables, subject to 12 sign restraints and $5 + 4 - 1$ specific restraints, 20 in all. The number of *possible* vertices is the number of ways in which 12 can be selected from 20; this is no less than 127,970. Thus if the thing were gone at bull-headed, more than an eighth of a million calculations, each of considerable size, would be necessary.

[2] Set out by that author in Chapter 21 of *Activity Analysis* (*op. cit.*). Versions are, of course, to be found in all the text-books.

[3] More accurately, it may be described as follows: As we have seen, any vertex A is a solution of n of the restraints (sign and specific) considered as equations. A vertex *neighbouring* to A can be defined as one which is a solution of $(n - 1)$ of A's equations, together with *one* of those which were not taken when A was determined. (A must, of course, be a true vertex, and the neighbouring vertices must be true vertices.) If A is an optimum the value of $V (= \Sigma px)$ at A must, of course, be no less than the value at any of the neighbouring vertices. It is less obvious, but it is true (as a result of convexity) that if A is not an optimum there must be at least one of the neighbouring vertices where the value of V is greater than it is at A. (This is the same principle as that which is familiar to economists, that—under universal diminishing returns—a maximum is sufficiently determined by looking at marginal conditions.) Thus in order to discover whether A is an optimum it is only necessary to look at its relations with its neighbouring vertices. And in order to proceed as rapidly as possible to the optimum, from a given vertex, it is only necessary to select that one of the neighbouring vertices along the " edge " to which V increases most rapidly; then to repeat the operation with the vertex so reached; continuing until a vertex has been found from which there is no increase to any neighbouring vertex. That is the Simplex method.

itself. By introducing extra variables into the original problem, a subsidiary problem can be written down which is such that: (1) a true vertex of the subsidiary can be found by inspection, and (2) an optimum of the subsidiary is a true vertex of the original problem. Thus the subsidiary can be solved by the Simplex method; once the subsidiary is solved, the Simplex method can be applied to the original problem without difficulty.[1]

Other methods are, however, in use. It is sometimes useful to begin by tackling the dual to the original problem; the dual can, of course, be written down immediately, and once the dual is solved, the primal can be solved at once. (An obvious case of this is when the primal has many variables but only two specific restraints; for the dual can then be reduced to two variables, and can be solved graphically.) There is also a Dual Simplex method, in which the dual is kept in sight all the time. A direct attack on the difficulty of finding a vertex from which to start is made by the " Multiplex method " (published in 1957 by Ragnar Frisch).[2] This requires only a feasible point (not a vertex) as a starting-point; from that it identifies a " centre " of the feasible region; if one moves from the centre, in the direction of increasing V, one should arrive somewhere near the optimum.

These are the basic tools which are at the disposal of the Linear Programmer; by these means a problem is soluble, if it can be cast into appropriate form, and of problems that can be so cast there appears to be an ample supply.[3] Most of them (like the diet problem and the transportation problem) are problems of the least cost method of carrying through a given programme; problems (both military and civil) of the public sector do often fall fairly naturally into that form. But since the coefficients in the weighted sum that is to be maximised (or minimised) may (when we have left the prototype) be either positive or negative, there is no reason why the determination of a maximum profit combination of inputs and outputs (prices of the inputs and outputs being given) should not be tackled in a similar way. Thus the uses of Linear Programming are not confined to the public sector, but can be extended, at least to some extent, to the field of private enterprise.

There is, however, a doubt which creeps in at this point; and it seems proper that in a survey like the present, such doubts should be mentioned. What is the relation between this new technique and the process of market adjustment by the price-mechanism, on which economists have been accustomed to rely for the solution of what are, after all, for the most part much the same problems? One can understand that there are problems of " economic maximisation " which are unsuitable, for social or institutional

[1] For a description of this device, see Gass, *Linear Programming*, pp. 61–66.

[2] It is briefly described by van Eijk and Sandee in *Econometrica*, January 1959, pp. 9–13.

[3] A fat bibliography has been published by Vera Riley and S. I. Gass (Johns Hopkins Press, 1958). It is summarised in nine pages at the end of Gass's book (above cited).

reasons, for solution by a competitive process; the " public sector " problems just mentioned are obvious examples of this, but no doubt there are others. Here, where the reason for the non-availability of the market mechanism is non-economic, it is an obvious gain to have found an alternative. What seems distinctly less clear is the usefulness of the technique in those cases which have so much troubled economists, where there are economic reasons why the market mechanism will not work. It looks only too likely that in these cases the Linear Programming technique will also be unsatisfactory.

Competitive theory (it has often been remarked by Linear Programmers) takes it for granted that the individual firm is maximising its profits; that, so they say, means that the Linear Programming problem, inherent in the firm's own production, has already been solved. That, they naturally maintain, is a big assumption. It has been shown by experiment that any complex problem of this sort requires a technique for its solution; without that technique it is too much to expect that the individual firm will be able to maximise its profits; now that the technique has been provided, the gap in the traditional theory can be filled. One would not deny the merits of this argument as a piece of salesmanship; but its deeper significance seems to come out more clearly if it is stood the other way up.

The traditional case for competition can be put into the form of saying that it is a way of avoiding the Linear Programming problem (the macro-problem, we might call it) which is involved in the co-ordination of production over the whole economy. The macro-problem is broken up, by the market, into little bits, each of which should be too simple to warrant the application of elaborate technique; the co-ordination between the bits (which would have otherwise to be provided by a supertechnician) is provided by the market mechanism. If this process were to be carried through fully there should be no scope for Linear Programming within the firm; for the firm's problem should be reduced to that of optimising against a set of restraints, so few and simple that the solution would be obvious. In practice, of course, the fragmentation is rarely carried so far as this; at the most, the market takes over a part of the task of co-ordination; a significant part is left to be done within the firm. The application of Linear Programming to business problems does therefore remain open as a useful possibility. We should, however, ask: why is it that the fragmentation does not proceed so far as to prevent this happening? What is it that stops the market from taking over the whole job?

Doubtless there are many reasons. But surely one should not overlook the reason which has, after all, most commended itself to economists: the diseconomies of small scale. Now if it is true that small-scale diseconomies are the main economic reason why fragmentation does not proceed to the limit it will follow that the same force which restricts the application of the market mechanism will also restrict the application of the linear technique. For the presence of scale economies implies the absence of convexity: some qualification (which may be more or less serious) to the convexity which Linear Programming requires.

One is driven to the conclusion that Linear Programming and the price mechanism are rather close substitutes—both in the things they can do and in those they cannot. But the fact that two things are close substitutes does not exclude the possibility that there may be a part for each to perform.

V. Activity Analysis

There is a wide sense of the term "Activity Analysis" in which it would include the whole of the theory (as opposed to the practical technique) of Linear Programming. I am using it here in a narrower sense, to which its title is (I think) more appropriate.

Let us go back to the prototype theory (which is subject to the Wald rules), and concentrate attention (this time) on its economic interpretation. As given so far, that economic interpretation was rather narrow. The prototype theory was presented as nothing more than a re-working of the Walras–Cassel system; the "fixed coefficients" and other basic restrictions, which notoriously limit the applicability of that system, were retained. It was, however, already shown by von Neumann[1] that there is an easy way in which they can be relaxed. All that is needed is a slight change in point of view.

It is convenient to begin with a rather special problem—that of products in joint supply. It is implicit in the Walrasian assumptions that the processes of production of the various products are *independent*: in the sense that the output of any product can be increased, by the absorption of additional units of the factors, without affecting the supplies of other products, except in so far as factors are withdrawn from the production of these other products. Though this independence assumption is not a bad approximation to reality, it is certainly not true universally; it is better, therefore, to do without it. There are indeed various ways by which that could be done.

It would, for instance, be possible to observe that joint supply relations can be reduced to (linear) equations connecting the various outputs (x); we have a regular technique for dealing with such equations. By their aid, for instance, some of the x's could be eliminated; we could then proceed, with the remaining x's, as before. That is the procedure which would be suggested by what has been said previously; but if we do proceed in that way, we are raising the question—what is the status of those x's, which remain as variables of the system, after the others have been eliminated? They are outputs, but they are not all the outputs—they *represent* both themselves and the others. The notion accordingly presents itself that it will be easier to work, from the start, with indices of output, which are to be distinguished from the actual outputs of the commodities, and which will spare us the

[1] In the article above cited.

(arbitrary) choice of which variables to eliminate. It is from that idea that Activity Analysis arises.

An *activity* is a process whereby certain quantities of inputs are transformed into certain quantities of outputs. There are *constant returns to scale* (this is an essential assumption of Activity Analysis) so that an activity can be carried on at any *intensity*; by increasing the intensity, one simply increases all inputs and all outputs in the same proportion. Thus the kth activity, carried on at unit intensity, transforms $a_{1k}, a_{2k}, \ldots a_{Mk}$ of the factors into $\alpha_{1k}, \alpha_{2k} \ldots \alpha_{Nk}$ of the products; if carried on at intensity X_k it transforms $a_{1k}X_k, \ldots a_{Mk}X_k$ of the factors into $\alpha_{1k}X_k, \ldots \alpha_{Nk}X_k$ of the products. (The a's and α's are non-negative constants, which define the activity. Of course, where there is no joint supply, all but one of the α's will be zero.)

If there are R activities, carried on at intensities (X_k) the total input of the ith factor is $\sum a_{ik}X_k$ (summed over all k); the total output of the jth product is $\sum \alpha_{jk}X_k$ (summed over all k). Thus V, the total value of output (at prices p_j), is $\sum\sum p_j\alpha_{jk}X_k$ (summed over all j and all k—all products and all activities); this may be written $\sum P_kX_k$, where P_k (being $\sum p_j\alpha_{jk}$ summed over all products) is nothing else but the value of the output of the kth activity, when that is carried on at unit intensity. Everything can now be expressed in terms of the X's. The sum to be maximised is $\sum P_kX_k$ (where the P's, since they depend upon given p's and given α's, are given constants). The specific restraints take the usual form

$$a_{11}X_1 + a_{12}X_2 + \ldots + a_{1R}X_R \leqslant b_1$$
$$\vdots$$
$$a_{M1}X_1 + a_{M2}X_2 + \ldots + a_{MR}X_R \leqslant b_M$$

there are the usual sign restraints. Thus the whole of the prototype theory can be reinterpreted, so as to allow for the possibility of joint products, without requiring any formal (or mathematical) change.

That, I think, is the best way to introduce the " activity "; but the idea would be much less important than it is if it could only deal with joint products. As a result of this restatement, there is a further extension, much more far-reaching, which is automatically at our disposal. In the prototype theory, we maintained the Walras–Cassel assumption of the " fixed technical coefficients "—that there is just one way of producing each product, so that the a_{ij}'s are all constants. It may well have appeared that we were putting too much weight upon this assumption (it was, after all, abandoned long ago by those who worked in the Walras tradition [1]); it was nevertheless convenient to maintain it, for purposes of exposition, and it was safe to do so, because it would be so easy to abandon it when the time came.

The Activity Analysis model, just described, is in fact no longer tied down by the assumption of fixed technical coefficients. Just as the possibility was left open, in the prototype, that some possible products would not be

[1] By Walras himself in his last edition; by Pareto already in the *Cours* (1898).

produced; so it is left possible here, for exactly the same reason, that some possible processes (for a product that is produced by another process) will not be employed, so that the intensities of these processes (X) are zero. The condition for this to happen can be worked out at once from the condition for zero output in the prototype. The intensity of the kth activity will be zero if $P_k < \sum w_i a_{ik}$; that is to say, if the activity is unprofitable at the imputed factor prices. Thus, while some of the disused activities will represent products that it does not pay to produce, others (and probably in practice these will be the more interesting) will represent methods of production that it does not pay to employ. Accordingly, by a sufficient widening of the range of possible activities, everything which economists are in the habit of saying about factor substitution can be brought in.

It must be emphasised that the resulting model is mathematically identical with our prototype model; the Wald rules are still in force; all that has happened is that it has been given a different economic dress. Nevertheless, by that simple change it has been converted into a general theory, with a range which is comparable to that of the Paretian theory of general equilibrium. The Activity Analysis approach is indeed in the end not so dissimilar from the Paretian approach; their strengths, and their weaknesses, are much the same. We get no help from Activity Analysis in dealing with increasing returns, the nut which is hardest to crack by Paretian methods; indeed, it may be said that the Activity Analyst is more completely dependent upon the hypothesis of constant returns to scale than the Paretian. There is nothing to prevent the Paretian from exploring the realms of increasing returns, to the very limited extent to which they can be explored by his methods; to the Activity Analyst they are forbidden territory. Each is beset by the temptation to make excessive use of the price parameters, which are associated on the one side with the assumption of perfect competition, on the other with convexity assumptions, which amount (in practice) to much the same thing. The possibility of methods that it does not pay to employ can be dealt with on either method; where Activity Analysis gains is in its more explicit attention to the possibility of products that it does not pay to produce, and of factors that it does not pay to use. For any problem where these latter possibilities are not important (and that is surely the case with the majority of economic problems) it will not matter which method one uses. If either is applicable, both will be applicable; each will give the same results.

This being so, it is not surprising to find that particular problems, for the solution of which the new method has a decided advantage, are far from common. It can indeed happen—it is already happening—that people who have learned to think in the new way will begin by getting their problems out in that way; but it usually appears in the end that they could have been got out in the old way just as well.[1] This is not to deny that there are things

[1] A nice example is to be found in the papers by Farrell and Champernowne (*Econometrica*, July 1954).

which it is easier to notice if one is thinking in the new manner; one wonders whether Samuelson would have put forward his famous Factor-price Equalisation Theorem just when he did, if he had not been working, at the same time, at the development of Activity Analysis.[1] It would, however, appear that (apart from Input–Output applications, which I shall be considering in the next section) the principal achievement of the new method has been the establishment of very general theorems, which are mainly valuable because, when we have them, we can go on in our old ways with a better conscience. The chief of these is the proof of the existence of a competitive equilibrium (the solution of Wald's problem) which is contained in a most remarkable passage of the DOSSO book.[2] The general character of this proof (too important a matter to be omitted from this survey) may be sketched out, very roughly, as follows.

From the Wald rules about the constants—a's, b's and p's (or P's)—which are carried over into Activity Analysis, it follows (as we have seen) that production is optimisable; there is a set of quantities of products (x) which maximises the value of output for given product prices (p), and there is a set of imputed factor prices (w) which belongs to that optimum. If production is organised (as it should then be possible for it to be organised) into firms which operate under perfect competition, the earnings of the factors will be such as correspond to these imputed factor prices. Thus on the "supply" side the equilibrium exists; but nothing has yet been said about the demands for the products. These must now be brought in. All we assume, at this stage, is that the demands depend, in some way, upon the product prices and factor earnings; then, since the factor earnings depend on product prices, both the demands (x') and the supplies (x) of the products have been shown to depend upon the product prices (p).[3] The difficulty is to show that there must be some set of product prices which makes demands equal to supplies. This is tackled in the following way.

Starting from any arbitrary set of product prices (and derived factor prices), we have an (x') determined by the demand functions; but this (x') may not be feasible, or, if feasible, it may not be efficient—there may be no (p) for which it would be optimum. What DOSSO then does is to diminish (or increase) all the x' in the same proportion, until the resulting set of quantities, $k(x')$, does lie on the frontier of the feasible region. To this $k(x')$ there will correspond a set of prices (p'), being a set of prices for which $k(x')$ is an optimum. (Usually, indeed, as when $k(x')$ is at a vertex, there will be many such sets of prices; but that does not—too much—matter.) These

[1] There is a family resemblance between the Factor Price Theorem and the Input–Output Substitution Theorem (see below, p. 107) due to the same author.

[2] Pp. 366–73. It appears that in its final form this proof is due to Solow; but it was built up by stages, that are to be associated with the names, first of Wald himself, then of Lionel Mackenzie, of Samuelson and of Harold Kuhn. (There is another discussion in Baumol, *op. cit.*, pp. 859–65.)

[3] The (p) are, of course, to be understood as *relative* prices; if all p's, and consequently w's, are multiplied by the same multiplier, they will generate the same (x)—and the same (x').

(p') prices are rather analogous to " supply prices," to be put against the " demand prices " (p) with which we began.

A rule has therefore been evolved by which a set (or sets) of supply prices can be associated with the given demand prices. At this point it is possible to invoke the aid of a powerful mathematical tool, *the fixed-point theorem*,[1] according to which (provided that a number of conditions, which can be shown to hold in this case, are satisfied) there must be some (p) which is itself included among the sets of (p') which, in this manner, it generates. Once that is established, the rest is simple. For since the total earnings of the factors (which, by " Walras' law," are all spent) are equal to the total value of output,[2] it follows that at this (p), $\sum px' = \sum p(kx')$. Since the k's are the same for all products, $k = 1$. The quantities demanded are optimum quantities; supplies and demands are equal. Thus the competitive equilibrium exists.

The most interesting thing about this proof, to the economist, is the little that has to be assumed about the demand functions.[3] It is necessary that there should be some set of demands, some (x'), that is generated by every (p) and the (w) that belongs to it; but little more is necessary.[4] There is nothing that corresponds to the " downward slope of the demand curve." The explanation of this rather surprising omission is that nothing has been said about the uniqueness of the equilibrium. Multiple equilibria are perfectly possible. Sufficiently strong " downward slope " assumptions (what Samuelson calls " the weak axiom of revealed preference "—what I should prefer to describe in terms of the absence of net-income effects) do, however, prove uniqueness. That is where they come in. It is, of course, familiar, from simple examples, that the presence of net-income effects may lead to such things as " upward sloping demand curves " and multiple equilibria.

VI. Input–Output

Throughout our discussion of Activity Analysis we have maintained the Wald rules; with the implication, which they carry, that factors and products (inputs and outputs) are fundamentally different sorts of things. Analysis

[1] The general idea of a fixed-point theorem is well explained in Courant and Robbins, *What is Mathematics?*, pp. 251–5. It should, however, be noticed that what is there described is the original Brouwer theorem, not the slightly more complicated Kakutani theorem, which is what is needed for the above purpose. See the passage in DOSSO, just cited; also Baumol, p. 859.

[2] See above, p. 88.

[3] It is quite unnecessary to make the peculiar assumption, which Wald made in 1934, that demands do not fall to zero, however high prices rise. As Kuhn has shown in the paper that was previously mentioned (*Linear Inequalities*, *op. cit.*), the reason why Wald made this assumption was that he did not have the duality theory. He took it for granted that all of a *given* list of outputs must have prices equal to costs; and that meant that he had to exclude the possibility of zero outputs. Though he allowed for the possibility of factors with zero prices, he did not allow for the other zero, which is dual to it.

[4] It has to be assumed that the demand functions are continuous—that there are no jumps in demand as prices change. This is necessary, if we are going to insist on making it a condition of equilibrium that demands should *equal* supplies. If we were prepared to be content with some sort of approximate equality this continuity condition could presumably be loosened a bit.

of that kind can deal with most aspects of a static system (under constant returns to scale); but it cannot deal with intermediate products, which are outputs from one angle and inputs from another. What it must be assuming about such products is that they have been " netted out " by vertical integration. It is, however, uncertain whether actual production is capable of such integration, without being involved in lateral integration also; in any case, the intermediate products which certainly exist are worthy of study on their own account. It will not be expected that any very serious discussion of the Input–Output theory, invented by Leontief as a means of studying such linkages,[1] can find a place at the end of this already lengthy survey; it has, however, proved so attractive a field [2] for the application of the developments which we have been considering that it cannot be left altogether on one side.

It is characteristic of Leontief's model that it reduces the primary factors to one only—homogeneous labour; apart from labour, the inputs of each industry are the outputs of other industries. We define x_i as the *gross* output of the ith commodity, including that which is absorbed as inputs of other industries, or indeed (for the seed-corn must come out of the harvest) as input in the production of x_i itself. The amount of the ith commodity which is needed as input of the jth (per unit of the latter) is taken as given, like the corresponding coefficients in the prototype; it will cause no confusion if we write it a_{ij}, as before. The demand for the product x_i, as input in the production of other commodities, will then come to $\sum a_{ij}x_j$ (summed over all j); the net, or final, output is the difference between this and gross output, that is to say, it is $x_i - \sum a_{ij}x_j$. The amount of labour that is required (per unit of product) for the jth product we will simply write a_j. Then the demand for labour is $\sum a_j x_j$ (over all products).

What are the restraints under which this system operates? There are, of course, first of all the usual sign restraints (all x_i non-negative). If we suppose that the supply of labour (b) is given, we have a specific restraint, of the usual kind, due to the limitation of the supply of that factor; here it will appear as $\sum a_j x_j \leqslant b$. It is, however, further necessary that the *net* outputs of the products should be non-negative. It is possible, that is, for the whole output of a particular product to be absorbed as inputs in the production of other products; but it is inconsistent with static equilibrium for more than the whole output to be so absorbed. Thus we have another set of specific restraints, of the form $\sum a_{ij}x_j \leqslant x_i$ (for all i), or, written in full,

$$a_{i1}x_1 + a_{i2}x_2 + \ldots + (a_{ii} - 1)x_i + \ldots + a_{in}x_n \leqslant 0$$

It is the appearance of these " Leontief restraints," as we may call them, in

[1] *Structure of the American Economy* (1st ed., 1941; 2nd ed., 1951); *Studies in the Structure of the American Economy* (1953). I have made extensive use of the chapters on Input–Output in DOSSO (IX and X); it does, however, take some effort to disentangle from these chapters the essential points.

[2] As will be apparent to anyone who turns the pages of *Econometrica* or the *Review of Economic Studies*, it is one of the fields of application on which interest has been centred in the most recent years.

addition to the labour restraint, which marks the Leontief system off from those we have considered hitherto.

It may be assumed, for the same reasons as before, that the *a*'s (of every kind) are non-negative; but that cannot mean that all of the coefficients in any Leontief restraint can be non-negative. If they were, it would follow at once (because of the zero on the right-hand side) that outputs of all commodities with non-zero coefficients must be zero. For the Leontief system to be feasible at all, it is first of all necessary that the " feedback coefficient " a_{ii} (of any output into its own production) should be less than unity. But that means that we are bound to have one negative coefficient in each of the

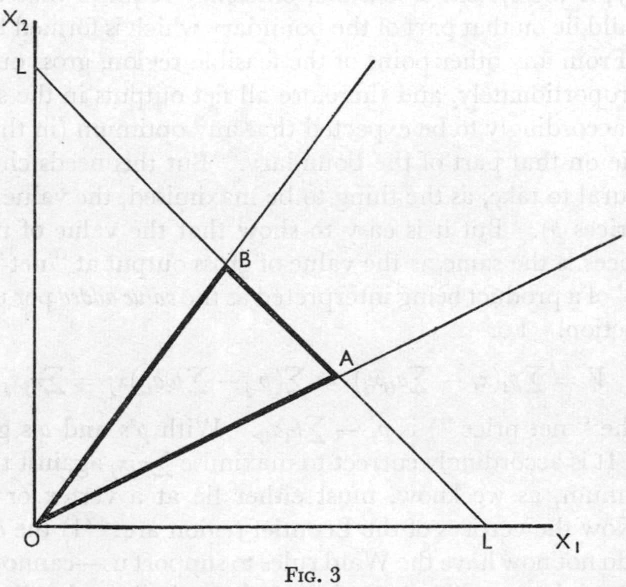

FIG. 3

Leontief restraints; accordingly, the Wald rules, and their consequence—assured feasibility—will not apply.

The situation which emerges can easily be illustrated diagrammatically (Fig. 3). If gross outputs x_1 and x_2 are measured on the two axes, the labour restraint will appear as a downward sloping line of the usual kind (*LL*); while the Leontief restraints will appear as upward-sloping lines (because of the negative coefficient) through the origin (because of the zero on the right-hand side). The feasible region is accordingly cut down to the triangle *OAB*. Evidently it will continue to take the same sort of form—a pyramid or " cone " with apex at the origin—in more than two dimensions.

There are two things, which are already visible in this construction, which require to be noticed. In the first place, the mere condition that $a_{ii} \leqslant 1$ (which keeps the Leontief lines upward sloping) is not sufficient to ensure that there exists a feasible region. The line *OA* could easily be swung up (or *OB* swung down) so that the feasible region disappeared. What this would mean (in the two-goods case) is that the amount of x_2 absorbed in making x_1 was greater than could be replaced by absorbing all of the x_1 in the x_2 industry (so that if net x_1 were zero, net x_2 would still be negative); with a coefficients chosen at random that would certainly be possible, and it would certainly mean that the system would not work. The same thing can naturally happen in more complicated ways when there are more than two commodities. The conditions (upon the a coefficients) for it *not* to happen are called the Hawkins–Simon conditions; [1] it is unnecessary to write them out here. It is sufficient to observe that some such conditions must be satisfied if the Leontief system is to be feasible.

Secondly, if the system is feasible, efficiency requires that the " point " selected should lie on that part of the boundary which is formed by the labour restraint. From any other point of the feasible region, gross outputs can be increased proportionately, and therefore all net outputs in the same proportion. It is accordingly to be expected that any optimum (in the sense so far used) will lie on that part of the boundary. But this needs checking up.

It is natural to take, as the thing to be maximised, the value of *net* output (at given prices p). But it is easy to show that the value of net output at " gross " prices is the same as the value of gross output at " net " prices—the " net price " of a product being interpreted as the *value added* per unit of output in its production. For

$$V = \sum p_i(x_i - \sum a_{ij}x_i) = \sum (p_j - \sum p_i a_{ij})x_j = \sum \pi_j x_j$$

where π_j (the " net price ") is $p_j - \sum p_i a_{ij}$. With p's and a's given, the π's are given. It is accordingly correct to maximise $\sum \pi_j x_j$ against the restraints.

An optimum, as we know, must either lie at a vertex or " between " vertices. Now the vertices of the Leontief region are: (1) the origin, which —since we do not now have the Wald rules to support us—cannot be excluded as a possible optimum; (2) the points such as A, B on the diagram, which are intersections of Leontief restraints with the labour restraint. At the origin, however, V is necessarily zero, while at the latter vertices V will necessarily be positive [2] (if there is a feasible region), so that it is only the latter vertices which we need consider. Each of these vertices will represent a position in which there is a zero net output of all but one of the commodities, and a maximum net output of the one that remains. Possible optima (all of which, it is now confirmed, must lie on the labour restraint part of the boundary) are weighted averages of these vertices.

If there are positive net outputs of all the n commodities, V must have an equal value at all of these vertices, so that $\sum \pi_j x_j$ must be the same all over the " plane " $\sum a_j x_j = b$. This can only happen if π_j bears the same proportion to a_j for all commodities. This we may write $\pi_j = wa_j$, where w is

[1] They were worked out, with a little trouble, by the eponymous authors, in *Econometrica* during the year 1949.

[2] We keep the " extra " Wald rule, that the p's are non-negative, and not all zero.

easily recognisable as the (imputed) price of labour. Thus we have n equations

$$p_j - \sum p_i a_{ij} = wa_j \quad \text{(for all }_j\text{)}$$

to determine the gross prices (p) relatively to the wage of labour. It will only be at these prices that the net outputs of all N commodities can be positive.

How do we know, it may, however, be asked, the prices (p) that are determined by these equations will be non-negative? It turns out that the conditions for this to be so are the same Hawkins–Simon conditions as we had formerly to invoke to establish feasibility. Thus, granted these conditions, the internal coherence of the Leontief model is established.

Substitutability in Leontief Models. There are a few more points to be noted. The prices which have just been determined are independent of the demands for the commodities; however demands change, the optimum point must keep on the " labour restraint " plane, so that the prices just determined must continue to hold. Thus, in spite of the " fixed coefficients " at which products are transformed into one another, the fact that there is (ultimately) only one scarce factor keeps the " labour theory of value " in operation, with the system operating under constant cost. It follows from this that even if the net outputs of some commodities are zero (so that they are pure intermediate products, only produced in order to be re-absorbed into the productive process) their " net prices " must still be equal to the value of their labour coefficients: the condition $\pi_j = wa_j$ must still hold for such products. Equality does not require, as seemed at first sight, that net output should be positive; it is sufficient that gross output is positive.

There is a more remarkable consequence of the same property, that has been pointed out by Samuelson—his " substitution theorem."[1] It is not necessary, in the Leontief model, to start, as hitherto supposed, with given technical coefficients—given methods of producing the commodities. There may be a choice of methods, and it will yet follow that there is one method which has to be adopted for each product; the method chosen is independent of the demands for the products. Thus the Leontief system produces under constant cost, even if methods are (in principle) variable.

This, it will be recognised, is again a generalisation of the labour theory of value. If all labour was applied directly to the making of finished products (and labour was the only factor), there might be a choice of methods, but efficiency would dictate that the most efficient method should be used for each product—as Marx (for instance) knew very well. The choice of method would be independent of the demand. What Samuelson has shown is that the same continues to hold, so long as labour is the only primary factor of production, even if labour is applied indirectly as well as directly. Put in this way, his result is by no means surprising.

[1] Originally stated in Chapter VII of *Activity Analysis* (ed. Koopmans).

There is, however, an exception to the classical doctrine, that has been familiar since the days of J. S. Mill. If some of the products are joint products, the relative prices of the joint products will depend upon demand; it is then possible that a shift in demand will lead to the substitution of one method of production for another, even though labour is the only primary factor. The Leontief system excludes such joint production, so that in the Leontief system this complication cannot arise. It is, however, to be expected that it will arise if we attempt to extend the Samuelson principle to cases in which joint production is allowed.[1]

It may be useful to show in detail how this is. In terms of Activity Analysis, the general problem may be posed as follows: There are R activities, capable of producing the N commodities (by input of some and output of others, and, of course, by input of labour). Since the activities include many alternative possible methods of producing the commodities, R may be supposed to be larger—if we like much larger—than N. We may generalise our notation, and write α_{ik} as the *output* of the ith commodity by the kth activity, when it is operating at unit intensity; inputs can be covered by the same symbol, α_{ik} being negative when the ith commodity is an input. Here we will write β_k for the input of labour. Then, if X_k is the intensity of the kth activity, the net output of the ith commodity, over the whole system, is $\sum\alpha_{ik}X_k$. We have to maximise $\sum\sum p_i\alpha_{ik}X_k$, subject to the restraints: $X_k \geqslant 0$ for all k; $\sum\alpha_{ik}X_k \geqslant 0$ for all i; $\sum\beta_kX_k \leqslant b$. Formally, the problem is almost the same as before. Since some α's are positive, and some negative, there is still the same question of determining whether or not there exists a feasible region; in order that it should exist the α's will have to be suitable. We will suppose that they are suitable.

Following the same argument as before, it would be necessary, if all activities were utilised, that $\sum p_i\alpha_{ik} = w\beta_k$ for every activity. But this gives us R equations to determine N prices; if $R > N$, as we have supposed, the system is over-determined.[2] Thus, in general, it will not be possible for more than N activities to be utilised; the rest will have $\sum p_i\alpha_{ik} < w\beta_k$, and intensity zero. Optimisation involves the selection of a particular set of not more than N activities, which are to be employed; an optimum set of activities must satisfy the conditions just stated. If the optimum set consists of the whole number of N activities the prices at which these activities can be employed will be determinate; any demands for final outputs which the system is capable of satisfying can be satisfied at these prices and with these activities. Now if there is no joint supply, at least N activities will be required to produce the N commodities; this therefore is Samuelson's case.

[1] The point of the elaborate investigations by Koopmans and Arrow (Chapters VIII and IX of the *Activity Analysis* volume) was to clear up this exception.

[2] This assumes (and it is assumed throughout the argument) that the activities are "linearly independent"—that we are not including any activity which is a mere combination of other activities. In economic applications that (I think) may be taken for granted.

But if there is joint supply it will be possible for the N commodities to be produced in positive quantities with less than N activities; the prices are then not determinate, and it is possible that as demands vary, the activities that are utilised may change.

The matter may be illustrated, and the argument made more precise with the aid of a diagram (Fig. 4). Suppose that there are two commodities being produced and three possible activities: $N = 2$ and $R = 3$. Measuring the intensities of the activities along three axes, the labour restraint becomes a plane; as we have seen, the optimum must lie upon that plane: let us therefore take it to be the plane of the paper. The intersections of this plane with the co-ordinate planes will accordingly appear on the paper as a triangle XYZ. The sign restraints and the labour restraints limit possible optima to points within or on the sides of this triangle. The *two*

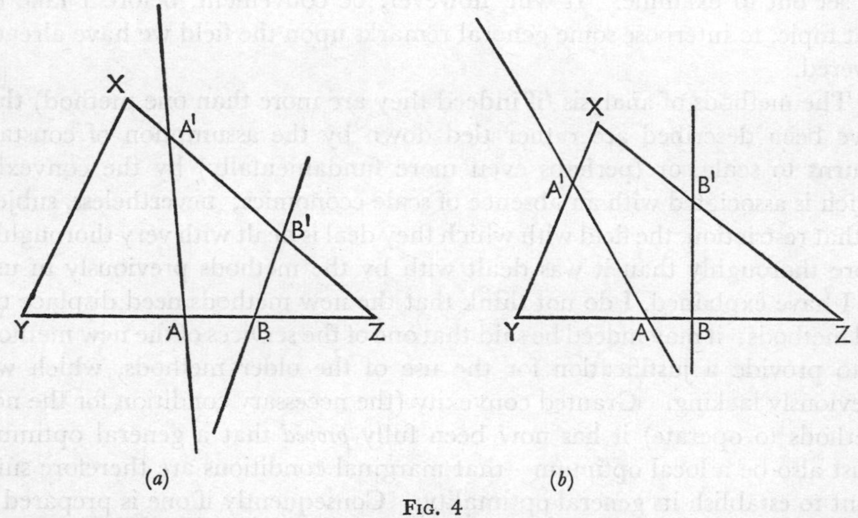

Fig. 4

Leontief restraints (which will also be shown as straight lines—the intersections of the Leontief planes with the labour plane) will limit the possible optima further. If they are to be operative at all they must intersect the triangle: there are then two main cases, in one of which they intersect the same two sides (Fig. 4 (*a*)); in the other there is only one side which they both intersect (Fig. 4 (*b*)).

Now in either case, for the reason above stated, it is not possible that all three activities should be used in an optimum position; the optimum cannot therefore lie *within* the triangle XYZ; it must lie *on* one of the sides. Accordingly, in Fig. 4 (*a*), possible optima lie along AB or along $A'B'$; one of these stretches will be more efficient than the other. If it is AB the system will be at A when the demand for one commodity is zero, at B when the demand for the other is zero; they can be combined (efficiently) in any proportions by moving along AB.

In this case, therefore, the Samuelson theorem is verified; but now consider Fig. 4 (*b*). Possible optima now lie along *AB*, or along the broken line *A'XB'*. If *AB* is optimum, all is as before; but if the other is the optimum stretch there is a change in the combination of activities as demand varies from one extremity to the other. But this exception can only arise if the point *X* is on the optimum path—if positive net outputs of the *two* commodities can be secured by using only *one* activity. Joint production is accordingly a necessary condition for the exception to arise.

VII. Conclusion—The Theory of Games

There remains one further topic which needs consideration before we have exhausted the list of specialisms which, in their relations to one another, we set out to examine. It will, however, be convenient, before I take up that topic, to interpose some general remarks upon the field we have already covered.

The methods of analysis (if indeed they are more than one method) that have been described are rather tied down by the assumption of constant returns to scale, or (perhaps even more fundamentally) by the convexity which is associated with an absence of scale economies; nevertheless, subject to that restriction, the field with which they deal is dealt with very thoroughly, more thoroughly than it was dealt with by the methods previously in use. As I have explained, I do not think that the new methods need displace the old methods; it may indeed be said that one of the services of the new methods is to provide a justification for the use of the older methods, which was previously lacking. Granted convexity (the necessary condition for the new methods to operate) it has now been fully *proved* that a general optimum must also be a local optimum—that marginal conditions are therefore sufficient to establish its general optimality. Consequently if one is prepared to grant (as in many cases one is) that the changes one wants to consider will not involve any change in the number or specifications of the kinds of goods that are to be produced, or of the resources that are used, the old-fashioned marginal rules are all that have to be considered. The occasions on which the economist will want to go further, so as to have to use the new methods in relation to particular problems (while being able to retain the convexity conditions which enable him to use them) are really rather infrequent.

It must nevertheless be recognised (and this is the point on which I now want to lay stress) that the new methods are a great advance upon the old in the understanding which they convey of the *raison d'être* of the price mechanism. The rather inappropriate mathematical methods, which have been employed (at all levels of mathematisation) by the school of Cournot and Walras—and of Marshall—did in this respect rather let us down. For they caused it to appear that the price system is just one way of organising an economy efficiently; that it is, in a sense, exterior to the economic problem, something that is brought in from outside. What the linear theory has shown—and this, speaking as a theoretical rather than as a practical economist, seems to me to have been its greatest service—is that, so long as the convexity assumptions hold (and though I have constantly emphasised that they do not hold universally, I would certainly admit that they hold, to a fair approximation, over a large part of the economic field), the price mechanism is something that is inherent. It did not have to be invented, or brought in from outside. It belongs.

This indeed is what was first perceived, after a fashion, by Menger and his followers; but they did not have the power of explaining, in a manner which would compel communication, the truth that they had seen. Now it has all been set down in black and white. It has been made apparent, not only that a price system is inherent in the problem of maximising production from given resources but also that something like a price system is inherent in any problem of maximisation against restraints. The imputation of prices (or " scarcities ") to the factors of production is nothing else but a measurement of the *intensities* of the restraints; such intensities are always implicit—the special property of a competitive system is that it brings them out and makes them visible. It is through its power of developing the intensities (in the photographic sense of developing), so that they are available for use as instruments in the process of maximisation, that the competitive system does its job.

To have taken so much of economics, and to have reduced it to a problem in pure mathematics, is no doubt in many ways a most notable achievement; to many economists it will be a rather shattering achievement, but it is (after all) the kind of thing that has happened in one after another of the natural sciences. It is not surprising that it should happen to us also. Nevertheless, the question persists: how much of economics is it that is being thus absorbed? If we take the famous definition, given so many years ago by Lord Robbins—" the relationship between ends and scarce means that have alternative uses " [1]—economics, in that sense, is very well covered by the linear theory. It has, however, been shown that in that sense it has very little to do with " human behaviour "—a phrase that Robbins did allow to creep in. The " logic of choice," now that it has been fully mathematised, appears as nothing else but pure technics—the distilled essence of a general technology.

Economics, surely, is a social science. It is concerned with the operations of human beings, who are not omniscient, and not wholly rational; who (perhaps because they are not wholly rational) have diverse, and not wholly consistent, ends. As such, it cannot be reduced to a pure technics, and may benefit by being distinguished from a pure technics; for we can then say that its concern is with the use that can be made of pure

[1] *Nature and Significance of Economic Science*, p. 15. The "Austrian" credentials which are presented in the footnote to that page should be noticed.

technics by man in society. And that looks like being a distinctly different matter.

But is it? Here I come to my last topic, on which I propose to be brief. In the Theory of Games we have a subject (evidently related to those which we have been discussing, at least in the sense that it uses some of the same mathematics) which is specially concerned with the analysis of behaviour when ends are different, either completely or partially opposed. Are we to say that the rest of economic theory, which is not pure technics, is nevertheless capable of being treated in much the same way by the sister subject—the Theory of Games?

I do not pretend to know the answer to that question. I am not equipped to answer it; the Theory of Games now covers a vast territory, and there is far too much of it that I make no pretence of understanding. I shall confine myself to one point which I think I do see clearly—namely that the relation of economics to the Theory of Games is an entirely different matter from those which we have been discussing. There is no doubt that the theory of optimisation (whether or not it *is* economics) is highly relevant to economics; it may well be that the Theory of Games is highly relevant; but one does not follow from the other.

This is worth stating, because it is easy to get the impression that the connection is closer. One of the neatest ways of proving the general Duality theorem [1] (which, it will be remembered, has not been proved in this paper) is to develop it as a consequence of the fundamental theorem of Game theory —the Minimax theorem, as it is called.[2] If this is done, it looks as if the theory of optimisation is being swallowed up by Game theory—as if the Theory of Games was not merely swallowing that part of economics on which it has obvious designs, but was ready to absorb the lot! But that, I am convinced, would be a mistake.

Though the Minimax theorem is usually stated as a theorem in Game theory (and no doubt it is that application which to mathematicians is the most fruitful), it is not necessary to state it that way. It can easily be stated in a more abstract manner—as a pure property of numbers that are arranged in a rectangular matrix. Any such matrix has a minimax (the minimum of row maxima) and a maximin (the maximum of column minima). It is easy to prove that the minimax must always be greater than, or equal to, the maximin. What von Neumann's Minimax theorem states is that there is a process of " enlarging " the matrix by which the gap between minimax and maximin (if it initially exists) can be so reduced that it ultimately disappears. This process of enlargement is simply the addition of new rows and columns which are weighted averages (in the sense in which we have been using that term) of the former rows and columns. By sufficient enlargement, minimax and maximin can be brought together.

[1] See above, p. 91.

[2] See, for instance DOSSO, Chapter 16.

What I want to emphasise is that this enlargement is a purely abstract operation, which can be given all sorts of meanings, that have nothing but a formal connection with one another. When the Minimax theorem is used as a means of proving Duality the matrix is a matrix of technical coefficients; the enlargement (in one direction) is carried out by varying outputs, in the other by varying factor prices. When it is used in Game theory the matrix is a matrix of pay-offs; the enlargement is performed by mixing strategies. The mixing of strategies has nothing necessarily to do with the Minimax theorem; it is one of the ways in which the theorem can be applied, and no more. That the Minimax theorem can be used in the theory of optimisation does not show that " Outputs *v.* Factor Prices " is in any sense a Game.

BIBLIOGRAPHICAL NOTE

So much bibliographical work has been done by others upon the subjects covered in this survey that there is no case for appending to it a formal bibliography. The wants of mathematicians and of Linear Programming technicians are catered for in the bibliography to Gass, *Linear Programming* (1958). There is a more selective bibliography, more directed to economists, in DOSSO (Dorfman, Samuelson and Solow, *Linear Programming and Economic Analysis*, 1958). The further reading that can be recommended to the non-mathematical economist is, however, rather limited; most of it has been mentioned already.

For an easy introduction, there is G. Morton, "Notes on Linear Programming" (*Economica*, 1951); with W. J. Baumol, "Activity Analysis in One Lesson" (*A.E.R.*, 1958) to follow. Valuable background is provided by Koopmans' introduction to *Activity Analysis of Production and Allocation*, and by the first essay in his *Essays on the State of Economic Science* (1957). After these, there is nothing for it but to plunge into the DOSSO book, so frequently mentioned.

On the side of technique, Charnes, Cooper and Henderson, *An Introduction to Linear Programming* (1953) remains the simplest account of the Simplex method; it should, however, be noticed that it is the original method that is there described, not the revised method, making use of the " subsidiary," that is mentioned on p. 96 above. If one uses DOSSO for this purpose, there is much to be said for beginning with their chapter on the transportation problem. It should however be recognised that the technique of linear programming is a practical subject, like practical statistics or practical accounting; though it can be taught in classes to students of quite average intelligence, it is a tiresome thing to work out for oneself from a book.

XII

RESEARCH ON HOUSEHOLD BEHAVIOUR

By

ROBERT FERBER[1]

THE purpose of this article is to survey the main empirical research of recent years on household behaviour. Although the emphasis is on empirical work, principal theoretical developments are also reviewed, partly because of their relevance to an understanding of current thinking in the field and partly to place the empirical studies in proper perspective.

It should be stressed that this article relates to consumer behaviour at the microeconomic level. Although various parts touch on problems of aggregation and of macroeconomic relations, comprehensive coverage of these areas is outside the present scope. Furthermore, the focus is on spending and saving behaviour rather than on the income or other economic or non-economic behaviour aspects of the consumer. At the same time this article necessarily transcends the usual boundaries of economics, in view of the growing importance of other disciplines to this area, particularly marketing, sociology and psychology.

Virtually all of the developments covered in this article relate to the period since the Second World War. This hardly constitutes much of a limitation considering the tremendous amount of research that has taken place during this period. As it is, this material is so extensive and diversified that only the highlights can be covered in a relatively short article such as this.

The great bulk of studies of household behaviour in the past fifteen years have dealt with one or more of the following aspects of the subject: (1) theories of spending, or saving, behaviour; (2) influence of variables other than income on spending and saving; (3) determinants of asset holdings; (4) determinants of specific expenditures; (5) decision processes.

This classification accordingly serves as the framework for this article. Admittedly, it focuses entirely on the determinants of household behaviour, and ignores the two other basic aspects of this subject, namely, the effects of household behaviour on other sectors of the economy, and the measure-

[1] The author is Research Professor of Economics, Bureau of Economic and Business Research, and Professor of Economics in the Department of Economics, University of Illinois. He would like to thank Margaret Reid, Marianne A. Ferber and Walter McMahon for their helpful comments. He would also like to express his appreciation to Anne Harper for assisting with the preparation of the bibliography on pp. 147–54.

ment of household behaviour. The fact remains, however, that relatively little work has been done in these areas, despite their great importance. They are considered briefly in the final section, dealing with future directions for research.[1] Excluded also are those studies dealing with the purchase behaviour of a particular population, or reference group, and studies dealing with the choice of brands or of shopping locations. Some of these studies are covered in connection with the determinants of specific expenditures. To cover all of them, however, is too much for this article, aside from the fact that these studies are primarily of a more routine nature.

I. General Theories of Spending or Saving Behaviour

Three general theories currently exist on the determinants of total consumer spending: the *absolute income hypothesis*, the *relative income hypothesis* and the *permanent income hypothesis*. Though radically different in interpretation, they nevertheless possess certain properties in common. One such property is their purported generality. Each has been used on time series as well as on cross-section data and to derive macro- as well as micro-relationships.[2] Each was advanced originally in terms of individual behaviour and then generalised to aggregate behaviour, sometimes with explicit recognition of the aggregation problem and at other times largely ignoring it on the apparent presumption that non-linearities or distributional effects are relatively unimportant.

Each hypothesis postulates a relationship between consumption and income though the concepts underlying these terms may vary substantially. In other words, the primary concern is to isolate the influence of income, and occasionally of wealth, on consumer spending, holding constant the effect of other possibly relevant, less important variables—age, family composition, location of residence, education, etc. Each is the subject of wide controversy, receiving support from some empirical studies but not from others. Finally, each when first presented appears deceptively simple, at least in theory, but when it comes to implementation proponents of the same hypothesis often disagree with each other on appropriate definitions and approaches. This will become clear from a consideration of each hypothesis in turn.

A. *Absolute Income Hypothesis.* ". . . men are disposed, as a rule and

[1] Omitted also is the normative aspect of how households *should* behave. Hardly any empirical research has been devoted to this question, with the possible exception of exploratory studies in the measurement of utility. In its more pedestrian aspects the normative question falls within the realm of home economics.

[2] In the latter case the application has often been to groups of households rather than to individual households, particularly in the case of the permanent income hypothesis, on the ground that the importance of erratic factors is so great for individual households as to obscure more basic relationships.

on the average, to increase their consumption as their income increases, but not by as much as the increase in their income " [92, p. 96]. Whether or not this is the original statement of the absolute income hypothesis, there is no doubt that this statement by Keynes stimulated much empirical work to test this hypothesis and to derive " the consumption function." Many of these studies were carried out on time series, the general practice being to correlate aggregate consumption expenditures over time with aggregate disposable income and various other variables. They need not concern us here except to note that invariably they " corroborated " the hypothesis, producing very high goodness of fit (adjusted correlation coefficients of 0·98 or more), with current income accounting for the bulk of the variation in consumption, the average and marginal propensities being less than unity, and with the marginal propensity less than the average propensity.[1]

One early modification of the absolute income hypothesis was brought about by a theoretical controversy regarding the existence of any automatic force to assure full-employment equilibrium. Keynes took a negative position, but others showed that a full-employment equilibrium position could exist if consumption expenditures depended on wealth as well as on income, the " Pigou real balance effect " [138].[2] It was only in the post-war period that data became available to test the relevance of a wealth variable. Such tests as were made did tend to show that aggregate consumption was influenced by this variable, though nowhere to the extent of the influence of current income [69] [95]. It is pertinent to note, however, that the early post-war years were characterised by high asset-income ratios, low stocks of durables and relatively little debt.

At the micro level many studies had been carried out prior to the advent of *The General Theory*, but their focus invariably was on ascertaining budget relations for different groups of families or deriving Engel curves for particular components of expenditure.[3] In retrospect, such of these studies as were applicable appeared to corroborate the absolute income hypothesis. Indeed, it was this hypothesis that served as the basis for the derivation of estimates of aggregate expenditures for different population groups in 1935–36, namely, by " blowing up " average consumption observed at each income level in the 1935–36 Consumer Purchases Study [161].[4] The absolute income hypothesis also served as a basis for the derivation of aggregate forecasts of post-war consumption patterns, particularly the consumption patterns that might be expected under full employment [28].

In its empirical applications the absolute income hypothesis has generally followed one of two forms. One form has been to express the level of saving,

[1] For a summary of these studies to 1950, see Ferber [41]. An extensive bibliography of these earlier studies has been compiled by Orcutt and Roy [135].

[2] For a somewhat different interpretation, see Hansen [71].

[3] These are reviewed in Stigler [148]. A fairly comprehensive listing of these studies will be found in Williams and Zimmerman [169].

[4] The actual aggregation procedure was more complicated, but was based on this principle.

or of consumption expenditures,[1] as a function of income and of other variables, *i.e.*:

$$S = a + bY + cZ + u \tag{1}$$

where S represents saving, Y is income, Z is a conglomeration of other variables, u is a stochastic term and the other letters represent parameters.[2]

The second form involves expressing the saving *ratio* as a function of the same independent variables, *i.e.*:

$$\frac{S}{Y} = a' + b'Y + c'Z + u' \tag{2}$$

Each of these forms has advantages and limitations. Thus, in equation (1) the marginal propensity is a constant and, if logarithms of the variables are used, the income elasticity is also constant, namely, b. Equation (2) does not possess this convenient property, but may be more realistic for this reason. Parameter estimates based on equation (1) are subject to the danger of bias from two sources: the parameter estimates may be dominated by extreme values, and u is not likely to be independent of S. Expressing dollar variables in logarithms (assuming absence of negative values) removes this tendency somewhat, but not altogether. In actual practice, both forms have been used.[3]

Questions about the adequacy of the absolute income hypothesis arose because of its apparent inability to reconcile budget data on saving with observed long-run trends. Estimates of national saving and other aggregates derived by Kuznets [105] [106] and later by Goldsmith [65, Vol. 1, pp. 75–87] indicated that the aggregate saving ratio had remained virtually constant since the 1870s. Yet budget studies showed that the saving ratio rose substantially with income level. Since incomes have risen tremendously since the 1870s by almost any standard, this would suggest, according to the absolute income hypothesis, that the aggregate saving ratio should have moved up noticeably over time.

B. *Relative Income Hypothesis*. An answer to this apparent inconsistency is provided by the relative income hypothesis, which seems to have been first propounded by Dorothy Brady and Rose Friedman [14]. Its underlying

[1] It is perhaps needless to note that consumption functions and saving functions are the same, in theory, one being the complement of the other. However, substantial differences can be obtained in empirical work according to which term is being measured.

[2] We shall follow the usual distinction between *saving* and *savings*, the former representing a flow, that is, the difference between income and consumption during a particular period, and the latter representing a stock as of a certain point in time. Unless otherwise specified, saving is defined as the amount set aside out of current income rather than as the net increment in wealth.

[3] For applications of these functions at the microeconomic level, see Mendershausen [119], Klein [94] [96], Fisher [50].

assumption is that the saving rate depends not on the level of income but on the *relative position* of the individual on the income scale, *i.e.*:

$$\frac{s}{y} = a + b\frac{y}{y} \tag{3}$$

where s and y represent individual saving and income, respectively, and y represents average income.

Much additional theoretical and empirical support of this hypothesis was provided by the work of Modigliani and of Duesenberry, carried out at about the same time [122] [35]. On a theoretical level, Duesenberry supplied psychological support for this hypothesis, noting that a strong tendency exists in our social system for people to emulate their neighbours and, at the same time, to strive constantly towards a higher standard of living. Hence, once a new, higher standard of living is obtained, as at a cyclical peak, people are reluctant to return to a lower level when incomes go down. In other words, people seek to maintain at least the highest standard of living attained in the past.

On the basis of this reasoning, Duesenberry inferred that from an aggregate time-series point of view the relative income hypothesis could be transformed into one expressing the saving rate as a function of the ratio of current income to the highest level previously reached, *i.e.*:

$$\frac{S}{Y} = a + b\,\frac{Y}{Y_0} \tag{4}$$

where Y_0 represents the highest level of income previously attained (after deflation for changes in prices and population).

The implication of this hypothesis is that the saving ratio in the long run is constant, independent of the absolute level of income, although in the short run (from one cycle to another) the rate depends on the ratio of current income to previous peak income.

One variation of this approach has been the suggestion by Davis: that previous peak consumption be substituted for previous peak income [33]. The rationale for this suggestion is that people become adjusted to a certain standard of *consumption*, rather than to a certain level of income, so that it is past spending that influences current consumption rather than past income. An additional argument for the substitution of consumption for income is that current income, referring to a period of one year or less, is likely to be less stable and less representative of a family's living standard than is current consumption [164, pp. 280–95].

The empirical support for the relative income hypothesis has proceeded along two lines. One consisted of showing that the aggregate relations of a form similar to (4) provide at least as good explanations and statistical " fits " to fluctuations in national personal saving over time as the various forms of the absolute income hypothesis [33] [35, pp. 89–92] [122, pp. 379–99]. Noteworthy in this respect was the finding of an independent evaluation that these functions yielded greater predictive accuracy outside of the period of observation than did various forms of the absolute income hypothesis [45].[1] In addition, of course, there was the constancy of the aggregate saving ratio over time which fitted in with the relative income hypothesis.

Second, a number of instances were demonstrated in which the relative income hypothesis was, and the absolute income hypothesis was not, able to explain differences in saving or consumption patterns observed in budget data. Thus, Brady and Friedman by this approach were able to reconcile the higher saving rates of village than city families at the same levels of income in 1935–36, and again in 1941; the similarly higher saving rates of farm families than non-farm families in 1935–36, and also in 1941; and various geographical differences in saving rates in 1935–36 [14]. Duesenberry used this hypothesis to reconcile the fact that dissaving at a given level of income was less frequent in 1941 than in 1935–36, that Negro families saved more than white families in 1935–36 at the same level of income, as well as to explain geographic differences in saving rates [35, Ch. 4, 5]. Brady showed that family saving varied not only with family income but also with the income level of the community in which it resided [10].

Findings such as these do not necessarily serve to rule out the absolute income hypothesis, and it is still very much of an open question whether the facts do indeed conflict with the absolute income hypothesis or whether the hypothesis has been misinterpreted. A basic tenet of the hypothesis is the *ceteris paribus* assumption for all variables other than (current) income. Yat, data availability in empirical studies has been too restricted to allow other principal relevant variables to be held constant; and if such variables are indeed not constant, failure of saving, or the saving rate, to fluctuate with income may represent simply the effects of these omitted variables. Thus, Tobin shows that the apparent failure of the absolute income hypothesis to explain Negro–White saving differentials at the same level of income can be reconciled if allowance is made for the smaller financial resources available to Negro families than to White families. Because of this difference in wealth, Negro families are unable to dissave as frequently or as much as White families at the same income level, and therefore require extra financial reserves to tide them over emergencies [154, pp. 145-9].

In a similar manner Tobin shows that wealth differentials may explain geographic differences in saving rates, and even the historical constancy of the saving ratio. The latter is based on the presumption that the substantial growth in asset holdings over time may have reduced the need for saving out of current income and contributed to raising the propensity to consume as real income increased. Admittedly, the evidence is rather

[1] However, the most accurate predictions of all were obtained when the functions were transformed into first-difference form, and it was then of little consequence which functional form was used.

sketchy, as is noted by Tobin [154, pp. 154–6] and is stressed by Milton Friedman [56, pp. 173–82]. However, if a variable such as wealth could be shown to have influenced the secular propensity to consume the absolute income hypothesis could be vindicated.

C. *The Permanent Income Hypothesis.* This most recent hypothesis on consumer behaviour grew out of the rising concern regarding the adequacy of current income as the most appropriate determinant of consumption expenditures.[1] Particularly among non-wage-earner families income receipts vary substantially from period to period, while consumption outlays exhibit much greater stability. This led to the belief that people geared their expenditures to average actual and anticipated income over a number of periods rather than only to income received in the current period. The central idea is as follows [56, p. 220]:

> " Consider a large number of men all earning \$100 a week and spending \$100 a week on current consumption. Let them receive their pay once a week, the pay days being staggered, so that one-seventh are paid on Sunday, one seventh on Monday, and so on. Suppose we collected budget data for a sample of these men for one day chosen at random, defined income as cash receipts on that day, and defined consumption as cash expenditures. One-seventh of the men would be recorded as having an income of \$100, six-sevenths as having an income of zero. It may well be that the men would spend more on pay day than on other days but they would also make expenditures on other days, so we would record the one-seventh with an income of \$100 as having positive savings, the other six-sevenths as having negative savings. Consumption might appear to rise with income, but, if so, not as much as income, so that the fraction of income saved would rise with income. These results tell us nothing meaningful about consumption behaviour; they simply reflect the use of inappropriate concepts of income and consumption. Men do not adapt their cash expenditures on consumption to their cash receipts, and their cash expenditures on consumption may not be a good index of the value of services consumed—in our simple example, consumption expenditures might well be zero on Sunday."

As is often the case with developments of this sort, a theoretical foundation for this hypothesis was developed more or less independently by two different people: by Milton Friedman and by Franco Modigliani, the latter with the collaboration of R. E. Brumberg and Albert Ando. The two versions are similar in principle, though different in certain respects. Whether it is because of its deceptively simpler formulation or because of its more provocative interpretations and assumptions, the Friedman form has gained wide attention. In what follows both forms are presented, with greater emphasis on the Friedman formulation.

The permanent income hypothesis of Friedman may be said to rest on three fundamental tenets. First, a consumer unit's measured (observed)

[1] For example, see Margaret Reid [142], Milton Friedman and Simon Kuznets [58].

income (y) and consumption (c) in a particular period may be segregated into " transitory " and " permanent " components, *i.e.*:

(5*a*) $$y = y_p + y_t$$

(5*b*) $$c = c_p + c_t$$

Permanent income, say, in a given year, is the product of two factors: the wealth of the consumer unit, estimated as the discounted present value of a stream of future expected receipts, and the rate, r (or weighted average of a set of rates), at which these expected receipts are discounted [57].

The second tenet is that permanent consumption is a multiple, k, of permanent income:

(6) $$c_p = ky_p$$

where k depends only on the interest rate, i, the ratio of non-human to total (non-human plus human) wealth, w, and a catchall variable, u, of which age and tastes are principal components. In other words, $k = f(i, w, u)$, but k is independent of the level of permanent income. It should be noted that consumption here is defined in the physical sense rather than in the monetary sense, *i.e.*, as the physical consumption of goods and services. Durables purchased in a current period are considered as saving to the extent that they are not used up in that period.

Third, transitory and permanent income are assumed to be uncorrelated, as are transitory and permanent consumption, and transitory consumption and transitory income:

(7) $$r_{y_t y_p} = r_{c_t c_p} = r_{y_t c_t} = 0$$

As a result, a consumer unit is assumed to determine its standard of living on the basis of expected returns from its resources over its lifetime. These returns are expected to be constant from year to year, though in actual practice some fluctuation would result over time with changes in the anticipated amount of capital resources, The expenditures of the consumer unit are set as a constant proportion (k) of this permanent level of income, the value of k varying for consumer units of different types and of different tastes.[1] Actual consumption and actual income deviate from these planned, or permanent, levels to the extent that transitory factors enter in, *e.g.*, a crop failure in the case of farm family income or unexpected medical bills in the case of spending. However, these transitory factors are essentially random and independent of each other, with the primary result of serving to obscure the true underlying relationship between the permanent components of income and of consumption.

The Modigliani–Brumberg–Ando (MBA) formulation is essentially a " permanent wealth " hypothesis rather than a " permanent income "

[1] A very similar formulation is provided by William Hamburger [70]. He postulates total current expenditures of consumers to depend principally on tastes, the interest rate and the discounted value of lifetime resources, the last being determined by the sum of wealth and a multiple of his current wage-rate.

hypothesis, though in practice the two approaches converge. In its most recent formulation, the household or consumer unit is assumed to determine " the amount available for consumption over life, which is the sum of the household's net worth at the beginning of the period . . . plus the present value of its non-property income . . . minus present value of planned bequests " [123, p. 78]. The amount allocated to consumption (defined in the same manner as by Friedman) is a certain proportion of these resources. Actual consumption, however, differs from this allocated amount by transitory expenditures and by certain stochastic factors (v), *i.e.*:

$$c_r = k_r^* x_r + v_r \tag{8}$$

Thus, this relationship is essentially the same as that derived by Friedman [by substituting (6) into (5*b*), with k^* in (8) corresponding to the product of r and k]. Note, however, that the variables in equation (8) have time subscripts, whereas those of Friedman's do not. In the MBA formulation k^* is assumed to vary explicitly with the age of the consumer unit, as is x, and possibly with other factors, such as family size. In the Friedman formulation, k is a constant for the same consumer unit over time.[1]

The MBA formulation is also more flexible in that the possibility is considered that transitory income and transitory consumption may be related to each other. In that event, Modigliani and Ando show that equation (8) turns into the following form:

$$c_r = f(k'_r, x_r, y_r) \tag{9}$$

so that current income as well as permanent income enter into this relation as determinants of current (observed) consumption. In their empirical work, however, Modigliani and Ando do not seem to have tested this relation.

In either formulation the central tenet is the assumption that the proportion of permanent income saved by a consumer unit in a given period is independent of its income (or its resources) during that period, and furthermore, that transitory incomes may have no (Friedman) or little (MBA) effect on current consumption.

Clearly, from an empirical point of view, this is a very difficult hypothesis to test, because of the difficulty of measuring permanent income and permanent consumption. Nevertheless, the permanent income hypothesis is analytically a very rich one and lends itself to a number of significant inferences regarding individual and aggregate behaviour. This is not the place to develop these inferences, particularly since they have been developed elsewhere [56, Ch. 3, 7] [124] [123, esp. pp. 74–109]. However, one theoretical inference of this hypothesis deserves special mention because of its basic importance to the empirical tests. Under the permanent income hypothesis, the slope of the relation between observed consumption and observed income, namely (assuming linearity) b in: $c = a + by$, can be

[1] Although k may vary among consumer units, as noted previously, *i.e.*, $k = f(i, w, u)$.

shown to be equivalent to kP_y, where P_y is the ratio of the variance of the permanent component of income to the total variance of income, *i.e.*:

$$P_y = \frac{\sum (y_p - \bar{y}_p)^2}{\sum (y - \bar{y})^2}$$

Since k is constant, by assumption, this means that fluctuations in the slope of measured income reflect fluctuations in the relative importance of the permanent component of income. Furthermore, P_y is equivalent to the income elasticity of consumption, if the elasticity is estimated at the sample means and if the transitory components of both income and consumption averago zero. The significance of this becomes clear when we list the principal empirical results and observations advanced to support the permanent income hypothesis.

1. From time series aggregates, Friedman notes that the following findings are in accord with the hypothesis [56, Ch. 5]: (*a*) The marginal propensity to consume is invariably less than the average propensity to consume. (*b*) The ration of permanent consumption to permanent income, k, appears to have been constant since at least 1897, after allowance for variability in the observed consumption–income ratio due to transitory factors.[1] (*c*) The income elasticity of consumption tends to rise as the period of observation to which a consumption function is fitted increases, thus confirming that transitory factors become less important over longer time spans. (*d*) Marginal propensities estimated from data deflated for price or population changes are less than those estimated from the corresponding undeflated data: permanent components are more important in the latter case because of the general positive correlation among output, prices and population.

2. From cross-section budget data, Friedman notes that [56, Ch. 4]: (*a*) Despite observed inequality of income distributions on a cross-section basis, long-run trends indicate that the income distribution is becoming, if anything, more equal—thereby suggesting that measured income is not a valid measure of wealth. (*b*) The average propensity to consume has been relatively constant in budget studies covering different times and different groups. Furthermore, the stability in the average propensities, and the values of less than unity of the income elasticities, contradict the stability of these cross-section relations—suggesting that the consumption–income ratio declines as income rises, which is inconsistent with the time-series aggregates. (*c*) Income elasticities are less for the United States than for Great Britain or Sweden, suggesting that transitory factors are more important in the United States, as one might expect. (*d*) The income elasticity, as well as the marginal propensity and k, are all lower for farm families,

[1] The allowance is rather arbitrary—seeing whether most of the annual points fall within 5 percentage points of a line going through the origin of the consumption–income graph and the long-run average of this ratio, 0·877. On the other hand, as Friedman notes, secular constancy of k is not an integral part of the permanent income hypothesis.

and for non-farm and own-business families, than for other non-farm families, in accord with the hypothesis. (*e*) Consumption–income regressions for groups of families classified by income change have steeper slopes than the overall regression: the transitory component is smaller for income-change classes.

3. Turning to work other than Friedman's, P_y estimated from income data for the same consumer units over time yields consistent results for different groups and different time periods. Such estimates also correspond with estimated income elasticities from budget data, which also estimate (independently) P_y [143].

4. Classification of families by income change appears to result largely in a manifestation of transitory income, rather than expenditure lags behind changes in permanent income; the consumption–income ratio varies most between years for families with substantial income change [146].

5. The estimated income elasticity for all households exceeds the weighted average of income elasticities for relatively homogeneous groups of households—variation due to transitory factors is less important in the former case [38] [123, pp. 123–66].[1] Furthermore, no systematic association is apparent between mean income and the consumption–income ratio for most criteria; education is a notable exception.

6. Increasing the importance of transitory income by classifying families by current income categories reduces income elasticity estimates—transitory components are more important among these presumably more homogeneous subgroups [37].

7. Groups with the more variable incomes have higher saving ratios [53, pp. 229–63].

8. The effect of age, or life cycle, is supported by the fact that the observed saving ratio is low for young age groups, highest in the later earning stages and negative or very low in retirement [124].

Despite these seemingly impressive arguments, the permanent income hypothesis is by no means established. Indeed, the evidence to the contrary seems at least as impressive. This opposing evidence, like the arguments for the theory, covers both theoretical and empirical considerations. On a theoretical plane, question is raised regarding the validity of the two central tenets of the theory, namely, the independence of k of the level of income, and the lack of correlation between transitory consumption and transitory income. Thus, Friend and Kravis note that the permanent income hypothesis implies " that low-income families will have no greater preference for purchase of future goods than will high-income families " [59, p. 538] while Duesenberry makes a similar criticism [36]. Such a concept they find to be seriously deficient on purely deductive grounds because of the

[1] " Relatively homogeneous groups " means households classified by characteristics unrelated to transitory factors, and for which permanent and transitory incomes are uncorrelated. Classifying criteria used were city size, education, occupation, age, tenure.

very different kinds of pressures and motivations acting on families at different income levels.

In a similar fashion, the assumption of a zero marginal propensity to consume out of transitory income is questioned, partly on the basis that low-come families are under strong pressures to spend any unexpected income to meet current needs [59, pp. 539–41], and partly because of the very unequal distribution of wealth which mitigates against dissaving by low-income families to maintain consumption in the face of temporary declines in income [156, p. 451].

Criticism of the permanent income hypothesis on empirical grounds has followed two lines. One line has been to note that much of the evidence advanced is either inconclusive or is not inconsistent with other principal hypotheses. Thus, under the absolute income hypothesis one would also expect the marginal propensity to consume to be less than the average propensity, groups with more variable incomes to have higher saving ratios, and consumption–income regressions for groups of families classified by income change to have steeper slopes than the overall regression. In addition, as was noted previously, Tobin has suggested how the constancy of the long-run propensity to consume might be reconciled with the absolute income hypothesis. Furthermore, the interpretation given by Friedman to many of his test results is not the only possible interpretation and is at times subject to considerable doubt [63] [72] [156], though some of the evidence can apparently be interpreted only in terms of it [143].

From a more direct point of view, various test results have been advanced as contradicting the permanent income hypothesis. Thus, Friend and Kravis show that the same variation in the saving rate occurs when families are classified by constancy of three-year income as by constancy of one-year income, based on recall data obtained in one-time interviews [59, pp. 544–5]. In addition, they show that saving rates of different occupational groups appear to be closely correlated with the average income of these groups [59, p. 546] [60, pp. 272–3].

To test the zero propensity to consume out of transitory income, Bodkin [8] analysed by correlation methods the extent to which consumption expenditures were made out of unexpected dividends paid in early 1950 out of National Service Life Insurance. This study yielded not only a statistically significant propensity but a propensity to consume out of these dividends much higher than out of regular income.[1] On the other hand, Kreinin [104A] obtained a low marginal propensity to consume out of

[1] Friedman attempts to reconcile the results with the permanent income hypothesis, on the assumption that these dividend receipts might have been anticipated and/or they created expectations of future dividend receipts, so that this windfall becomes a proxy for permanent income [57A, pp. 191–206]. In view of the circumstances surrounding the payment of these dividends, however, such an assumption is highly questionable. A more likely explanation is one offered by Margaret Reid (unpublished) that the receipts may have stimulated purchase of homes, thereby setting off a long-run programme of saving but a short-run programme of spending.

*

restitution payments made by Germany to former citizens in Israel. However, these payments could hardly have been unexpected.

Admittedly, these negative findings are themselves subject to question. For example, the reliability and representativeness of budget data collected in a partial wartime period such as 1950 is a matter of doubt [136]. In any event, the permanent income hypothesis is far from proven. However, whether or not the permanent income hypothesis turns out to be valid, there is little doubt that, to quote Tobin, " This is one of those rare contributions of which it can be said that research and thought in its field will not be the same henceforth " [156, p. 447]. Most of all, it has led to widespread recognition of the possible effects of variability in income on consumption patterns and has provided a theoretical basis for measuring these effects as a springboard for a more realistic theory of consumer behaviour.[1]

II. Influence of Variables Other than Income

A number or studies have been undertaken in recent years to ascertain the effect of particular variables entering into the *ceteris paribus* assumption of the consumption, or saving, function. These studies have focused generally on three sets of variables: socio-economic characteristics of the household, particularly age and life cycle; financial characteristics; and attitudes and expectations. Principal work in each of these sub-areas is reviewed in this section.

Focus on the *ceteris paribus* assumption does not necessarily abstract from the effect of income, for two principal reasons. First, most socio-economic as well as other variables are related to income. Since most of these " *ceteris paribus* studies " are carried out either by cross tabulation or by some multivariate method such as analysis of variance or multiple regression, part of the effect attributed to the particular variable may actually be due to income, particularly when interactions and other non-linear effects are present. Second, to the extent that the permanent income hypothesis is valid, even holding constant the effect of current income (the only basis on which income data are available) means that these other variables act to some unknown extent as proxies for permanent income, thereby leading to biased estimates of the effect of these other variables. The fact remains, however, that the *ceteris paribus* variables are of interest in their own right, and even biased effects can be useful.

A. *Socio-economic Characteristics*

Virtually every budget study presents breakdowns of expenditures and data on such characteristics as age, education, family size, etc. However, the isolation of the effects of these variables on total expenditures or on total

[1] For an interesting application of the permanent income hypothesis to analysing consumer behaviour, see the study by Jacob Mincer relating labour activity to family income and consumption [121].

saving has received relatively little attention until recently. The availability of the Surveys of Consumer Finances and the various BLS consumer expenditures studies, particularly the 1950 study, and the advent of the relative income and permanent income hypotheses have spurred new interest in these variables. As a result of the latter interest, various studies have attempted to derive saving–income ratios for different population groups. One such study, by Harold Watts, ascribes a central role to occupation and education in the determination of expenditures [165]. Watts attempts to explain expenditures on the basis of a person's expected future income, which is related to a " cross-section profile " holding occupation, education and age constant. Among other things, he finds that, at a given level of income, those with more education expect higher incomes and spend more.

An attempt by James Morgan to isolate the effects of socio-economic factors on the saving ratio [126]—in this study saving is defined as changes in net worth, including purchases of durable goods—uses residuals from regressions of saving on income to examine the effect of a large number of additional socio-economic variables, partly by further regressions and partly by application of analysis of variance.[1] Among other things, these results show that the self-employed, including farmers, had very different saving patterns from other families, that home owners saved more than renters, that dwellers in open country areas saved more than metropolitan dwellers and that life cycle was highly relevant to understanding saving patterns.

In the case of family size, considerable attention has been given to the problem of allowing for variations in expenditures due to differences in family size, either by deflating by a family-size variable or by including family size as a separate factor. The principal work in this area has been concerned with converting family size into an equivalent-adult unit basis. This problem goes back many years, and an extensive literature has grown up around it, with more recent emphasis on the incorporation of this adjustment within a multi-variate framework (for example, [140, Ch. 9] [55]).

Attention has also been given to the effect on saving and spending of owning an unincorporated business. Various studies in recent years have thrown considerable light on the saving habits of unincorporated business families, as well as on aggregate saving trends in this area [60] [101]. Thus, both Klein–Margolis and Friend–Kravis show that such families have much larger than average negative saving at low incomes and much higher than average positive saving at high incomes than other families, and that the same is true of both farm and non-farm entrepreneurs. Friend–Kravis show that the self-employed exhibit much the same consumption

[1] Aside from purely statistical considerations, the validity of this methodological procedure depends on whether the absolute income hypothesis or the permanent income hypothesis is correct. If the latter is the case the procedure is a biased one because, as noted previously, only measured income is then held constant, while the effect of permanent income is intermingled with the other socio-economic variables. See Friedman [56, p. 86 ff.].

pattern as that of other families; though another study by L. R. Klein suggests that the self-employed are more frequently home-owners and tend to spend less for rental costs and more for household operations than families of salaried professionals and officials [99, pp. 331–5]. Klein also shows that the self-employed save more than other families, principally because of their business saving; they do not save appreciably more in other forms.

Age and the Life Cycle. Perhaps the main analytical work in recent years relating to socio-economic characteristics has been with age and the life cycle. Although various early budget studies were concerned in part with the influence of age in one or more of these respects, it was primarily the 1935–36 Consumer Purchases Study with its extensive tabulations that served as a springboard for analysis of the influence of the age factor on consumption. In that study, attempts were made to examine variations in income and in consumption not only by different age groups but by different family types, reflecting to a large extent different stages of the family life cycle [158] [159].

The substantial variations observed in income and consumption by age and family composition led to further study of these variables in the post-war years. The initial studies focused primarily on the effects of age or of family composition. Many of these studies were carried out at the Survey Research Center of the University of Michigan, based on data collected in the Survey of Consumer Finances. Using these data, Janet Fisher was able to develop much useful information on the role of the age factor in consumer behaviour [50] [51] [52]. These studies provide empirical data on the manner in which income increases from youth to about middle age and then declines thereafter (though with considerable variation by occupation and wealth); on the manner in which liquid assets rise from youth through middle age and decline thereafter; and on the different purchasing patterns of families in different age levels. Especially notable in the last category is the tendency for younger families to be heavy purchasers of durable goods, even though they may have to dissave to do so, whereas older families with the necessary assets make relatively few durable-goods purchases.[1]

In a very interesting exploratory study of the determinants of saving, Dorothy Brady finds that to a large extent age comparisons of saving rates are confounded with the effects of income changes, so that " the variation among the age groups in expenditures and saving within the current income bracket will accordingly be a reflection of changes in the direction and magnitude of income . . . " [12, p. 193]. Holding income constant, saving is found to increase uniformly as the age of the wife rises. In addition, Brady shows that family saving is influenced not only by socio-economic variables such as age, family size and occupation but may also be

[1] Of particular interest from this point of view is the article by Dorothy Brady on the influence of age on saving and spending patterns [11]. More recently, a wealth of descriptive data on the consumption patterns of the aged will be found in the study by Sidney Goldstein [66].

influenced substantially by the general level of income in the community where the family resides.

These and other results on the effect of family composition on spending and saving have brought into focus the importance of a life-cycle variable, a variable which would reflect the simultaneous influence of a number of different socio-economic characteristics.[1] This interest led, among other things, to the convening in 1954 of a conference by Consumer Behavior, Inc., on the life cycle as related to economic, marketing and sociological behaviour of consumer units. The volume that grew out of this conference provides a wealth of data on the subject [23], ranging from provocative discussions of the role of age and U.S. culture on consumer purchases (by David Riesman and Howard Roseborough) to the first really thorough empirical study of consumer finances over the life cycle (by John B. Lansing and James N. Morgan). The latter study is particularly noteworthy because it uses as the basis for the analysis a classification of consumer units by stage of life cycle rather than by age alone, as was the case for virtually all of the previous studies. The article demonstrates the analytical values of such a classification and presents empirical data on the manner in which income, spending and assets vary over the life cycle. Related studies in this volume present information on the manner in which purchasing interest and purchasing trends vary by the life cycle, and on the possible impact of the life cycle on advertising [5] [120].

Some studies have also been conducted on the effect of the life cycle on consumer behaviour in Great Britain. Thus, Harold Lydall has traced the life-cycle pattern in income receipts, in savings and in net worth, finding the pattern roughly similar in Great Britain to that in the United States [112].[2] At the same time net worth does not appear to decline as much in Great Britain after income has turned down. In addition, a comparative study by Janet Fisher shows that durable-goods purchases were much more prevalent in the United States than in Great Britain for the same age groups, and that incomes began to decline at an earlier age in the United States than in Great Britain [52, pp. 33–5].

B. *Financial Factors*

Income Change. A number of studies of the effects of income change have been made in the post-war years. The findings of these studies are generally similar, but the interpretation of the findings has differed at times substantially, as noted in the discussion of the permanent income hypothesis. Thus, in several studies based on data collected in the Surveys of Consumer Finances high saving rates are found to be associated, at the same income level, with recent increases in income, while those whose incomes have fallen

[1] Actually, life cycle as a variable had for some time previous been a principal topic in the study of the sociology of the family, and had also been of interest in studying the spending patterns of farm families. For example, see Kirkpatrick [93], Glick [64].

[2] Although life cycle is the focus of this study, only age is used as a classifying variable.

tend to save less. Dissaving was more common among those whose incomes had either declined or risen substantially than among consumer units with relatively stable incomes. Furthermore, an inverse correlation was found between the purchase of durable goods and saving, consumer units having major outlays for durable goods being much more likely to dissave [82] [83] [87] [98] [126]. Morgan notes that the effect of income change varies with asset ownership: among those with small amounts of liquid assets, saving does not vary so much with income change [96, p. 124].

Similar findings on the effect of income change on spending behaviour were obtained by Ruth Mack in analysing budget data of 600 farm families [114]; and she suggests that the effect of changes in income is likely to differ for different expenditure categories. On the other hand, as noted earlier (p. 30), Margaret Reid shows that the same data can be interpreted as highlighting the importance of transitory income in distorting expenditure–income relationships.

The incorporation of income change as a variable in multiple regressions explaining household saving rates leads to mixed results. Studies by Klein, Morgan and Katona indicate that the effects of this variable may interact partly with income expectations and partly with liquid assets [82] [94] [96] [98]. Furthermore, the effect may be asymmetrical, being more pronounced for income decreases than for income increases. Households experiencing income decreases and who expect further decreases appear to save more, at the same level of income, than households experiencing decreases but expecting an upturn in the near future [94, p. 446].

In a unique study of short-run effects of income change upon saving, savings and expenditures in a relatively isolated New England community, George Brinegar finds that household behaviour serves to amplify rather than to dampen the effects of income change upon purchases of goods and services [17] [18]. Thus, following a sharp income decrease, milk purchases first declined, then rose above the earlier level and finally levelled off. In addition, correlations between payrolls and bank balances indicated greater stability between payrolls and savings-account balances than between payrolls and saving in these accounts, thus providing some support for the Pigouvian analysis of income determination.

Wealth. The relevance of wealth to consumption and saving has been recognised in the theoretical literature for some time. As noted earlier, Pigou [138], as well as Lerner in a different sense [110, pp. 44–9], had stressed the importance of increases in wealth in maintaining full employment by causing the consumption–income schedule to shift to the right. Tobin has suggested that increases in wealth may be responsible for the constancy of the aggregate propensity to save over time. Ackley has ascribed a crucial role to wealth in the determination of the cyclical consumption function [1]. In addition, wealth, it will be recalled, plays a central role in the permanent income hypothesis: In the Friedman formulation the ratio of permanent consumption to permanent income is assumed to rise with increases in the ratio of wealth to income; in the MBA formulation wealth serves as the basis for estimating permanent income. However, empirical work has been, and continues to be, hampered by lack of data. This has been particularly true with regard to wealth and individual behaviour, since data on liquid assets have been available only since the Second World War.

Although not conclusive, the weight of empirical evidence points to a positive, though erratic, relationship of liquid assets to consumption and saving, at least in the post-war years. Under the much less prosperous pre-war conditions it is doubtful whether liquid assets exerted much influence on the consumption–income relationship, at least in the aggregate [26]; on a cross-section basis there do not seem to be any data. In the post-war years the effect of liquid assets appears to have varied with time. A strong positive relationship with durable-goods expenditures existed in the late 1940s and a much weaker effect in the early 1950s [96].

As a general rule, the saving rate for individual households appears to vary inversely with the ratio of liquid assets to income, and the influence of liquid assets on saving tends to diminish as the level of income rises [94] [95, pp. 210–27]. Households with a given amount of liquid assets that experience a decline in income tend to save less than households with the same income decline but with less liquid assets, or than households with the same amount of liquid assets but no income decline.

In his study, Morgan found the liquid-asset effect to interact with income change, the saving rate increasing with liquid assets for those experiencing a substantial income increase, and the saving rate varying inversely with liquid-asset holdings among those experiencing substantial income declines [126].

Various students of the problem have suggested that net worth is a more relevant concept than liquid assets [113] [155]. This concept is also much closer to the definition of wealth in the MBA formulation of the permanent income hypothesis, in which wealth plays a basic role. Unfortunately, data on net worth are difficult to collect, and hypotheses based on net worth or on total resources have yet to be subjected to direct examination.

C. *Expectations and Intentions-to-buy*

Although the role of expectations in consumer behaviour has been discussed in the economic literature for many years, empirical research in this area has been purely a post-war development, and is attributable largely to the activity of one man, George Katona. His interest in economic behaviour supplemented by a strong psychological background led him to stress, in the 1940s, the importance of expectations and attitudes in a high-level economy. He noted the importance of studying the factors underlying decision processes in economic behaviour as well as the growing discretionary aspects of consumer spending, in the case of which attitudes and expectations might be expected to exert a dominant role [81]. Such factors influence *willingness* to buy, which for spending and saving other than that which is habitual would seem to be about as important as *ability* to buy.[1] With the aid of data collected under his supervision in the annual Surveys of Consumer Finances, he has been able to present considerable support for this point of view, showing that durable-goods purchases were related to a number of individual attitudes as well as to an index of attitudinal variables [90, pp. 91–106].

On the basis of such analyses, Katona and his associates at the Survey Research Center were able to conclude that " motives, attitudes, and expectations often change at about the same time and in the same direction among large groups of consumers. Such changes commonly occur prior to changes in the rate of postponable spending and of saving " [85, p. 67], and hence attitudinal data were valuable for predicting consumer spending and saving behaviour. As a result of these studies, the Survey of Consumer Finances has been collecting such data every year and using them as a basis for analysing and also predicting consumer behaviour.

Data on intentions-to-buy were also collected in the annual Surveys of Consumer Finances, as part of the attitudinal section. It soon became evident, however, that not only did these data differ conceptually from that obtained with the other attitudinal questions (representing in effect an *ex ante* expression of consumer purchases) but exhibited at times a marked relationship to actual purchases apart from the attitudinal data. Such relationships were apparent both over time and on a cross-section basis, even though these intentions referred to a year or more ahead [109, pp. 405–40]. In addition, experimentation with the collection of plans-to-buy data on a quarterly basis showed that meaningful quarterly data could be collected and, furthermore, that an even more marked relationship existed between plans to buy reported quarterly and later purchases [43, pp. 42–51] [42].

Considerable additional support for the value of plans-to-buy data has been provided by a project of the National Bureau of Economic Research, under the direction of F. T. Juster, to analyse the value, as a forecasting tool, of buying plans as reported by Consumers Union subscribers. Although Consumers Union subscribers are not typical of the total population, and although buying plans were collected on an annual basis, year-to-year changes in buying plans for selected major durable goods were found to foreshadow closely corresponding changes in actual purchases for the post-war years [77] [78]. In addition, these studies indicated that plans-to-buy data made a net contribution to predictive accuracy even after income was taken into account [76].

Partly as a result of these findings and partly because of the intercorrelation between plans to buy and attitudinal variables, a lively controversy

[1] The main theoretical arguments are presented in Katona's early volume [84, pp. 63–81]. Also, see the study by George Katona and Eva Mueller [88].

has arisen regarding the relative superiority of these two types of data for forecasting purchases. Katona and some of his associates at Michigan maintain that attitudinal data provide insight into underlying motives and buying forces apart from socio-economic factors (age, income, wealth, etc.), and that such information can help improve forecasts. Others feel that plans-to-buy, though perhaps not as fundamental in a psychological sense, is the relevant overt variable for forecasting purposes, and that once such data have been taken into account, no net additional contribution can be expected from information on expectations or attitudes.[1]

To date, the empirical tests provide strong evidence in favour of the second hypothesis. After reviewing the evidence then available, the Federal Reserve Consultant Committee on Consumer Survey Statistics under the chairmanship of Arthur Smithies concluded, in 1955, that " buying intentions, properly interpreted, appear to have predictive value. . . . Other attitudes are highly correlated with buying intentions, both over time and as among spending units, and there is so far no convincing evidence that they make an independent contribution to ability to predict . . ." [160, pp. 137–8]. Klein and Lansing found plans-to-buy to help significantly in multiple regressions discriminating between buyers and non-buyers of durable goods—in addition to age, income and marital status—while other attitudinal variables were either not effective or much less effective [100, pp. 115–26]. In a fundamental test, Tobin showed by regression analysis that plans-to-buy, in addition to socio-economic variables, made an appreciable net contribution to explaining durable-goods purchases, whereas this was not true of an attitudinal index; and, when combined in the same equation, plans-to-buy was significant, but not the attitudinal index [157]. Similar results were obtained by Okun [133].

Eva Mueller, though espousing the other side, shows that buying intentions but not an attitudinal index contribute significantly to multiple regressions explaining major durable-goods purchases [130]. The only evidence to the contrary presented so far is also in this study, which shows that an attitudinal index contributes more than buying plans, or than the same index including buying plans, to explaining aggregate semi-annual fluctuations in durable-goods expenditures from 1952 to 1957. However, this test is not as comprehensive as Tobin's, including only income as an independent variable and making no allowance for heteroscedasticity.

The findings regarding the value of buying intentions as a predictive tool have been impressive enough that such data are now collected on a continuing, short-run basis. Consumer-spending plans for major durables and other large expenditures have been collected bimonthly by telephone by the National Industrial Conference Board since 1958 [27], while the Federal Reserve Board in conjunction with the U.S. Bureau of the Census has been

[1] An excellent source for recent arguments and evidence pro and con is [162].

collecting quarterly buying intentions data on a much more comprehensive basis since 1959 [167].

Attitudinal data have not been ignored. Indeed, virtually everybody is agreed that " the primary reason for collecting data on psychological factors influencing behaviour is to improve the diagnosis of the prevailing situation " [79, p. 455]. Many of the studies reviewed here, particularly those of Katona and Mueller, have shown how expectations and attitudes are related to buying plans and to economic events, and have thrown light on their nature and characteristics.[1]

III. Determinants of Asset Holdings

The growing stock of consumer assets has led to investigation not only of the influence of assets on saving behaviour but also on the factors associated with holding particular assets. With these more recent studies, the focus shifts from flows out of income to the investment decisions of the household and to explaining differences in the total stock of assets and their distibution among households and over time.

Reasons for holding particular types of assets have been discussed in the theoretical literature for some time [*e.g.*, 92, Ch. 16]. More recently, Katona has attempted to merge these reasons with motivational and other psychological factors as a basis for empirical study [84, pp. 98–107].

Empirical studies are, as yet, relatively few. In a comprehensive study of the factors influencing the composition of the " capital account " of the household (essentially financial assets, durables, business capital), Watts and Tobin concluded that " households tend to maintain some sort of balance in their capital accounts both between assets yielding direct service and financial assets, and between liquid funds and liabilities " [166, p. 48]. Ownership of different assets was positively correlated, while assets and debts were negatively correlated: apparently as households moved up the economic status scale, more of all kinds of assets were acquired and debt was reduced.

By means of a series of multiple regressions on the 1950 Consumer Expenditures data, Watts and Tobin find the composition of particular portfolios to be influenced by a number of " fundamental but unobserved measures of social, economic, and biological, and environmental characteristics " [166, p. 48]. In particular, households headed by people with more education tended to have larger stocks of assets and lower debt, with income and other relevant variables held constant. Older households had less invested in durables and less debt as well. Occupational differences are pronounced, though erratic. Larger families generally had more in durables and less cash than other households. Regional and city-size differences

[1] In the former respect, see in addition to the previously cited publications, Katona [86] and Calla Van Syckle [163]. In the latter connection, see Ferber [44] and Katona [80].

were also apparent. Higher-income households had more in financial assets and less in durables.

Despite the large number of significant relationships, however, in most instances less than 10% of the variation in the dependent variable was explained.

In a study of factors influencing the holding of liquid assets by British households, Lydall finds total wealth (measured as net worth) rather than income level to be the primary determinant of such holdings [113].[1] Applying multiple regressions to data from the Surveys of Consumer Finances, Harold Guthrie shows that liquid assets relative to income tend to rise with age and fall as the size of the consumer unit increases. In addition, the liquid-assets ratio is higher for those who appear to have permanently depressed incomes and is less for those anticipating income increases [67].

Two other U.S. studies, by Butters *et al.* and Claycamp, found that the proportion of total assets held in liquid form declined substantially as wealth increased [19, pp. 299–316] [25]. The proportion of assets in liquid form also declined with income level, but a multiple regression study including both income and total assets indicated, as in the case of Lydall's study, that wealth was by far the dominant factor [25, Ch. 4].

Using data from the Consumer Savings Project,[2] Claycamp applied multiple-regression analysis to test the relevance of a wide range of socio-economic and psychological variables to the proportion of total financial assets held in variable-dollar form, that is, assets whose value fluctuates with changes in prices (common stocks, marketable bonds, real estate, etc.). Age, home ownership, total assets and occupation were significantly related to various forms of this variable-dollar ratio. Attitudinal variables, such as price expectations and other economic expectations, were not significant.

A major part of Claycamp's work was the investigation of the apparent lack of substitution between different types of assets. Such a lack of substitution had been noted by Guthrie between liquid assets and equity in homes; and he had suggested that " consumers do not shift between asset forms while maintaining some normative level of security in total wealth " [67, p. 478]. Tobin and Watts had also advanced the same idea with their hypothesis that consumers, in the handling of their capital accounts, attempted to balance assets and debts against each other [166]; while in a more recent study Phillip Cagan found an absence of substitution between pension contributions and other savings [20].

Claycamp's investigation of the frequency of different asset holdings provided strong support for this phenomenon, extending it to different combinations of thirteen assets and debts, two or more at a time, using ownership frequencies and dollar amounts in turn. The results led to the

[1] It is not clear, however, to what extent this finding is affected by the fact that liquid assets averaged overall about one-fourth of net worth, but over 100% in the lower net-worth classes.

[2] Sponsored by the Inter-University Committee for Research on Consumer Behavior with financial assistance from the Ford Foundation and the U.S. Department of Agriculture.

so-called "independence hypothesis," namely, that "there is no significant difference between the actual proportion . . . owning a combination of holdings and the expected proportion which is found by multiplying each of the proportions in the combination" [25, p. 1]. Confirmation of this hypothesis would have major implications for economic analysis.

Various studies have been made by Kreinin with Survey Research Center data of the factors influencing ownership of specific assets, notably, liquid assets, life insurance, and common stock [102] [103] [104]. In these studies, which were carried out by analysis of variance, a number of socio-economic factors were found to be associated with ownership of these assets, particularly income and occupation. In the case of liquid assets, age and region were also significant; while education and liquid assets appeared to influence stock ownership. In the latter case an optimistic outlook and willingness to take risk also showed some relationship to the dependent variable. In all of these studies, however, price expectations were not significantly related to the dependent variable, though other attitudinal variables were significant.[1]

IV. Determinants of Specific Expenditures

Two different lines of approach have been used to ascertain the factors influencing the consumption of specific consumer products, reflecting the conceptual equality between purchases of goods by consumers and sales of these goods by retailers or manufacturers. One approach has attempted to explain static differences in product purchases of different households in terms of household characteristics, largely to the exclusion of prices and other market variables; while the other approach has attempted to explain temporal differences in aggregate sales in terms of market variables, largely to the exclusion of household characteristics (though aggregate income does appear in such functions).

Paralleling the consumption function, the first approach has been characterised by the search for so-called Engel curves—relationships between specific expenditures (or forms of saving) and income level, holding other relevant variables constant. The second general approach has utilised sales data and related information from industry sources. This approach has necessarily had to be aggregative in nature and, for this reason, has generally focused on the derivation of time-series relationships; it is

[1] Unfortunately, the method used in these studies is subject to serious question. In each case the analysis of variance was carried out by treating the cell means as the unit of observation rather than the individual consumer unit. Since the cell sizes in consumer surveys are decidedly unequal, such a procedure is an immense time saver. However, the procedure is also likely to distort seriously the significance of different factors, particularly of interaction effects, since the variance among the cell means is treated as equivalent to the random sampling variance. Some experimental computations made by the writer indicate that such an assumption is clearly unjustified, and that the use of the individual consumer unit as the unit of observation is likely to produce very different results, especially bringing out unexpected significant variables and interaction effects.

exemplified by the search for demand curves, to ascertain how sales fluctuate in response to changes in price, holding other relevant factors constant.

Empirical work on both approaches had its beginning about the mid-nineteenth century, with the work of Engel on household budgets and, some time later, with the work of a number of U.S. and British statisticians on demand relationships.[1] Since then empirical studies in both areas have multiplied enormously, spurred by the growing interest in statistical methods (and the ease with which a demand study can be used as the basis for a thesis). With both approaches, the past two decades have witnessed numerous empirical studies of specific commodities—and, more recently, of services—which have added considerably to knowledge of the effect of different variables on purchases, or sales. At the same time, this period has witnessed a growing emphasis on methodological improvements, and it is here that the principal developments in this area have taken place. For this reason, the present review is relatively brief and, in view of the orientation of this paper, focuses primarily on the use of household budget data.

In the area of demand analysis, considerable progress has been made in the specification and estimation of relationships. Recognition that price and possibly other relevant variables are not always independent of quantity led to more careful specification of demand relationships and to the development of more appropriate methods of estimation. Interdependence was taken into account by the equation-systems approach, using limited-information or reduced-form methods of estimation [*e.g.*, 152]. For situations where the interdependence was not instantaneous, the simpler recursive method of estimation was developed and has been shown to yield highly effective results [170]. Although least squares is still probably the most widely used method of estimating the parameters of demand functions, in many instances justifiably so, and the controversy on the relative efficiency of the different estimation methods is by no means settled [*e.g.*, 22], a wide variety of effective estimation procedures are currently available. (Perhaps the most recent innovation is the use of both income and total expenditures as intrumental variables in deriving Engel Curves [111A].)

Considerable progress has also been made in specifying the *ceteris paribus* of demand functions. A major innovation has been the introduction, and the significance revealed, of quality as a determining variable [15, pp. 36–46] [149, pp. 388–9]. Another innovation has been the attempt to allow discontinuity in reaction to changes in income and prices. One such attempt is exemplified by the "ratchet effect" of Modigliani and Duesenberry, according to which people continually adjust upward their living standards in response to peak standards attained in the past. A somewhat different approach has been that of Farrell, who allows for the possibility that demand relationships may be irreversible over time, that responses to a given change

[1] For a brief description of these early studies, see G. J. Stigler [148].

may depend not only on the amount of the change but also on the direction of change [39].

Further realism has been added through the use of lagged reactions, which have been shown to aid considerably in explaining fluctuations in demand [21, pp. 49–74] [151]. Distributed lags, and the so-called quasi-accelerator (in which demand is assumed to depend upon the rate of increase, as well as upon the prevailing level, of income), have also been introduced successfully in demand analysis [132].[1]

Attempts have been made to derive demand functions not only for a single commodity at a time but for a large range of commodities. This technique has been used by the U.S. Department of Commerce as well as by Richard Stone in explaining fluctuations in consumer demand [137] [149]. Unfortunately, the use of a standardised equation for a wide range of commodities serves to place the demand function essentially in a statistical strait-jacket, and at least one experimental study suggests that biased estimates of income elasticities may result [46, pp. 410–13].

Turning to the use of household-budget data, Engel's " Law "—that the proportion of household expenditure on food declines as household income rises—has by now been verified literally hundreds of times.[2] Generally, most studies also provide strong support for what is known as Schwabe's Law, namely, that the per cent of income spent for housing declines as income rises, although using permanent income concepts Margaret Reid alleges that high-quality housing in reality is one of the main luxuries of consumers [142] [144]. Further support for both laws was obtained in a study by Houthakker in which he derived Engel curves for four expenditure groups based on data from each of forty surveys from seventeen countries [73]. It is interesting that the function used in this study, as in many others, was essentially the same as used by Engel in his original paper, namely, a log–log relationship between the specific expenditure and total expenditures.

Recent studies reflect a growing interest in ascertaining the determinants not only of food expenditures but of a wide range of household purchases, such as housing, clothing, house furnishings and services.[3] These studies show that these consumer purchases are influenced by a wide variety of socio-economic characteristics; but, nevertheless, the proportion of variance in individual household purchases explained by these numerous factors is small, often the order of 0·3 or less. In addition, these studies tend to bear out earlier findings on income elasticity, yielding low elasticities for

[1] A general description of these and other innovations in demand analysis will be found in the recently published book by Robert Ferber and P. J. Verdoorn [49, Ch. 8, 9].

[2] For a partial list of studies, see the bibliography by James N. Morgan [127]. There has also been an abortive tendency to mangle the principle by refuting its applicability with time-series data, something that would make Engel turn over in his grave.

[3] On clothing, see Dorothy S. Brady [13] and Morris Hamburg [68]; on house furnishings, see Vernon Lippitt [111]; on services, see Robert Ferber [47]; on housing, see Sherman Maisel and Louis Winnick [116].

food and housing, elasticities close to unity for clothing and education, and higher elasticities for various types of recreation, personal care, home operation and other services.[1]

Special attention has been given to the relationship between durable-goods expenditures, financial saving and other variables; and strong evidence now exists that to a large extent purchase of durables is a substitute for financial saving [62A] [97] [118]. All of these studies find purchase of durable goods related to a variety of socio-economic characteristics, particularly age, income change, size of consumer unit and various expectations. Studying the characteristics of a host of such purchases combined into "consumer investment" expenditures (purchases of cars, other durables, household equipment, and additions and repairs to houses), Morgan finds this category to have constituted a relatively constant proportion (between 12 and 16%) of disposable income at all income levels, except the lowest and the highest, during each of the post-war years, 1947–56 [128].[2] Such expenditures are found to be influenced, as in other studies, by a variety of demographic and attitudinal variables, and are found to be sticky downward and flexible upward with respect to changes in income.

As in the area of demand analysis, linear (in some cases, logarithmic) single-equation forms have been used to derive from the same data marginal propensities and income elasticities for a wide range of consumption categories. This was the approach used by Prais and Houthakker on English data, and by Crockett and Friend on American data [32] [140]. The Friend–Crockett study analyses by multiple regression analysis the effects on all major consumption categories of a large number of family characteristics including income. Among other things, their results indicate that family size and age, next to income, appear to exert the main influence on family consumption, particularly through the influence of family size on food expenditures and of age on durable-goods purchases. The study also finds that income elasticities are reduced substantially once variables reflecting other family characteristics are introduced into the relationships.[3]

At the same time dissatisfaction has been expressed over the rigid assumptions inherent in this approach. This dissatisfaction was crystallised to some extent by the findings of Prais and Houthakker that a semi-logarithmic form is preferable for necessities and a log–log form is preferable

[1] For a summary of these earlier studies, see the review article by Ruth P. Mack [115].

[2] Morgan suggests that this proportion might have been constant at the highest income level too, if purchases of such items as summer homes, motor boats and fur coats had been included.

[3] A basic question underlying many of these studies is whether they do provide reasonably accurate estimates of the income effect on particular expenditures. To the extent that the permanent income hypothesis is correct, income effects estimated by relating current expenditures to current income can be understated substantially. Thus, in the case of housing, Margaret Reid obtains income elasticities of close to 2 by using average incomes for groups instead of data for individual households [144]. On the other hand, as noted earlier, Friend and Kravis obtained much the same income elasticities using three-year averages of household income as from one-year figures [59].

for luxuries [140, pp. 87–103]; and by Stuvel and James that the use of only one form of equation to explain variations in food expenditures over the entire range of incomes and social classes is unsatisfactory [150].

One result of this dissatisfaction has been some interesting attempts to modify the Engel-curve approach. One approach has been to introduce non-linearities into the expenditure–income relationship to allow for the possibility that a commodity may behave as a luxury in one range of income and as a necessity in a different range [139]. A Sigmoid response curve, which has an upper asymptote and at the same time passes through the origin, appears to yield realistic results in such instances [2].

Another approach, one that uses linear equations, has been to explain consumer purchases of specific goods on the basis of relationships between stocks and wealth rather than between income and expenditure. Quasi-Engel curves relating inventories to a measure of wealth have been derived by Cramer for a wide variety of household goods based on two Dutch surveys [29], and by Houthakker and Haldi for automobiles based on panel data for U.S. families [74]. The latter study is particularly interesting, showing that at a given level of income gross investment in automobiles varies inversely with beginning-of-the-year inventory, and that at a given level of beginning inventories gross investment rises with income level.[1]

Dissatisfaction with the linear-equation approach has also led to the use of variance analysis rather than multiple regression to ascertain the net effect of different variables on household expenditures. Variance analysis offers a more flexible approach to the estimation of relationships, since no assumption is necessary regarding the form of the functional relationship. As a result, studies using this technique do not always give the clear-cut simple results yielded by multiple regression, but in many ways appear to be more realistic, bringing out effects of various characteristics not only singly but in combination with each other (*e.g.*, [31] [47] [111]). Unfortunately, as noted previously, several of these studies have utilised group averages rather than individual families as the unit of observation, thereby greatly reducing the chances of detecting interaction effects.

Another post-war development has been emphasis on obtaining and analysing the expenditure and saving behaviour of the same households over time. Popular for many years in marketing and advertising circles, the value of the consumer panel technique to economic analysis, and as a connecting link between time-series aggregates and cross-section budget surveys, has only recently been recognised, stimulated in part by the emphasis of the permanent income hypothesis on the life history of the household. Panel studies undertaken so far have clearly demonstrated

[1] It might be noted that a somewhat similar approach was used by Hans Brems on time-series data to predict the long-run equilibrium demand for automobiles based on a model relating stock of automobiles to the equilibrium rate of growth and the average age at which cars are scrapped [16]. An extension of this model, incorporating time lags, has been presented by Marc Nerlove [131].

their value. In addition to studies discussed earlier [43] [87] [1] Houthakker and Haldi, in their automobile investment study, which was based on panel data, were able to isolate family taste as a separate variable. In another study based on panel data, Jean Crockett showed that income elasticities based on continuous panel data were much closer to time-series elasticities than the usual cross-section elasticities [31].

The introduction of panel data in budget studies highlights the growing interest in recent years in integrating the techniques of demand analysis and of household budget analysis. Time-series aggregates have serious disadvantages because of the frequently unstable estimates of income and of demand elasticities obtained as a result of the high correlation between income and prices. On the other hand, cross-section data are essentially static and are difficult to use as a basis for prediction. Hence, a combination of the two types of data would seem to offer a much more powerful technique for understanding consumer behaviour.

Initial efforts made to integrate these two sets of data have been directed towards deriving independent estimates of income elasticities from budget data, inserting these estimates into an aggregate time-series demand relation, and estimating the parameters of the other variables from the time-series data [40] [153] [149, esp. Ch. 18]. An alternate approach has been to search for cross-section functions that might be expected to remain stable over time. This approach was used by Eleanor Snyder in a study finding a cross-section consumption relationship for food to yield essentially the same estimates of the parameters when applied to eight different cross-section studies between 1888 and 1950 [147]. A more elaborate variation of this same general approach is the Crockett–Friend attempt to derive a complete set of consumer demand relationships [32]. Derivation of stable relationships of this sort could be used for prediction *if* distributional changes in these variables could be anticipated and *if* stability were assured.

This general approach has been carried one step further by Vernon Lippitt [111]. He applied analysis of variance to measure the effect of relevant cross-section variables on the particular item of expenditure. Estimates of the aggregate effects of these variables were derived for years for which the necessary cross-section data were available; estimates for intervening years were obtained by interpolation. These aggregate effects were then incorporated into a time-series function relating expenditures to these variables as well as to other pertinent time-series variables. Although details of the procedure may be questioned, and although this procedure still requires an independent estimate of distributional effects for predictive purposes, Lippitt demonstrates convincingly that this procedure is practicable and, in particular, that the distributional effect exerts a pronounced influence on estimated expenditures.

[1] Another study still being analysed is a food purchase panel operated by Michigan State University. See G. G. Quackenbush [141].

V. Household Decision-making

The household can be viewed as a decision-making organisation engaged in much the same activities as is a business firm. From this perspective, the household becomes a separate organisation that receives income and other money receipts and that dispenses this money in accordance with certain criteria. Entering into these criteria are the wants and desires of different household members, the structure of the household and the interpersonal relationships existing among the different family members, all subject to various economic restraints. The explanation of consumer behaviour then becomes a matter of identifying and measuring the relative importance of the factors that enter into the decision processes.

To borrow an analogy advanced by March and Simon in organisation theory [117, pp. 178–82], the decision process can be subdivided into three distinct stages: (1) the manner in which the possibility of a particular action, *e.g.*, purchase, comes to the attention of the household; (2) specification of, and deliberation among, alternative forms of action; and (3) the actual choice.

To illustrate, before a car is purchased, its desirability must first somehow come to the attention of the household. Then, different types of cars (brands, body-styles, etc.) as well as different forms (cash *vs.* borrowing) and times of making the purchase must be specified, however implicitly, and a certain amount of deliberation among these alternatives must take place. Finally, one alternative is selected as best and the decision is made to purchase (or not to purchase).

The usual consumer surveys and budget studies reflect the last stage of this process, namely, decisions in the form of actual purchases. Past empirical research on household behaviour, as reviewed in the preceding sections, has been concerned with the measurement of these purchases and with the extent to which they appear to have been influenced by socio-economic characteristics of the household and, to a lesser extent, by its attitudes and expectations. In the latter sense, empirical research may be said to be reaching back into the second stage of the decision process. Nevertheless, from the point of view of decision theory, such results are of limited interest because no light is thrown on the dynamics of the decision process and, clearly, no knowledge is provided about decisions that were *not* consummated as purchases.

In recent years an increasing amount of activity has focused on the second stage of the decision process, particularly on the extent of deliberation entering into consumer purchases. Thus, the previously cited works by Juster, Ferber and Katona and his associates serve to reinforce the notion that many durable-goods purchases are planned and thought out carefully in advance. Particularly interesting in this respect is a study by Katona and Mueller on the extent of deliberation entering into purchase decisions of four major household durables (TV, refrigerator, washing machine and stove) [89]. This study found considerable variation in the extent of advance deliberation among households. The actions of only about one-fourth of the group appeared to conform with the idea of the economic man, who considers a purchase very carefully and investigates numerous possibilities before making a final decision. An almost equal proportion were found to have made these purchases with virtually no advance deliberation, largely as a result of some fortuitous event. Extent of deliberation was more frequent among those with higher education, higher income, older people and those in professional occupations, as well as among people expressing a liking for shopping. Deliberation was less frequent when the product was inexpensive relative to the buyer's income, when a special deal was offered or when the product was needed urgently (as when the currently owned model broke down). Families under some financial stress did not appear to consider alternatives any more thoroughly than other families.

Attempts have also been made to explain the decision process in terms of accumulation of desires for and against making a particular purchase, based on the approach to social psychology of Kurt Lewin. This approach has been used by Warren Bilkey on consumer panels to obtain periodic measures from the same families of the psychic tensions arising at various stages of the purchase decision. Intensity of desire for and against a particular purchase is measured in terms of positive and negative " valences " registered by the household; the more the excess of positive valences over negative valences, the closer is the decision to action [6] [7].

More recently, this theory has been extended into a general model of household buying-decisions by Joseph Clawson, who represents such decisions as the quantitative interplay of different motivations, status dimensions and intensities [24]. Except for isolated experiments, no general application has yet been made of such a model. Indeed, it remains to be shown that such an approach adds anything more to the explanation of the decision process than could be obtained from more straightforward data on buying intentions, attitudes and preferences.[1]

Very little empirical work has been carried out on the attention-directing stage of the purchase process. This is not surprising in view of the more ephemeral nature of the problem. However, two interesting studies can be mentioned. One study, by Eva Mueller, attempts to ascertain the role of innovation in household purchases [129]. Among other things, it finds that innovators, defined as those who are among the first to purchase new types of appliances, are scattered throughout the population, but, as a rule, are generally found among the young, among the well-educated, among married couples with children and among those who are financially optimistic.

[1] The little work that has been done on the subject indicates that preferences may be very similar to purchase intentions, and that preferences are related to later purchases, at least as far as brand selection is concerned. See Seymour Banks [4].

People who already own similar appliances are more likely to be attracted to the new products, though this may reflect the interaction effect of assets and incomes.

The other study, carried out from a sociological point of view, traces how people through interpersonal contact become interested in purchasing air conditioners [168]. Based on block observations, this article shows rather strikingly how air-conditioner purchases spread by means of neighbourhood communication—among neighbours on the same block, over back alleys and over fences. The study suggests that this pattern of communication, particularly if catalysed by the presence of a "leader," accounts for differences in ownership rates of air conditioners among blocks of the same socio-economic status. In addition, the study stresses the importance of the group in motivating people to purchase new products, inferring that "it is the group that determines when a luxury becomes a necessity" [168, p. 117].[1] Other sociological studies have also affirmed the importance of the group, and of leaders, in influencing purchase behaviour [9] [91, pp. 234–47].

VI. Directions for Future Research

The review of empirical work on decision processes of consumers in the preceding section is brief only partly because of the survey nature of this article. That empirical work in this area is only just beginning is highlighted by recent publication of a symposium volume on household decision-making which reflects in many ways a good picture of current thinking [54]. The bulk of this volume is devoted to exposition of theoretical approaches to various types of household decisions, ranging from changes in family composition and career choices to saving versus borrowing, and the allocation of expenditures. Empirical results, however, are meagre and, with the exception of relationships between buying intentions and purchases presented by Juster, are largely inconclusive. As is evident from this volume, workable models of consumer purchase decisions have yet to be developed.

There is little doubt that empirical work in this area will be greatly expanded in the future, partly for its own sake and partly because of the stimulus provided by simulation and by game theory. Thus, before realistic simulation models of the consumer sector can be obtained, as is being attempted by Guy Orcutt and his associates at Wisconsin, knowledge must be available of the manner in which consumers make decisions and of the factors that enter into these decisions [134]. In a somewhat similar fashion, game theory has led to attempts to reduce consumer decisions to basic elements and to reproduce these decisions under laboratory conditions. Experimental work along this line by Wroe Alderson and his associates tends to support the feasibility of such an approach [3].

[1] Much the same conclusion on the importance of community effects is reached by Dorothy Brady using an economic approach [10] [12].

Among other things, this review serves to highlight the need for reconciling the different theories of the consumption function. In addition, much greater attention may be expected to the effect on spending and saving of the variables entering into the *ceteris paribus* assumption of the consumption function, particularly to non-linear and irregular effects. Primary attention may be expected to be given to the role of assets, both their effect on the consumption function and as constituting a separate study area in itself. With asset ownership expanding tremendously year by year, even in recession, it would not be surprising to see a body of literature spring up on the study of " asset functions " to take its place alongside the study of the consumption function and the saving function.

Another area that can be expected to receive even more attention is the role of intentions, expectations and attitudes on consumer behaviour. In the past these variables have been tested almost exclusively on their ability to predict durable-goods purchases. However, there is no reason why modifications of these variables might not be equally effective in predicting other types of purchases and even, as suggested by a recent exploratory study, in predicting saving [75].

The integration of cross-section with time-series data in explaining consumer demand is yet another area where significant advances can be expected in coming years. The means for such integration has been available for some time, namely, through the use of continuous consumer panels. By keeping continuous records, a comprehensive picture can be obtained not only of the factors influencing a household's purchasing and saving behaviour but also of the manner in which decisions are made. Furthermore, this technique enables comparable cross-section distributions to be formed at different points of time and the joint distribution of these cross-sections to be studied over time. In addition, if the geographic scope of the panel operation coincides with an area that serves as a basis for aggregate statistics on incomes and expenditures a basis is obtained for comparing and combining the data from these two very different sources.

Still another area where major expansion may be expected, and which has been the subject of relatively little empirical work in the past, is the study of the effect of household behaviour on other sectors of the economy. The post-war experience has brought out rather dramatically that in a high-income economy consumers are no longer a passive force in business fluctuations, but constitute an autonomous force of their own. Thus, several of the recessions during the 1950s were mitigated considerably by the maintenance of consumer expenditures while activity in other sectors was turning down. Furthermore, the experience of more recent recessions suggests that one of the basic tenets of consumer behaviour in the business cycle may be violated, namely, the positive relationship between the saving rate and economic activity. At least in a moderate recession, it appears that consumers may be treating various categories of expenditure rather than saving as residual

have been made, principally by the Survey Research Center, the Federal Reserve Board and other government agencies, but except for the project mentioned above, no concentrated effort has been made to deal with this problem or to develop new approaches to it. It is in the improvement of data-collection techniques that perhaps the greatest strides of all are yet to be made. The sooner such strides are taken, the sooner a really firm basis will be reached for the analysis of household behaviour.

REFERENCES

1. Gardner Ackley, " The Wealth–Saving Relationship," *Jour. Pol. Econ.*, Apr. 1951, **59**, 154–61.
2. J. Aitchison and J. A. C. Brown, " A Synthesis of Engel Curve Theory," *Rev. Econ. Stud.*, 1954–55, **22** (1), 35–46.
3. Wroe Alderson, Comments on " Decision-making Regarding Allocation and Spending," in [54, pp. 184–5].
4. Seymour Banks, " The Relationship Between Preference and Purchase of Brands," *Jour. Marketing*, Oct. 1950, **15**, 145–57.
5. S. G. Barton, " The Life Cycle and Buying Patterns," in L. H. Clark, ed., *The Life Cycle and Consumer Behavior*, New York 1955, pp. 53–7.
6. W. J. Bilkey, " A Psychological Approach to Consumer Behavior Analysis," *Jour. Marketing*, July 1953, **18**, 18–25.
7. ———, " Consistency Test of Psychic Tension Rating Involved in Consumer Purchasing Behavior," *Jour. Soc. Psych.*, Feb. 1957, **45**, 81–91.
8. Ronald Bodkin, " Windfall Income and Consumption," [62, pp. 175–87].
9. F. S. Bourne, " Group Influences in Marketing and Public Relations," in Rensis Likert and S. P. Hayes, ed., *Some Applications of Behavioral Research*, UNESCO, New York 1957, pp. 205–57.
10. D. S. Brady, " Family Saving in Relation to Changes in the Level and Distribution of Income," Nat. Bur. Econ. Research *Studies in Income and Wealth*, Vol. 15, New York 1952, pp. 103–30.
11. ———, " Influence of Age on Saving and Spending Patterns," *Mo. Lab. Rev.*, Nov. 1955, **78**, 1240–4.
12. ———, "Family Saving, 1888–1950," in R. W. Goldsmith, D. S. Brady and Horst Mendershausen, *A Study of Saving in the United States*, Vol. 3, Princeton 1956, pp. 139–276.
13. ———, " Quantity and Quality of Clothing Purchases," [62, pp. 137–42].
14. ——— and Rose Friedman, " Savings and The Income Distribution," Nat. Bur. Econ. Research Stud. in Income and Wealth, Vol. 10, New York 1947, pp. 247–65.
15. Hans Brems, *Product Equilibrium Under Monopolistic Competition*. Cambridge, Mass. 1951.
16. ———, " Long-Run Automobile Demand," *Jour. Marketing*, Apr. 1956, **21**, 379–84.
17. G. K. Brinegar, " Short-run Effects of Income Change Upon Expenditure," *Jour. Farm Econ.*, Feb. 1953, **35**, 99–109.
18. ———, " Income, Savings Balances and Net Saving," *Rev. Econ. Stat.*, Feb. 1953, **35**, 71–74.
19. J. K. Butters, L. D. Thompson and L. L. Bollinger, *Investment by Individuals*. Boston 1953.

20. Phillip Cagan, *Pension Plans and Aggregate Saving.* Unpublished manuscript, 1961.
21. Gregory Chow, *Demand for Automobiles in the United States.* Amsterdam 1957.
22. Carl Christ, Clifford Hildreth, Ta-Chung Liu and L. R. Klein, in "A Symposium on Simultaneous Equation Estimation," *Econometrica*, Oct. 1960, **28**, 835–71.
23. L. H. Clark, ed., *The Life Cycle and Consumer Behavior.* New York 1955.
24. J. W. Clawson, "Family Composition, Motivation, and Buying Decisions," [54, pp. 200–17].
25. H. J. Claycamp, Jr., *The Composition of Consumer Savings Portfolios.* Ph.D. thesis, University of Illinois, 1961. To be published in series, Studies in Consumer Savings, University of Illinois Bur. Econ. and Bus. Research.
26. Morris Cohen, "Liquid Assets and the Consumption Function," *Rev. Econ. Stat.*, May 1954, **36**, 202–11.
27. ——— and M. R. Gainsbrugh, "Consumer Buying Plans: A New Survey," *Conf. Board Bus. Rec.*, Nov. 1958, **15**, 449–67.
28. J. Cornfield, W. D. Evans and M. Hoffenberg, "Full Employment Patterns, 1950," *Mo. Lab. Rev.*, Feb. 1947, **70**, 163–90.
29. J. S. Cramer, "Ownership Elasticities of Durable Consumer Goods," *Rev. Econ. Stud.*, Feb. 1958, **25**, 87–96.
30. Jean Crockett, "Population Change and the Demand for Food," in *Demographic and Economic Change in Developed Countries*, Universities—Nat. Bur. Com. Econ. Research, Princeton 1960, pp. 457–83.
31. ———, "A New Type of Estimate of the Income Elasticity of the Demand for Food," *Proc. Am. Stat. Assoc.*, Bus. Econ. Stat. Sec., 1957, pp. 117–22.
32. ——— and Irwin Friend, "A Complete Set of Consumer Demand Relationships," [62, pp. 1–92].
33. T. E. Davis, "The Consumption Function as a Tool for Prediction," *Rev. Econ. Stat.*, Aug. 1952, **34**, 270–7.
34. Jean M. Due, "Postwar Family Expenditure Studies in Western Europe," *Jour. Farm Econ.*, Aug. 1956, **38**, 846–56.
35. James Duesenberry, *Income, Saving and the Theory of Consumer Behavior*, Cambridge, Mass. 1949.
36. ———, Comments on "General Saving Relations" [62, pp. 188–91].
37. Marilyn Dunsing and M. G. Reid, "Effect of Varying Degrees of Transitory Income on Income Elasticity of Expenditures," *Jour. Am. Stat. Assoc.*, June 1958, **53**, 348–59.
38. Robert Eisner, "The Permanent Income Hypothesis: Comment," *Am. Econ. Rev.*, Dec. 1958, **48**, 972–90.
39. M. J. Farrell, "Irreversible Demand Functions," *Econometrica*, Apr. 1952, **20**, 171–86.
40. ———, "Demand for Motor Cars in the United States," *Jour. Royal Stat. Soc.*, Pt. 2, 1954, **117A**, 171–201.
41. Robert Ferber, *A Study of Aggregate Consumption Functions.* Nat. Bur. Econ. Research Tech. Paper 8. New York 1953.
42. ———, "The Role of Planning in Consumer Purchases of Durable Goods," *Am. Econ. Rev.*, Dec. 1954, **44**, 854–74.
43. ———, *Factors Influencing Durable Goods Purchases*, Bur. Econ. Bus. Research, Univ. of Illinois 1955; reprinted in [23, pp. 75–122].
45. ———, "The Accuracy of Aggregate Savings Functions in the Postwar Years," *Rev. Econ. Stat.*, May 1955, **37**, 134–48.

46. Robert Ferber, " A Statistical Study of Factors Influencing Temporal Variations in Aggregate Service Expenditures," in L. H. Clark, ed., *Consumer Behavior: Research on Consumer Reactions*, New York 1958, pp. 394–414.
47. ———, " Service Expenditures at Mid-Century," [62, pp. 436–60].
48. ———, " Making Less and Saving More," *Illinois Bus. Rev.*, Sept. 1961, **18**, 2, 8.
49. ——— and P. J. Verdoon, *Research Methods in Economics and Business.* New York 1962.
50. Janet Fisher, " Income, Spending, and Saving Patterns of Consumer Units in Different Age Groups," in Nat. Bur. Econ. Research *Studies in Income and Wealth*, Vol. 15, New York 1962, pp. 75–102.
51. ———, " Postwar Changes in Income and Savings Among Consumers in Different Age Groups," *Econometrica*, Jan. 1952, **20**, 47–70.
52. ———, " Family Life Cycle Analysis on Research on Consumer Behavior," [23, pp. 28–35].
53. M. R. Fisher, " Explorations in Savings Behavior," *Bull. Oxford Univ. Inst. Stat.*, Aug. 1956, **18**, 201–78.
54. N. N. Foote, ed., *Household Decision-Making.* New York 1961.
55. Milton Friedman, " A Method of Comparing Incomes of Families Differing in Composition," in Nat. Bur. Research, *Studies in Income and Wealth*, Vol. 15, New York 1952, pp. 9–20.
56. ———, *A Theory of the Consumption Function.* Nat. Bur. Econ. Research, Princeton 1957.
57. ———, *Windfalls, the " Horizon " and Related Concepts in the Permanent Income Hypothesis.* Unpublished memorandum.
57A. ———, " Comments on Windfall Income and Consumption," [62, pp. 191–206].
58. ——— and Simon Kuznets, *Income from Independent Professional Practice.* New York 1945.
59. Irwin Friend and I. B. Kravis, " Consumption Patterns and Permanent Income," *Am. Econ. Rev., Proc.*, May 1957, **47**, 536–55.
60. ——— and I. B. Kravis, " Entrepreneurial Income, Saving and Investment," *Am. Econ. Rev.*, June 1957, **47**, 269–301.
61. ——— and Stanley Schor, " Who Saves ?," *Rev. Econ. Stat.*, May 1959, Pt. 2, **41**, 213–48.
62. ——— and Robert Jones, ed., *Proceedings of the Conference on Consumption and Saving*, Vol. 2. Philadelphia 1960.
62A. ——— and ———, " The Concept of Saving," [62, pp. 336–59].
63. ———, " Discussion of Milton Friedman's ' A Theory of the Consumption Function,' " in L. H. Clark, ed., *Consumer Behavior: Research on Consumer Reactions*, New York 1958, pp. 256–58.
64. Paul Glick, " The Family Cycle," *Am. Soc. Rev.*, Apr. 1947, **12**, 164–74.
65. Raymond Goldsmith, *A Study of Saving in the United States.* Princeton 1955.
66. Sidney Goldstein, *Consumption Patterns of the Aged.* Philadelphia 1960.
67. H. W. Guthrie, " Consumers' Propensities to Hold Liquid Assets," *Jour. Am. Stat. Assoc.*, Sept. 1960, **55**, 469–90.
68. Morris Hamburg, " Demand for Clothing," in I. Friend and R. Jones, *Proceedings of the Conference on Consumption and Saving*, Vol. 1, Philadelphia 1960, pp. 311–58.
69. William Hamburger, " The Relation of Consumption to Wealth and the Wage Rate," *Econometrica*, Jan. 1955, **23**, 1–17.
70. ———, " The Determinants of Aggregate Consumption," *Rev. Econ. Stud.*, No. 57, 1954–55, **22**, 23–35.

71. A. H. HANSEN, " The Pigouvian Effect," *Jour. Pol. Econ.*, Dec. 1951, **49** 535–36.
72. H. S. HOUTHAKKER, " The Permanent Income Hypothesis," *Am. Econ. Rev.*, June 1958, **48**, 396–404.
73. ——, " An International Comparison of Household Expenditure Patterns, Commemorating the Centenary of Engel's Law," *Econometrica*, Oct. 1957, **25**, 532–51.
74. —— AND JOHN HALDI, " Household Investment in Automobiles: An Intemporal Cross-Section Analysis," in I. Friend and R. Jones, *Proceedings of the Conference on Consumption and Saving*, Vol. I, Philadelphia 1960, pp. 175–225.
75. Inter-University Committee for Research on Consumer Behavior, *Anticipation of Saving Behavior*, Intermim Report No. 6, 1961.
76. F. T. JUSTER, " Predictions and Consumer Buying Intentions," *Am. Econ. Rev. Proc.*, May 1960, **50**, 604–17.
77. ——, " The Predictive Value of Consumers Union Spending-Intentions Data," in *The Quality and Economic Significance of Anticipations Data*, Nat. Bur. Econ. Research, Princeton 1960, pp. 263–89.
78. ——, *Consumer Expectations, Plans, and Purchases: A Progress Report*, Nat. Bur. Econ. Res., Occas. Paper 70, New York 1957.
79. GEORGE KATONA, in *The Quality and Economic Significance of Anticipations Data*, Nat. Bur. Econ. Research, Princeton 1960, p. 455.
80. ——, " Attitude Change: Instability of Response and Acquisition of Experience," *Psych. Monogr.*, Vol. 72 (10). Am. Psych. Assoc., Washington, D.C. 1958.
81. ——, " Contribution of Psychological Data to Economic Analysis," *Jour. Am. Stat. Assoc.*, Sept. 1947, **42**, 449–59.
82. ——, " Effect of Income Changes on the Rate of Saving," *Rev. Econ. Stat.*, May 1949, **39**, 95–103.
83. ——, " Analysis of Dissaving," *Am. Econ. Rev.*, June 1949, **39**, 673–88.
84. ——, *Psychological Analysis of Economic Behaviour*. New York 1951.
85. ——, " The Predictive Value of Data on Consumer Attitudes," [23, pp. 66–74].
86. ——, *The Powerful Consumer*. New York 1960.
87. —— AND J. A. FISHER, " Postwar Changes in the Income of Identical Consumer Units," in Nat. Bur. Econ. Research, *Studies in Income and Wealth*, Vol. 13, New York 1951, pp. 61–122.
88. —— AND EVA MUELLER, *Consumer Attitudes and Demand*, 1950–52, Survey Research Center, University of Michigan, Ann Arbor 1953.
89. —— AND ——, " A Study of Purchase Decisions," in L. H. Clark, ed., *Consumer Behavior: The Dynamics of Consumer Reactions*, New York 1954, pp. 30–87.
90. —— AND ——, *Consumer Expectations, 1953–56*, Survey Research Center, University of Michigan. Ann Arbor 1956.
91. ELIHU KATZ AND P. F. LAZARSFELD, *Personal Influence*. Glencoe, Ill. 1955.
92. J. M. KEYNES, *The General Theory of Employment Interest and Money*. New York 1936.
93. E. L. KIRKPATRICK, *The Life Cycle of the Farm Family*. Wisconsin Agric. Exper. Sta. Research Bull. 121. Madison 1934.
94. L. R. KLEIN, " Estimating Patterns of Savings Behavior from Sample Survey Data," *Econometrica*, Oct. 1951, **19**, 438–54.
95. ——, " Assets, Debts, and Economic Behavior," in Nat. Bur. Econ. Research, *Studies in Income and Wealth*, Vol. 14, New York 1951, pp. 195–227.

96. L. R. Klein, "Statistical Estimation of Economic Relations from Survey Data," in George Katona, L. R. Klein, J. B. Lansing and J. N. Morgan, *Contributions of Survey Methods to Economics*, New York 1954, pp. 189–240.
97. ———, "Major Consumer Expenditures and Ownership of Durables," *Bull. Oxford Univ. Inst. Stat.*, Nov. 1955, **17**, 387–414.
98. ———, "Patterns of Savings," *Bull. Oxford Univ. Inst. Stat.*, May 1955, **17**, 173–214.
99. ———, "Entrepreneurial Saving," [62, pp. 297–335].
100. ——— and J. B. Lansing, "Decisions to Purchase Consumer Durable Goods," *Jour. Marketing.*, Oct. 1955, **20**, 109–32.
101. ——— and J. Margolis, "Statistical Studies of Unincorporated Business," *Rev. Econ. Stat.*, Feb. 1954, **36**, 33–46.
102. M. E. Kreinin, J. B. Lansing and J. N. Morgan, "Analysis of Life Insurance Premiums," *Rev. Econ. Stat.*, Feb. 1957, **39**, 46–54.
103. ———, "Factors Associated with Stock Ownership," *Rev. Econ. Stat.*, Feb. 1959, **41**, 12–23.
104. ———, "Analysis of Liquid Asset Ownership," *Rev. Econ. Stat.*, Feb. 1961, **43**, 76–80.
104A. ———, "Windfall Income and Consumption," *Am. Econ. Rev.*, June 1961, **51**, 388–90.
105. Simon Kuznets, *National Product Since 1869*. Nat. Bur. Econ. Research, New York 1946.
106. ———, "Proportion of Capital Formation to National Product," *Am. Econ. Rev.*, May 1952, **42**, 507–26.
107. Helen Lamale, *Methodology of the Survey of Consumer Expenditures in 1950*. Philadelphia 1959.
108. J. B. Lansing, *An Investigation of Response Error*. Univ. of Illinois, Bur. Econ. Bus. Research, Stud. in Consumer Savings, No. 2, 1961.
109. ——— and S. B. Withey, "Consumer Anticipations: Their Use in Forecasting Behavior," Nat. Bur. Econ. Research *Studies in Income and Wealth*, Vol. 17, Princeton 1955, pp. 381–453.
110. A. P. Lerner, "Fiscal Finance and the Federal Debt," *Soc. Research*, Feb. 1943, **10**, 38–51.
111. Vernon Lippitt, *Determinants of Consumer Demand for Housefurnishings and Equipment*. Cambridge, Mass. 1959.
111A. Nissan Liviatan, "Errors in Variables and Engel Curve Analysis," *Econometrica*, July 1961, **29**, 336–62.
112. Harold Lydall, "The Life Cycle in Income, Saving, and Asset Ownership," *Econometrica*, Apr. 1955, **23**, 131–50.
113. ———, "Income, Assets, and the Demand for Money," *Rev. Econ. Stat.*, Feb. 1958, **40**, 1–14.
114. R. P. Mack, "The Direction of Change in Income and the Consumption Function," *Rev. Econ. Stat.*, Nov. 1948, **30**, 329–58.
115. ———, "Economics of Consumption," in B. F. Haley, ed., *A Survey of Contemporary Economics*, Vol. 2, Homewood, Ill. 1952, pp. 39–78.
116. Sherman Maisel and Louis Winnick, "Family Housing Expenditures: Elusive Laws and Intrusive Variances," in I. Friend and R. Jones, ed., *Proceedings of the Conference on Consumption and Saving*, Vol. 1, Philadelphia 1960, pp. 359–435.
117. J. G. March and H. A. Simon, *Organizations*. New York 1959.
118. E. S. Maynes, "The Relationship Between Tangible Investment and Consumer Saving," *Rev. Econ. Stat.*, Aug. 1959, **41**, 287–93.
119. Horst Mendershausen, "Differences in Family Saving between Cities of Different Sizes and Locations, Whites and Negroes," *Rev. Econ. Stat.*, Aug. 1940, **22**, 122–37.

120. D. L. MILLER, "The Life Cycle and the Impact of Advertising," in [23, pp. 61–5].
121. JACOB MINCER, "Labor Supply, Family Income and Consumption," *Am. Econ. Rev., Proc.*, May 1960, **50**, 574–83.
122. FRANCO MODIGLIANI, "Fluctuations in the Saving-Income Ratio: A Problem in Economic Forecasting," Nat. Bur. Econ. Research *Studies in Income and Wealth*, Vol. 11, New York 1949, pp. 371–443.
123. ——— AND ALBERT ANDO, "The 'Permanent Income' and the 'Life Cycle' Hypotheses of Saving Behavior: Comparison and Tests," [62, pp. 49–174].
124. ——— AND ———, "Tests of the Life Cycle Hypothesis of Savings," *Bull. Oxford Univ. Inst. Stat.*, May 1957, **19**, 99–124.
125. ——— AND R. E. BRUMBERG, "Utility Analysis and the Consumption Function: An Interpretation of Cross-Section Data," in K. K. KURIHARA, ed., *Post-Keynesian Economics*, New Brunswick, N.J. 1954, pp. 388–436.
126. J. N. MORGAN, "Factors Relating to Consumer Saving when It Is Defined as a Net-worth Concept," in L. R. Klein, ed., *Contributions of Survey Methods to Economics*, New York 1954, Ch. 3, 4.
127. ———, "A Review of Recent Research on Consumer Behavior," in L. H. Clark, ed., *Consumer Behavior: Research on Consumer Reactions*, New York 1958, pp. 93–219.
128. ———, "Consumer Investment Expenditures," *Am. Econ. Rev.*, Dec. 1958, **48**, 874–902.
129. EVA MUELLER, "The Desire for Innovations in Household Goods," in L. H. Clark, ed., *Consumer Behavior: Research on Consumer Reactions*, New York 1958, pp. 13–37.
130. ———, "Consumer Attitudes: Their Influence and Forecasting Value," in *The Quality and Economic Significance of Anticipations Data*, Nat. Bur. Econ. Research, Princeton 1960, pp. 149–75.
131. MARC NERLOVE, "A Note on Long-Run Automobile Demand," *Jour. Marketing*, July 1957, **22**, 57–64.
132. ———, *Distributed Lags and Demand Analysis*, U.S. Dept. Agric., *Washington* 1958.
133. A. M. OKUN, "The Value of Anticipations Data in Forecasting National Product," in *The Quality and Economic Significance of Anticipations Data*, Nat. Bur. Econ. Research, Princeton 1960, pp. 411–28.
134. GUY ORCUTT AND OTHERS, *Micro-Analysis of Socio-Economic Systems: A Simulation Study*. New York 1961.
135. ——— AND A. D. ROY, *A Bibliography of the Consumption Function*. Cambridge University, Dept. of Applied Economics, 1949. Mimeographed.
136. A. R. OXENFELDT, "Comments on the article by Friend and Kravis," in *Am. Econ. Rev., Proc.*, May 1957, **47**, 571–4.
137. L. J. PARADISO AND CLEMENT WINSTON, "Consumer Expenditure–Income Patterns," *Surv. Curr. Bus.*, Sept. 1955, **35**, 23–32.
138. A. C. PIGOU, "The Classical Stationary State," *Econ. Jour.*, Dec. 1943, **53**, 343–51.
139. S. J. PRAIS, "Nonlinear Estimates of the Engel Curve," *Rev. Econ. Stud.*, Pt. 2, 1952–53, **20**, 87–104.
140. ——— AND H. S. HOUTHAKKER, *The Analysis of Family Budgets*. Cambridge, Eng. 1955.
141. G. G. QUACKENBUSH AND J. D. SHAFFER, *Collecting Food Purchase Data by Consumer Panel*, Michigan State Univ. Agric. Exper. Sta. Tech. Bull. 279. East Lansing 1960.
142. M. G. REID, "Effect of Income Concept Upon Expenditure Curves of Farm Families," Nat. Bur. Econ. Research *Studies in Income and Wealth*, Vol. 15, New York 1952, pp. 133–74.

143. M. G. Reid, " The Relation of the Within-group Transitory Component of Income to the Income Elasticity of Family Expenditure." Unpublished paper, 1952.
144. ———, " Capital Formation in Residential Real Estate," *Jour. Pol. Econ.*, Apr. 1958, **66**, 131–53.
145. ———, Comments in I. Friend and R. Jones, eds., *Proceedings of the Conference on Consumption and Saving*, Vol. 1, Philadelphia 1960, pp. 143–55.
146. ——— and Marilyn Dunsing, " Effect of Variability of Incomes on Level of Income–Expenditure Curves on Farm Families," *Rev. Econ. Stat.*, Feb. 1956, **38**, 90–5.
147. E. M. Snyder, " Impact of Long-term Structural Changes on Family Expenditures, 1888–1950," in L. H. Clark, ed., *Consumer Behavior: Research on Consumer Reactions*, New York 1958, pp. 359–93.
148. G. J. Stigler, " The Early History of Empirical Studies of Consumer Behavior," *Jour. Pol. Econ.*, Apr. 1954, **42**, 95–113.
149. Richard Stone, *The Measurement of Consumers' Expenditure and Behaviour in the United Kingdom*. Cambridge, Eng. 1954.
150. G. Stuvel and S. F. James, " Household Expenditures of Food in Holland," *Jour. Royal Stat. Soc.*, Ser. A, **113**, Pt. 1, 1950, 59–80.
151. D. B. Suits, " The Demand for Automobiles in the United States, 1929–1956," *Rev. Econ. Stat.*, Aug. 1958, **40**, 273–80.
152. Gerhard Tintner, " Static Econometric Models and Their Empirical Verification," *Metroeconomica*, 1951, **2**, 172–81.
153. James Tobin, " A Statistical Demand Function for Food in the U.S.A.," *Jour. Royal Stat. Soc.*, Ser. A, **113**, Pt. II, 1950, 113–41.
154. ———, " Relative Income, Absolute Income, and Saving," in *Money, Trade, and Economic Growth, Essays in Honor of John Henry Williams*, New York 1951, 135–56.
155. ———, " Asset Holdings and Spending Decisions," *Am. Econ. Rev.*, May 1952, **42**, 109–23.
156. ———, " Discussion of Milton Friedman's ' A Theory of the Consumption Function,' " in L. H. Clark, ed., *Consumer Behavior: Research on Consumer Reactions*, New York 1958, pp. 447–54.
157. ———, " On the Predictive Value of Consumer Intentions and Attitudes," *Rev. Econ. Stat.*, Feb. 1959. **41**, 1–11.
158. U.S. Dept. of Agriculture, *Family Incomes and Expenditures* (titles vary). Misc. Pubs. between No. 339 and No. 489, 1939–41.
159. U.S. Bureau of Labor Statistics, *Family Income and Expenditures in (selected areas)*. U.S. Dept. of Labor Bull. 642–49, 1938–41.
160. U.S. Federal Reserve Board, *Report of Consultant Committee on Consumer Survey Statistics*. July 1955.
161. U.S. National Resources Planning Board, *Family Expenditures in the United States*. Washington 1941.
162. Universities-Nat. Bur. Com. Econ. Research, *The Quality and Economic Significance of Anticipations Data*. Princeton 1960.
163. Calla Van Syckle, " Economic Expectations and Spending Plans of Consumers," *Rev. Econ. Stat.*, Nov. 1954, **36**, 451–5.
164. W. S. Vickrey, " Resource Distribution Patterns and the Classification of Families," Nat. Bur. Econ. Research *Studies in Income and Wealth*, Vol. 10, New York 1947, 260–329.
165. H. W. Watts, *Long-run Income Expenditure and Consumer Savings*. Cowles Foundation Paper No. 123. New Haven 1958.
166. ——— and James Tobin, " Consumer Expenditures and the Capital Account," [62, pp. 1–48].

167. G. S. Weiss, Tynan Smith and T. G. Flechsig, " Quarterly Survey of Consumer Buying Intentions," *Fed. Res. Bull.* Sept. 1960, **46**, 977–1003.
168. W. H. Whyte, Jr., " The Web of Word of Mouth," in [23, pp. 113–122]; this article first appeared in the November 1954 issue of *Fortune* Magazine.
169. F. M. Williams and C. C. Zimmerman, *Studies of Family Living in the United States and Other Countries.* U.S. Dept. of Agriculture, Misc. Pub. 223, Washington 1935.
170. Herman Wold and Lars Jureen, *Demand Analysis.* New York 1953.

XIII

COST-BENEFIT ANALYSIS: A SURVEY[1]

By

A. R. PREST AND R. TURVEY

The order of discussion in this survey article will be as follows: in I we shall outline the development and scope of the subject in general terms; II will be concerned with general principles; in III we shall survey particular applications of cost-benefit techniques, examining the uses made of them in a variety of fields—water-supply projects, transport, land usage, health, education, research, etc. We shall proceed to a general summing up in IV, and conclude with a bibliography.

I. Introduction

Cost-benefit analysis[2] is a practical way of assessing the desirability of projects, where it is important to take a long view (in the sense of looking at repercussions in the further, as well as the nearer, future) and a wide view (in the sense of allowing for side-effects of many kinds on many persons, industries, regions, etc.), *i.e.*, it implies the enumeration and evaluation of all the relevant costs and benefits. This involves drawing on a variety of traditional sections of economic study—welfare economics, public finance, resource economics—and trying to weld these components into a coherent whole. Although the subject of cost-benefit analysis has come into prominence among economists only in recent years, it has quite a long history, especially in France, where Dupuit's classic paper on the utility of public works, one of the most original path-breaking writings in the whole history of economics, appeared as long ago as 1844 [19]. In the present century cost-benefit analysis first came into prominence in the United States. Here, according to Hammond [32], it was "in origin an administrative device owing nothing to economic theory and adapted to a strictly limited type of Federal activity—the improvement of navigation" (*op. cit.*, p. 3).

The River and Harbor Act 1902 required a board of engineers to report on the desirability of Army Corps of Engineers' river and harbour projects, taking into account the amount of commerce benefited and the cost. Another Act further required a statement of local or special benefits as a means for

[1] The authors are indebted to M. E. Beesley, J. L. Carr, O. Eckstein, M. J. Farrell, M. S. Feldstein C. D. Foster, R. N. McKean, E. Mishan, A. T. Peacock, M. H. Peston and C. S. Shoup for most valuable comments and suggestions on an earlier draft.

[2] Alternatively christened "investment planning" or "project appraisal."

*

charging local interests with part of the cost. So the Corps of Engineers worked out valuation techniques confined to tangible costs and benefits.

In the thirties, with the New Deal, the idea of a broader social justification for projects developed. The Flood Control Act of 1936 thus authorised Federal participation in flood-control schemes "if the benefits to whomsoever they may accrue are in excess of the estimated costs." The practice of making analyses then spread to the other agencies concerned with water-development projects. The purpose was not only to justify projects but also to help to decide who should pay.

By the end of the war, agencies had broadened their approaches by:

(*a*) bringing in secondary or indirect benefits and costs;
(*b*) including intangibles.

In 1950 an inter-agency committee produced the "Green Book" [40], an attempt to codify and agree general principles. It was noteworthy as bringing in the language of welfare economics.

Interest among economists in this technique has grown tremendously in the last few years, as can be seen from the number of references cited in the bibliography and the years in which these works appeared.[1] There seem to be several reasons for this. One has been the growth of large investment projects—absorbing a large amount of resources, having repercussions over a long period of time or substantially affecting prices and outputs of other products, etc. Another obvious reason is the growth of the public sector, *e.g.*, the Central Government, local authorities and public enterprises such as nationalised industries accounted for 45% of gross fixed investment in the United Kingdom in 1963, compared with 33% in 1938. A technique which is explicitly concerned with the wide consequences of investment decisions is obviously of much more interest to-day than it was twenty-five years ago. Another reason for increasing interest by economists is the rapid development in recent years of such techniques as operations research, systems analysis, etc., both in the public and the private sectors of the economy. This is a point on which McKean [53] has laid particular emphasis.

It is always important, and perhaps especially so in economics, to avoid being swept off one's feet by the fashions of the moment. In the case of cost-benefit analysis, one must recognise that it is a method which can be used inappropriately as well as appropriately. There are two very clear general

[1] Alternatively, one can look at earlier works to see what their authors had to say about the principles of public investment expenditures. If one selects Dalton [16] for this purpose—and in doing this one can hardly be accused of selecting someone uninterested in the subject—one finds the following kind of statement:

> "There is thus a large field for the intervention of public authorities to increase economic provision for the future and to create a better balance between its component elements. These two objects furnish the key to nearly all public expenditure designed to increase productive power" (*op. cit.*, p. 157).

This is unexceptionable but hardly a complete guide to policy-makers.

limitations of principle (as distinct from the many more of practice) which must be recognised at the outset. First, cost-benefit analysis as generally understood is only a technique for taking decisions within a framework which has to be decided upon in advance and which involves a wide range of considerations, many of them of a political or social character. Secondly, cost-benefit techniques as so far developed are least relevant and serviceable for what one might call large-size investment decisions. If investment decisions are so large relatively to a given economy (*e.g.*, a major dam project in a small country), that they are likely to alter the constellation of relative outputs and prices over the whole economy, the standard technique is likely to fail us, for nothing less than some sort of general equilibrium approach would suffice in such cases. This means that the applicability of the technique to underdeveloped countries is likely to be less than is sometimes envisaged, as so many investment projects involve large structural changes in such areas. Of course, this does not rule out all applications of this technique in such countries, as a number of valuable studies (*e.g.*, Hawkins [34], Farmer [22]) bear witness. Nor should it do so, given the shortage of capital resources in such countries. The point is simply that one must remain more acutely aware of the limitations of the technique in these cases.

So much for the general limitations of cost-benefit analysis. It must be made clear at this point that this survey has particular limitations as well. First, cost-benefit analysis has many facets and many applications [1] which we cannot hope to cover fully. There are therefore gaps in both subject matter and references. Secondly, a good deal of the material in the field lies unpublished in the files of government departments or international agencies and is therefore inaccessible. Third, there is no discussion of such maximisation methods as linear and non-linear programming, simulation, game theory, etc. Finally, we shall confine ourselves to the applications of these techniques in economies which are not centrally planned and where there is a reasonable amount of recognition of the principle of consumer sovereignty. This should not be taken to mean that we think that cost-benefit analysis has no relevance at all in centrally planned economies, but simply that we are not attempting to deal with such cases.

II. General Principles

1. *Preliminary Considerations*

(a) *Statement of the Problem*

As we have seen, cost-benefit analysis is a way of setting out the factors which need to be taken into account in making certain economic choices. Most of the choices to which it has been applied involve investment projects

[1] The bibliography cited by McKean [53] contains references to works on, *e.g.*, government budgeting, capital budgeting, strategy, investment theory, welfare economics, highway pricing, operational research, staff and management control.

and decisions—whether or not a particular project is worthwhile, which is the best of several alternative projects, or when to undertake a particular project. We can, however, apply the term "project" more generally than this. Cost-benefit analysis can also be applied to proposed changes in laws or regulations, to new pricing schemes and the like. An example is furnished by proposals for regulating the traffic on urban roads. Such schemes involve making economic choices along the same lines as investment schemes. As choice involves maximisation, we have to discuss what it is that decision-makers want to maximise. The formulation which, as a description, best covers most cost-benefit analyses examined in the literature we are surveying is as follows: the aim is to maximise the present value of all benefits less that of all costs, subject to specified constraints.

This formulation is very general, but it does at least enable us to set out a series of questions, the answers to which constitute the general principles of cost-benefit analysis:

1. Which costs and which benefits are to be included?
2. How are they to be valued?
3. At what interest rate are they to be discounted?
4. What are the relevant constraints?

Needless to say, there is bound to be a certain degree of arbitrariness in classifying questions under these four headings, but that cannot be helped.

(b) *A General Issue*

Before we can take these questions seriatim it is convenient to discuss an issue which involves more than one of these questions. It arises because the conditions for a welfare maximum are not likely to be fulfilled throughout the economy. If they were, and so resource allocation were optimal, the marginal social rate of time preference and the (risk-adjusted) marginal social rate of return from investment would coincide. A single rate of interest would then serve both to compare benefits and costs of different dates and to measure the opportunity cost of that private investment which is displaced by the need to provide resources for the projects in question. As things are, however, no single rate of interest will fulfil both functions simultaneously; in a non-optimal world there are two things to be measured and not one.

The problem has been discussed by a number of authors, including Eckstein [20, 21], Steiner [80], Marglin [48] and Feldstein [23, 24, 25]. They suggest that the costs and benefits of a project are the time streams of consumption foregone and provided by that project. The nature of this approach emerges clearly from Feldstein's remarks on the social opportunity cost of funds transferred from the private sector to the public sector in [25]:

> "Part of the money taken from the private sector decreases consumption immediately, while the rest decreases investment and therefore

future consumption. A pound transferred from consumption in a particular year has, by definition, a social value in that year of £1. But a pound transferred from private investment is worth the discounted value of the future consumption that would have occurred if the investment had been made. The original investment generates an income stream to investors and workers. Some of this income is spent on consumption and the remainder is invested. Each of these subsequent investments generates a new income stream and thus consumption and further investment. The final result is an aggregate consumption time-stream generated by the original investment. It is the current value of this aggregate that is the social opportunity cost of a one pound decrease in private investment."

The application of this approach to both costs and benefits produces a complicated expression for the present worth of a project's benefits less its costs. Nobody has as yet succeeded in quantifying such expressions, however,[1] so at present the approach can only serve as a reference-standard for judging simpler but more practicable ways of tackling the problem. Meanwhile, we note that the problem arises to the extent: (i) that a project's benefits are reinvested or create new investment opportunities, or (ii) that some of the funds used for the project would otherwise have been invested or that the project renders impossible some other and mutually exclusive investment project. If neither of these conditions is fulfilled; if, in other words, benefits and costs both consist exclusively of consumption (directly provided and, respectively, precluded by the project), then these complications do not arise, and the problem is reduced to one of choosing an appropriate social time preference rate of discount.

2. *The Main Questions*

(a) *Enumeration of Costs and Benefits*

(i) *Definition of a Project.* In most cases the scope and nature of the projects which are to be submitted to cost-benefit analysis will be clear. For the sake of completeness, however, we must make the point that if one authority is responsible for producing A goods and B goods, then in judging between A goods investment projects of different sizes it must take into account the effect of producing more A goods on its output of B goods. There are all sorts of complications here: relationships between A and B goods may be on the supply or demand side, they may be direct (in the sense of A influencing B) or indirect (in the sense of A influencing C, which influences B) and so on. One illustration is the operations of an authority responsible for a long stretch of river; if it puts a dam at a point upstream this will affect the water level, and hence the operations of existing or potential dams downstream. Construction of a fast motorway, which in

[1] " Estimating many of the variables and parameters needed to calculate net social benefit may indeed be difficult " (Feldstein [23], p. 126).

itself speeds up traffic and reduces accidents, may lead to more congestion or more accidents on feeder roads if they are left unimproved. All that this amounts to saying is that where there are strong relationships on either the supply or the demand side, allowances must be made for these in cost-benefit calculations. We shall return to this point later (see p. 176 *infra*), when discussing investment criteria.

(ii) *Externalities*. We now come to the wide class of costs and benefits which accrue to bodies other than the one sponsoring a project, and the equally wide issue of how far the sponsoring body should take them into account. We shall discuss the general principles at stake and then apply them to particular cases.

McKean [53, Ch. 8] discusses the distinction between technological and pecuniary *spillovers* at length. The essential points are that progenitors of public investment projects *should* take into account the external effects of their actions in so far as they alter the physical production possibilities of other producers or the satisfactions that consumers can get from given resources; they *should not* take side-effects into account if the sole effect is via prices of products or factors. One example of the first type is when the construction of a reservoir by the upstream authority of a river basin necessitates more dredging by the downstream authority. An example of the second type is when the improvement of a road leads to greater profitability of the garages and restaurants on that road, employment of more labour by them, higher rent payments to the relevant landlords, etc. In general, this will *not* be an additional benefit to be credited to the road investment, even if the extra profitability, etc., of the garages on one road is not offset by lower profitability of garages on the other, which are now less used as a result of the traffic diversion. Any net difference in profitability and any net rise in rents and land values is simply a reflection of the benefits of more journeys being undertaken, etc., than before, and it would be double counting if these were included too. In other words, we have to eliminate the purely transfer or distributional items from a cost-benefit evaluation: we are concerned with the value of the increment of output arising from a given investment and not with the increment in value of existing assets. In still other words, we measure costs and benefits on the assumption of a given set of prices, and the incidental and consequential price changes of goods and factors should be ignored.[1]

No one can pretend that this distinction is a simple one to maintain in practice; there may well be results from investment which are partially technological and partially pecuniary. Nor is the task of unravelling made easier by the fact that some of the transfers occasioned by investment projects may affect the distribution of income significantly, and hence the pattern of demand. But as a general guiding principle the distinction is most valuable.

We now consider the application of this principle. First of all, an invest-

[1] Apart from allowances necessary to get a measure of the change of surplus (see p. 163 *infra*).

ing agency must try to take account of obvious technological spillovers, such as the effects of flood control measures or storage dams on the productivity of land at other points in the vicinity. In some cases no explicit action may be needed, *e.g.*, these effects may be internal to different branches of the same agency, or some system of compensation may be prescribed by law. But in others there should at least be an attempt to correct for the most obvious and important repercussions. Although in principle corrections are needed whatever the relationship between the interacting organisations, it must be expected that in practice the compulsion to take side-effects into account will be much greater if similar organisations are involved, *e.g.*, one local authority is more likely to take account of the costs it imposes on other bodies if those mainly affected are one or two other local authorities than if they are a large multitude of individuals.

(iii) *Secondary Benefits*. The notion that some pecuniary spillovers are properly included in benefits has appeared in a particular guise in arguments about secondary benefits. The American discussion of this matter has centred on the benefit estimation procedures used by the Bureau of Reclamation in respect of irrigation projects. In their analysis of the problem, McKean [53], Eckstein [20] and Margolis [52] all start by describing these procedures. The essential principle can be made clear by taking the case of irrigation which results in an increase in grain production, where the direct or primary benefits are measured as the value of the increase in grain output less the associated increase in farmers' costs.

The increased grain output will involve increased activity by grain merchants, transport concerns, millers, bakers and so on, and hence, it is asserted, will involve an increase in their profits. If the ratio of total profits in all these activities to the value of grain at the farm is 48% then secondary benefits of 48% of the value of the increase in grain output are credited to the irrigation project. These are called "stemming" secondary benefits. "Induced" secondary benefits, on the other hand, are the extra profits made from activities which sell to farmers. The profit rate here has been computed as averaging 18% of farmers' purchases.

All the three authors mentioned are highly critical of these notions, as they were set out by the Bureau of Reclamation in 1952. We shall not give a blow-by-blow account of the arguments of each author, but instead attempt to provide our own synthesis.

Where the output of a project has a market value this value plus any consumers' surplus can be taken as the measure of the gross benefit arising from the project. But where the output either is not sold or is sold at a price fixed solely with reference to cost-sharing considerations, it is necessary to impute a value to the output. Thus, in the case of irrigation water, a value is obtained by working out what the water is worth to farmers as the excess of the value of the increased output which it makes possible over the cost of the necessary increase in all the farmers' other inputs. The question now arises whether we should not impute a value to the increased farm output just as we have imputed one to the water instead of taking the market value of that output. Thus, supposing (to simplify the argument) that wheat is the only farm output, that all the wheat is used to make flour and that all the flour is used to make bread, why should we not value the water by taking the value of the increased output of bread and deducting the increase in farmers', millers' and bakers' costs? Consumption is, after all, the end of all economic activity, so is not what matters the value of the increase in consumption of bread made possible by the irrigation project less the sacrifice of alternative consumption involved—as measured by increased farming, milling and baking costs?

The answer must be that a properly functioning price mechanism performs the function of imputing values for us. It does so not only as regards the increase in farmers' costs (as the argument implicitly assumes) but also as regards the increase in their output (as it seems to deny). The market demand for wheat is a derived demand, and so reflects the value of extra bread and the marginal costs of milling, baking, etc. Imputation of values by the analyst is thus necessary only where there is no market for a product, *i.e.*, only for the water itself.

We conclude, therefore, that if the conditions for optimal resource allocation are fulfilled in the rest of the economy the estimate of benefits obtained by using the price of wheat and the price of farming inputs constitutes an adequate measure. Putting the matter the other way round, we need worry about secondary benefits (or, for that matter, costs) only to the extent that market prices fail to reflect marginal social costs and benefits. The real problem concerning secondary benefits (and costs) is thus a matter of second-best allocation problems.

(iv) *Project Life.* Estimation of length of life is clearly a highly subjective process depending on assessments of the physical length of life, technological changes, shifts in demand, emergence of competing products and so on. The effect of any error will depend on the rate of discount adopted; the higher this is, the less do errors of estimation matter. Some investigations seem to show that different assumptions about lengths of life do not affect the viability of schemes to an enormous extent (Foster and Beesley [28]). We have here, incidentally, one example of the scope for sensitivity analysis, where the calculations are repeated many times for different values of variables. This is an extremely important tool when estimates of costs and benefits are uncertain.

(b) *Valuation of Costs and Benefits*

(i) *The Relevant Prices.* When we are dealing with costs and benefits which can be expressed in terms of money it is generally agreed that adjustments need to be made to the expected prices of future inputs and outputs to allow for anticipated changes in relative prices of the items involved (including expected changes in interest rates over time), but not for expected changes in the *general* price level. The essential principle is that all prices must be reckoned on the same basis, and for convenience this will usually be the price-level prevailing in the initial year.[1] Future developments in output levels have also to be taken into account, *e.g.*, it is customary in cost-benefit studies of highway improvements to allow for the long-term trend of traffic growth.

(ii) *Non-marginal Changes.* With the exceptions discussed below, market prices are used to value the costs and benefits of a project. Difficulties arise when investment projects are large enough to affect these prices. In the case of final products, the benefits accruing from investment cannot be measured by multiplying the additional quantum of output either by the old or the new price. The former would give an over-estimate and the latter an underestimate. What is needed, as has long been recognised (Dupuit [19]), is a measure of the addition to the area under the demand curve, which, on the assumption that the marginal utility of money remains unchanged, is an appropriate measure of the money value of the benefits provided, in the sense of assessing what the recipients would pay rather than go without them. When the demand curve is linear an unweighted average of before and after prices will suffice; but more complicated techniques are necessary for other forms of demand function—when they are known. In the case of intermediate products, the demand curve is a derived one, and so it can only be a perfect reflector of social benefit if the optimum welfare conditions are met all along the line. If this condition is satisfied the gross benefit arising from a project concerned with intermediate products is measured by the market value of sales plus any increase in consumers' and producers' surplus in respect of any final products based on the intermediate ones.

On the costs side there is a double problem, clearly distinguished in Lerner's treatment of indivisibilities [45]. First, it is necessary to adjust prices of factors so as to eliminate any rental elements, which will be measured by excesses over transfer earnings in their next best alternative use. Second, one has an exactly analogous problem to the demand side, in that as more and more of a factor is absorbed in any one line of output the price of the alternative product which it might have been making rises further and further. Therefore we are faced with the choice between valuation of factors at the original price (*i.e.*, that ruling prior to the expansion of output of the commodity in question), the ultimate price, or some intermediate level. On the assumption of linearity, a price half-way between the original and ultimate levels will meet the bill, as on the demand side. Obviously, either or both of these two types of adjustments may be necessary at any

[1] Hirshleifer [37, p. 143] argues that, since the " true " interest rate lies below the " monetary " one when prices are expected to rise, a downward adjustment should be made to market rates to allow for this.

particular time, and so to this extent the adjustments for indivisibilities on the costs side are likely to be more complex than those on the benefit side.

(iii) *Market Imperfections.* Departures from Pareto-optimum situations arise when monopolistic elements or other imperfections in goods or factor markets are such as to twist relative outputs away from those which would prevail under competitive conditions. In cases of this kind investment decisions based on valuations of costs and benefits at market prices may not be appropriate; failure to correct for these distortions is likely to lead to misallocations of investment projects between different industries.

The relevance of this point for public decisions concerning investment is several-fold. First, if a public authority in a monopolistic position behaves like a private monopolist in its pricing and output policy its investment decisions will not comply with the principles of efficient allocation of resources unless the degree of monopoly is uniform throughout the economy. Secondly, complications may arise when there is monopolistic behaviour at a later stage in the production process. This can be illustrated by the example of an irrigation project which enables more sugar-beet to be grown, and hence more sugar to be refined. If the refiners enjoy a monopolistic position the sugar-beet farmers' demand for irrigation water will not be a sufficient indication of the merits of the irrigation project. If the refiners were producing at the (higher) competitive level they would absorb more beet, and this would in turn react back on the demand for irrigation water.

A third illustration is in respect of factor supplies. If the wages which have to be paid to the labour engaged on an investment project include some rental element and are greater than their marginal opportunity costs, then a deduction must be made to arrive at an appropriate figure: conversely, if wages are squeezed below marginal opportunity costs by monopsony practices.

Fourthly, there may be an excess of average over marginal costs. This raises the well-known difficulty that if prices are equated to short-run marginal costs, as they must be to ensure short-period efficiency, the enterprise will run at a loss. Various ways (see, *e.g.*, Hicks [36]) of getting over the problem have been suggested, but there are snags in all of them. Charges can be made, *e.g.*, by means of a two-part tariff, but this is likely to deter some consumers whose marginal valuation of the output exceeds its marginal cost. Various systems of discriminatory charges can be devised, but these may imply inquisitorial powers on the part of the authorities. Voluntary subscriptions can be asked for, but this runs into the Wicksell objection in respect of collective goods.[1] If none of these solutions are acceptable one must be prepared to countenance losses. So this is still another case where investment decisions have to be divorced from accounting computations of profits. Instead, they must be based on notions of what people would be willing to

[1] See *infra*, p. 168.

pay or what the project " ought to be " worth to customers, as Hicks [36] puts it. It must be emphasised that this is not a case where prices of goods or factors are imperfect measures of benefits and costs *per se*, but where the present value of net receipts no longer measures benefits.

These are all examples of what is fundamentally the same problem: the inapplicability of investment decision rules derived from a perfectly competitive state of affairs to a world where such a competitive situation no longer holds. It should be noted that there are two possible ways of making the necessary accounting adjustments: either a correction can be made to the actual level of costs (benefits), or the costs (benefits) arising from the market can be taken as they stand but a corresponding correction has to be made to the estimation of benefits (costs). Normally, the first of these two methods would be less complicated and less liable to cause confusion.

(iv) *Taxes and Controls*. Imperfect competition constitutes only one case of divergence between market price and social cost or benefit. Another is that of taxes on expenditure. Most economists prefer to measure taxed inputs at their factor cost rather than at their market value, though the latter would be appropriate when the total supply of the input in question has a zero elasticity of supply, *e.g.*, an imported item subject to a strict quota. A possible extension of this particular example relates to the cost of imported items in an economy with a fairly high level of tariff protection where it could be argued that price including duty is the best measure of social cost, because in the absence of protection the country's equilibrium exchange rate would be lower. Perhaps the most important example of a tax which it has been decided to exclude from costs occurs in the estimation of fuel savings resulting from road improvements [14].

Public decisions may properly differ from private ones in the investment field in respect of direct tax payments too. While private profit-making decisions should allow for income and profits tax payments, this is not apposite in the public sector. What one is primarily concerned with here is a measurement of cost which corresponds to the use of real resources [1] but excludes transfer payments. Hence profits or income taxes on the income derived by a public authority from its project are irrelevant.

As an example of government controls, we may take agricultural price supports and production controls. There seem to have been cases in the past in the United States (*e.g.*, the Missouri Basin project) where estimates of the benefits from sugar-beet production were made without taking any notice of existing sugar-beet quotas or considering whether sugar-beet production would actually be allowed to increase! Hard as it is to cope with refinements

[1] Additional government expenditures necessitated by a public authority project should be included as part of its costs. But whether these expenditures are, or are not, financed by taxes on that authority is irrelevant.

When public projects are being compared with private ones there must obviously be a common standard of comparison in respect of transfers to and by government, the simplest being to ignore them.

of this sort, obviously some attempt must be made to take cognisance of the more blatant discrepancies.

(v) *Unemployment.* A divergence of social cost from private cost which is sometimes of major importance arises when there is unemployment. When there is an excess supply at the current market price of any input that price overstates the social cost of using that input. Furthermore, when there is general unemployment, expenditure upon a project, by creating a multiplier effect, will create additional real incomes in the rest of the economy. Hence the use of market values to ascertain direct costs and benefits of a project overstates its social costs and underestimates its total benefits (by the amount of " induced benefits "). Under these conditions almost any project is better for the countıy than no project, so that, to achieve sub-optimisation, autonomous public agencies should bring these considerations into their benefit and cost calculations, while agencies subject to central government control over their expenditure should either choose the same or be told to do so. This simple picture only holds, however, when there is but one issue to decide: shall a particular project be initiated or not? But such a choice never exists in this solitary state. The Government can choose between public works and other methods of curing unemployment. The agencies responsible for the public works can choose between a number of possible projects, some of them mutually exclusive (*e.g.*, the choice between building a four- or six-lane motorway along a particular alignment). And it is not at all obvious that unemployment-adjusted estimates of costs and benefits constitute the right tool for making these choices.

The arguments against correcting costs for an excess of the market price of factors over the price which would clear the market for them and against including multiplier effects in benefits are largely [1] practical (cf. McKean [53]):

(*a*) It is easier to allow for the overpricing of labour which is to be used in constructing or operating a project than to allow for the overpricing of equipment, fuel, materials, etc., which are overpriced because they, too, include in their costs some overpriced labour. Yet if correction is made for project labour costs only, the relative social costs of project labour and of other inputs may be more poorly estimated than if no correction at all is made.

(*b*) Correcting future costs requires estimates of future unemployment. Government agencies are not usually equipped to make such forecasts, and governments may be reluctant to provide them on a realistic basis in view of the difficulty of keeping them out of public notice.

[1] But not entirely: it is possible to conceive of an unemployment situation in which shadow cost pricing would make a very large number of investment projects pass a cost-benefit test—in fact, a larger number than would be needed to reach full employment. The problem is to fix the shadow prices so that one can select the best projects but not so many of them that one has more than full employment.

(*c*) The effect of a project upon unemployment depends not only upon the expenditure which it involves but also upon the way it is financed, and this may not be known to the people doing the cost-benefit analysis (*e.g.*, in the case of an agency financed by government grants).

These arguments suggest that in most cases it is best for unemployment policy to be left to the central government and for the agencies responsible for public works to confine their corrections of market prices on account of under-employment (*i.e.*, overpricing) to divergences which are local or which relate to some specialised factor of production. National unemployment, to take an example, should be no concern of the National Coal Board, but the alleged lack of alternative employment opportunities for miners in certain coalfields should.

(vi) *Collective Goods.* Market prices clearly cannot be used to value benefits which are not capable of being marketed. Thus we meet the collective goods issue (Samuelson [72, 73, 74], Musgrave [60], Head [35]). The essential point is that some goods and services supplied by Government are of a collective nature in the sense that the quantity supplied to any one member of the relevant group cannot be independently varied. For example, all members of the population benefit from defence expenditure, all the inhabitants of any given district benefit from an anti-malaria programme, and all ships in the vicinity benefit from a lighthouse. The difference between separately marketable goods and such collective goods can be shown as in Figs. 1 (*a*) and 1 (*b*), following Bowen [8].

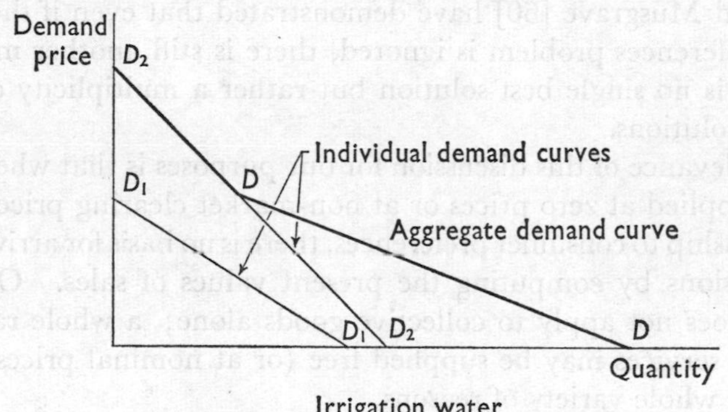

Fig. 1 (*a*).—Marketable Goods.

Whereas aggregation of individual demand curves is obtained by *horizontal* summation in the Fig. (1) (*a*) case, it is obtained by *vertical* summation in the Fig. 1 (*b*) case. This reflects the fact that though individuals may differ in their marginal valuation of a given quantity of a commodity, they all consume the same amount, in that each unit is consumed by all of them. For example, flood control afforded to different individuals is a joint product.

Ever since Wicksell, it has been recognised that any attempt to get consumers to reveal their preferences regarding collective goods founders on the rock that the rational thing for any individual consumer to do is understate his demand, in the expectation that he would thereby be relieved of part or all of his share of the cost without affecting the quantity obtained. Although a number of people (notably Lindahl) have attempted to find ways

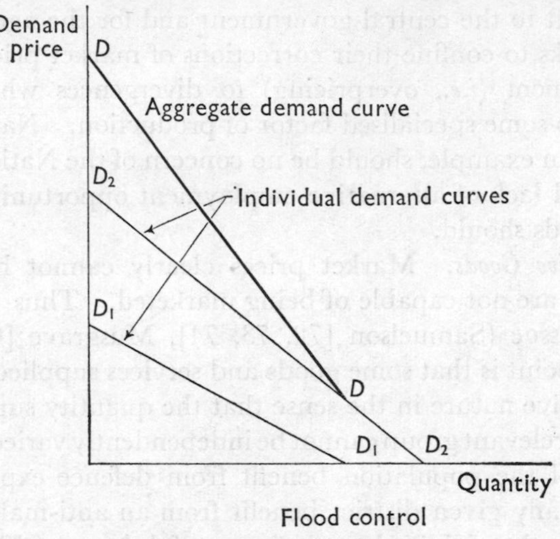

FIG. 1(*b*).—Collective Goods.

out of this impasse, it seems safe to say that no one has succeeded. In fact, the difficulties have multiplied rather than diminished, as Samuelson [72, 73, 74] and Musgrave [60] have demonstrated that even if the non-revelation of preferences problem is ignored, there is still another major snag, in that there is no single best solution but rather a multiplicity of alternative optimum solutions.

The relevance of this discussion for our purposes is that where commodities are supplied at zero prices or at non-market clearing prices which bear no relationship to consumer preferences, there is no basis for arriving at investment decisions by computing the present values of sales. Of course, the problem does not apply to collective goods alone; a whole range of other goods and services may be supplied free (or at nominal prices) by government for a whole variety of reasons.

(vii) *Intangibles*. Some costs and benefits (such as the scenic effect of building electricity transmission lines) cannot be quantified, and others, although they can be quantified, cannot be valued in any market sense (*e.g.*, a reduction in lives lost). Such costs and benefits have been called intangible costs and benefits. They are obviously important in many cases and, equally obviously, have to be presented to the decision-maker in the prose which accompanies the cost-benefit arithmetic, since they cannot be incorporated in the arithmetic itself. It may be possible to gain some idea of their importance on the basis of consumer questionnaires, but one has to be careful of the well-known difficulties inherent in such efforts (Yates [90]).

There is one possible exception in the case of quantifiable items. Consistency requires that the net marginal cost of, say, saving an average citizen's life be the same whether it be achieved by hiring more traffic police or by having more ambulances. If there were consistency and if the marginal cost were known, then it would measure how much decision-makers were ready to pay to save a life, and hence it could be used for valuing lives saved. So the importance attached to particular " intangibles " may sometimes be inferred from private or public behaviour. Thus, one might suggest that British public standards of visual amenity are higher than the private standards manifest in most back gardens!

(c) *Choice of Interest Rate*

(i) *The Social Time Preference Rate.* The literature on the choice of appropriate interest rates for public investment projects is voluminous, and we cannot hope to survey it in detail. But starting from the constellation of rates that one finds in the private sector, various questions have to be raised. Even if one can select a single or average risk-free long-term rate, it is not clear what significance can be attached to it. Straightaway we come up against all the old arguments about whether market rates of interest do bear any close relationship to the marginal productivity of investment and time preference or whether the relationship is so blurred as to be imperceptible. This is partly a matter of different interest theories (neo-Classical, Keynesian, Robertsonian, etc.) and partly a matter of how particular economies tick at particular times—do governments intervene in capital markets with any effectiveness, how well organised and unified is the capital market in a country, etc.? Both pure theory and imperfections in the capital market are thus involved.

Another issue is whether any market-determined interest rate would suffice for community decisions even if neo-classical theory is accepted and a perfectly functioning capital market assumed. Some writers believe that social time preference attaches more weight to the future than private time preference and that it is the former which is relevant for determining the allocation of society's current resources between investment and consumption. A number of arguments in favour of such a proposition have been produced over the years. Pigou [65], for instance, suggested that individuals were short-sighted about the future (" defective telescopic faculty ") and that government intervention might be needed to give adequate weight to the welfare of unborn generations (*op. cit.*, pp. 24–30). More recently, other arguments, which seek to avoid the objection that the Pigou position is a fundamentally authoritarian one, have been put forward (Eckstein [21], Marglin [49]). One point made really relates to a special kind of externality. It is that any one individual's preference for current consumption, relatively to future consumption by himself or his successors, will be less if there is some sort of government-organised programme for imposing sacrifices on everybody—or at least on a large section of the population—than if the solution is left to the market. More generally, one might follow the lines indicated by Feldstein [24] and distinguish between: (1) market preferences; (2) preferences expressed through the ballot box; (3) what the Government in its wisdom thinks is good for this generation; and (4) what the Government thinks is good for this generation and future generations taken together.

Whatever the ultimate pros and cons of these arguments, there are two difficulties, if one tries to give effect to them. The first is actually to determine the social rate of discount. Marglin accepts that this does pose serious difficulties, but goes on to suggest that one can set about it by choosing the growth rate for an economy and thence (on the basis of the marginal capital/output ratio) determine the rate of investment; the social rate of discount must then be equated with the marginal productivity of investment. The practicability of such a procedure does not commend itself to us; but we must leave this to others to judge.

Another difficulty of operating with a social rate of discount is that we have the very awkward problem that different rates of interest would be used in the public and private sectors. There is then likely to be considerable inefficiency in the allocation of funds inside the investment sector—in the sense that if the Government is, say, responsible for electricity and the private sector for oil, inferior projects of the former kind will supplant superior projects of the latter kind.[1] This particular difficulty leads us right back to the point discussed at the beginning of Section II, *i.e.*, that one rate of interest cannot perform two functions in a non-optimal situation. One way out of this is to recommend making the situation an optimal one. For instance, Hirshleifer [37] has suggested that the Government should take action to push down market rates of interest to the social rate, so that all investment decisions, whether in the public or private sectors, should be taken on the same basis. While applauding this idea in principle, other writers quite reasonably feel that in practice economists will still have to deal with sub-optimisation problems.

(ii) *The Social Opportunity Cost Rate*. The government borrowing rate is a popular and easily applicable measure of costs, both because it is a financial cost in the case of government financed investment and, more academically, because it can be regarded as " the " risk-free rate of interest.[2] Yet despite the recent empirically founded recrudescence of belief in the interest elasticity of private investment, no one has demonstrated that the latter's marginal efficiency does actually equal the interest rate. A direct attempt to measure marginal rates of return on private investment is therefore required. Even if such a measure were made, however, it would be

[1] Defining " inferior " and " superior " in terms of present values of net benefits.

[2] Abstracting from uncertainty about the price level.

relevant only in so far as the costs being evaluated consisted exclusively of displaced private investment.

Recognising this problem, Krutilla and Eckstein [43] assumed that the alternative to public investment would be a tax cut, considered the ways in which a likely tax cut would affect income groups, and then asked how the notional recipients would utilise their hypothetical receipts, thus finally arriving at a weighted average rate of return. An alternative postulate was that the additional public investment would be offset by tighter monetary policy; it was then asked which individuals would suffer and what sort of weighted interest rate could thence be derived. The general result from both assumptions was that Federal capital in the United States in the late 'fifties had an opportunity cost of 5–6%. Quite apart from the logical and statistical problems associated with the techniques of assigning tax cuts to the different income groups, etc., as Eckstein himself has noted [21], this approach deals with only two out of many relevant alternatives (*e.g.*, more public investment might be met instead by less public consumption). It has also been severely criticised by Hirshleifer [37] on the grounds that the composite interest rate finally derived has an unknown allowance for a risk premium in it. Feldstein has also commented on this approach [25].

(iii) *Adjustment for Uncertainty*. The various ways in which uncertainty impinges upon cost-benefit analysis are discussed by Dorfman [48, Ch. 3], McKean [53, Ch. 4], Eckstein [21, Section 5], Hirshleifer [37, pp. 139–41] in their admirable surveys, and we need only add two remarks here. The first point is that there is no reason to argue that public investment projects are free of uncertainty (see, especially, Hirshleifer [37]). The second is that allowances for uncertainty can be made: (1) in the assessments of annual levels of benefits and costs; (2) in the assumptions about length of life; and (3) in the discount rate. The first is most appropriate if the risk of dispersion of outcomes (or inputs) is irregularly, rather than regularly, distributed with time. If the main risk is that there may be a sudden day of reckoning when benefits disappear or costs soar, the second type of adjustment is needed. The third correction, a premium on the discount rate, is appropriate where uncertainty is a strictly compounding function of time.

(iv) *The Need for an Interest Rate*. When the problem of choice involves no opportunity cost of capital—as happens when all of a fixed budget is to be spent—there is obviously no need for an opportunity-cost rate of interest. It has been argued by some authors, *e.g.*, McKean [53], that in this case there is no need for a social discount rate of interest either. This can be generally true, however, only if the maximand is not the present worth of benefits less costs, for if it is, some rate of discount is obviously required. We shall not elaborate this point here, since one of us has already published a purely expository note on the subject in this JOURNAL [83].

(v) *Principles* vs. *Practice*. Discussions about social rates of time preference, social opportunity cost, etc., do not cut very much ice in most empirical work, and we have not been able to discover any cases where there was any convincingly complete application of such notions.[1] Nor do ideas about allowing for future changes in interest rates seem to receive much attention. In practice, the most usual kind of procedure is to select an interest rate or rates, on the basis of observed rates ruling at the time, for calculating present values, etc. For example, Weisbrod [86] takes a rate of 10% to represent the opportunity cost of capital in the private sector (on the basis that the observed yield of 5% for corporate stocks should be grossed up to approximately double that figure to allow for the corporate profits tax) [2] and one of 4% to represent the cost of Federal Government borrowing. He then makes his present value calculations on both bases. It can obviously be said that this may give ambiguous results, *e.g.*, that project A is preferable to project B on one basis, but project B is preferable on the other. This is indisputable; but there are also examples to show that the choice of varying discount rates does not, within the 4–8% band, make much difference to assessments of a project (Foster and Beesley [28]), though the same conclusions do not necessarily hold for a rather wider band. The truth of the matter is that, whatever one does, one is trying to unscramble an omelette, and no one has yet invented a uniquely superior way of doing this.

(d) *Relevant Constraints*

(i) *Introduction.* Eckstein [21] has provided a most helpful classification of constraints. First, there are physical constraints. The most general of these is the production function which relates the physical inputs and outputs of a project, but this enters directly into the calculation of costs and benefits. Where choice is involved between different projects or regarding the size or timing of a particular project, external physical constraints may also be relevant. Thus, one particular input may be in totally inelastic supply, or two projects may be mutually exclusive on purely technological grounds.

Next there are legal constraints. What is done must be within the framework of the law, which may affect matters in a multiplicity of ways, *e.g.*, rights of access, time needed for public inquiries, regulated pricing, limits to the activities of public agencies and so on. Third, there may be administrative constraints, related to limits to what can be handled administratively. Fourth, uncertainty can be introduced by constraints, for example, by the introduction of some minimum regret requirement. Finally, there are distributional and budgetary constraints; these need more extended discussion.

(ii) *Distributional Constraints.* The notion that the choice between projects can be made solely on the grounds of "economic efficiency," because

[1] Eckstein [21] concluded after several pages of discussion "thus the choice of interest rates must remain a value judgment" (*op. cit.*, p. 460).

[2] It might be argued that a further correction should also be made to bridge any gap between earnings yield and dividend yield. This would make for a wider spread of the rate band.

any unfavourable effects on income distribution can be overcome by making some of the gainers compensate some of the losers, is rarely applicable in practice.

It is perfectly possible to compensate property-owners not only for property which is expropriated but also for property which is reduced in value. Similarly, it is possible to levy a charge in respect of property which has been enhanced in value. These payments of compensation and charges, being lump sums, are not likely to have any direct effects upon resource allocation. Another way in which extra money can be raised from the beneficiaries of a project without affecting resource allocation arises where some of the project outputs are sold and intra-marginal units of these outputs can be priced at more than marginal units. (Thus electricity consumers may be charged on a two-part tariff.)

In general, however, attempts to get beneficiaries to pay more than the marginal social cost of the project outputs they consume will affect the allocation of resources. Such attempts may be made either because of a desire not to raise the real income of the beneficiaries to an extent regarded as unfair or because of a desire to raise funds to compensate a group who are made worse off by the project or simply because of a general belief that projects ought to break even. Whatever the reason, the pricing policy adopted will affect project outputs, and hence project costs. Tolls on a motorway, for instance, will affect the volume of traffic, and this may affect the appropriate width at which it should be constructed. Thus, benefits and costs are not independent of pricing policy.

This can affect cost-benefit analysis in either of two ways. The first is relevant when pricing rules have been laid down in advance in the light of political or social notions about income distribution. Here the task is to maximise the present value of benefits less costs subject to certain specified financial requirements, *i.e.*, subject to one or more constraints. The second way in which income distribution requirements may affect cost-benefit analysis occurs when the authorities have not laid down any specific financial rules but do clearly care about income distribution. In this case it is up to the analyst to invent and present as alternatives a number of variants of a project which differ both as regards the particular people who pay (or are paid) and the prices charged and, in consequence, as regards outputs and inputs. For each alternative, the analyst will have to set out not only total costs and benefits but also the costs and benefits for those particular groups whose economic welfare is of interest to the decision-maker.

In cases like this the choice can be formalised—if the decision-taker allows it—by expressing it in terms of maximising the excess of total benefits over total costs subject to constraints on the benefits less costs of particular groups. Alternatively, it can be expressed in terms of maximising the net gain (or minimising the net loss) to a particular group subject to a constraint relating to total benefits and costs. Whether or not this is helpful in practice is not known, but at least it may explain why income distribution considerations have been brought into this survey under the heading of constraints.

It should be noted that these considerations may relate to many different kinds of groups. In one context notions of " fairness " to workers may predominate, while in another it may be notions of " equity " between different geographical areas which are important. If one is taking a regional, rather than a national, viewpoint the assessment and measurement of costs and benefits may be quite markedly different. For instance, it has been argued that one of the benefits of the Morecambe Bay barrage scheme would be the attraction of more industry to the Barrow area. This would no doubt benefit Barrow; but it is perfectly conceivable that there would be equivalent or even greater losses to South Lancashire, or for that matter other regions of the United Kingdom. Therefore one gets an entirely different picture of benefits and costs, if one looks at them from the viewpoint of the Barrow area, from that prevailing for the whole of the North-west or the whole of the United Kingdom.

(iii) *Budgetary Constraints*. Discussions of this topic combine (and sometimes confuse) three issues: first, ought such constraints to exist; second, what form do they take; and third, how can they be incorporated into investment criteria? We shall deal with the third issue shortly when we reach the general subject of investment criteria. We do not propose to discuss the first point, but might note that Hirshleifer [37] has argued that if the budgeting authorities are worth their salt the amount allocated to the sub-budgets will take account of the productivity of the projects available to them and the costs of obtaining the necessary funds. If this is not done, it is argued, the answer is to recast the system of budget allocation rather than to go into python-like contortions at the sub-budget level. This argument, however, is rather unrealistic. For the present, at any rate, many decisions are in fact taken within the framework of a budget restraint, and the economist might as well help people to sub-optimise within this framework, even if, as a long-run proposition, he thinks in his private capacity that it should be changed.

On the second issue there is not much to be said in general terms. There may be a constraint upon total capital expenditure over one or more years, as, for instance, when the projects undertaken by a public agency have to fit within a budget framework determined in advance. The sums involved may be either maxima which do not have to be reached or amounts which are to be spent entirely.[1] In the first case, but not the second, the expenditure in question has an opportunity cost, since once the decision is made to use funds, they are effectively a bygone. There can be other kinds of constraint applying to capital expenditure, such as a prescribed percentage of self-financing, and constraints can also apply to current expenditure and/or to revenue, for example, a financial target for gross or net accounting profits.

[1] " Maximum " or " specific " rationing to use the convenient terminology of Hirshleifer [37].

3. *Final Considerations*

(a) *Investment Criteria*

We believe that the most common maximand where projects involve only costs and benefits expressed in terms of money is the present value of benefits less costs. Other maximands are possible, however, such as capital stock at a final date. We shall not attempt to argue the relative merits of different maximands, but, continuing to accept present value, now introduce the subject of investment criteria or, as they are sometimes called, decision algorithms.

Where no projects are interdependent or mutually exclusive, where starting dates are given and where no constraints are operative, the choice of projects which maximises the present value of total benefits less total costs can be expressed in any of the following four equivalent ways: [1]

(1) select all projects where the present value of benefits exceeds the present value of costs;

(2) select all projects where the ratio of the present value of benefits to the present value of costs exceeds unity;

(3) select all projects where the constant annuity with the same present value as benefits exceeds the constant annuity (of the same duration) with the same present value as costs;

(4) select all projects where the internal rate of return exceeds the chosen rate of discount.

Once the various complications just assumed away are introduced, more complicated rules are required. We shall explain the impact of these

[1] Symbolically, these criteria can be summarised as follows.

Let $c_1, c_2, \ldots c_n$ = series of prospective costs in years 1, 2, . . . n;
c = constant annuity with same present value as $c_1, c_2, \ldots c$;
$b_1, b_2, \ldots b_n$ = series of prospective benefits in years 1, 2, . . . n;
b = constant annuity with same present value as $b_1, b_2, \ldots b_n$;
s = scrap value;
i = appropriate rate of discount for annual compounding;
r = internal rate of return.

Then we may write the rules as follows: select projects where

(1) $$\frac{b_1}{(1+i)} + \frac{b_2}{(1+i)^2} + \ldots + \frac{b_n + s}{(1+i)^n} > \frac{c_1}{(1+i)} + \frac{c_2}{(1+i)^2} + \ldots + \frac{c_n}{(1+i)^n}$$

(2) $$\frac{\dfrac{b_1}{(1+i)} + \dfrac{b_2}{(1+i)^2} + \ldots + \dfrac{b_n + s}{(1+i)_n}}{\dfrac{c_1}{(1+i)} + \dfrac{c_2}{(1+i)^2} + \ldots + \dfrac{c_n}{(1+i)^n}} > 1$$

(3) $$b > c$$

Finally, select projects where $r > i$, where r is given by

(4) $$\frac{b_1 - c_1}{(1+r)} + \frac{b_2 - c_2}{(1+r)^2} + \ldots + \frac{b_n - c_n}{(1+r)^n} = 0$$

complications in terms of the present-value approach without claiming that it is always the most convenient one. Which approach is most convenient will vary with the facts of the case. Where a rule which is not algebraically equivalent to the present value approach is used, the issue is not one of convenience, but involves either error [1] or a different maximand.

Where the costs and/or benefits of two schemes A and B are interdependent in the sense that the execution of one affects the costs or benefits of the other (see pp. 159–60 *supra*), they must be treated as constituting three mutually exclusive schemes, namely A and B together, A alone and B alone. Thus, if one wants to improve communications between two towns one has the choice between a road improvement, a rail improvement and a combination of road and rail improvements.

Mutual exclusivity can also arise for technological reasons. Thus, a road intersection can be built as a cross-roads, a roundabout or a flyover. Similarly, a large or a small dam, but not both, may be put in one place. Whatever the reason for mutual exclusivity, its presence must be allowed for in formulating investment rules.

Where there is a choice of starting date it must be chosen so as to maximise the present value of benefits less costs at the reference date.

Constraints cause the biggest complications, particularly when there is more than one of them and when mutual exclusivity and optimal timing are also involved. Indivisibilities also complicate matters when constraints are involved.

We shall not venture into the algebraic jungle of constructing decision algorithms. Anyone who seeks examples can turn to Marglin's discussion of income distribution and budgetary constraints in his exemplary synthesis of much of cost-benefit analysis [48] or to his monograph on dynamic investment planning [51]. A most useful discussion is also to be found in an article on capital budgeting by Dryden [18].

(b) *Second-best Matters*

Since cost-benefit analysis is essentially a practical tool for decision-making, it is not worth our while pursuing the second-best problem into the higher reaches of welfare economics. The non-fulfilment of the conditions for a welfare maximum elsewhere in the economy is relevant to cost-benefit analysis only in so far as it makes the market values of outputs and inputs obviously biased measures of benefits and costs. Small and remote divergences from the optimum will cause biases in these measures which fall within their margin of error, while large divergences of an unknown sort create unknowable biases which are necessarily irrelevant to action. Only those divergences which are immediate, palpable and considerable thus deserve

[1] A naïve error in early writings was the use of benefit–cost ratios to choose between two mutually exclusive projects. One project may have the lower benefit–cost ratio, yet will be preferable if the *extra* benefits exceed the *extra* costs. This is clearly brought out by McKean [53, pp. 108 ff.].

our attention. We have discussed some of these already, and will bring in further examples in our survey of particular applications of cost-benefit analysis.

Ideally, all such divergences should be taken into account, for otherwise a sub-optimum will not be achieved. Yet it does not follow that public agencies ought always to take account of them; the ideal involves administrative costs. It has to be recognised that public agencies have defined spheres of competence and that the responsibility for wide issues lying outside these spheres rests not with them but with the Government which created them and their tasks. It is not the business of, say, the Scottish Development Department to decide whether or not the currency is overvalued, for instance, and it is not within its competence to put a shadow price upon the foreign-exchange content of proposed expenditure. Either it must value imports at their import price or it must be told to adopt a shadow rate for planning purposes by the central government, whose function it is to consider such matters. The division of labour in administration which is necessary if the public sector is to avoid monolithic sluggishness requires each part of the machine to act as if the rest were doing its job properly. After all, to continue with this example, it may be better if all government agencies value foreign exchange at a uniform but incorrect exchange rate than if they each have their own different shadow rates.

III. Particular Applications

We now come to illustrations of the ways in which the principles previously set out have been employed in cost-benefit studies. We shall first look at some water projects and then turn to transport—these being the two areas where cost-benefit studies have been most common. Subsequently, we shall survey the application and applicability of these techniques in land-usage schemes (urban renewal, recreation and land reclamation), health, education, research and development, and defence. Throughout, we shall be illustrative rather than comprehensive—both in the sense that we are concerned only with the main features of, say, irrigation schemes rather than detailed case studies, and in that we shall emphasise the differences in treatment rather than the similarities. This means that we examine general techniques for enumerating and evaluating costs and benefits rather than "standard" items, such as the choice of appropriate discount rates, the exclusion of superogatory secondary benefits, etc.[1] We are not reproducing any examples in full detail, but good ones can be found in Krutilla and Eckstein [43, Pt. II] on water-resource projects, Foster and Beesley [28] on transport and Borus [6] on labour retraining.

[1] As general sources of reference on all these matters see the U.S. "Green Book" [40] and a Canadian contribution (Sewell *et al.* [77]).

1. Water Projects

Water projects take many different forms. They may differ enormously in respect of their engineering characteristics, *e.g.*, an estuarine barrage or a dam in the hills. Similarly, the purposes of water investment are many—provision of more water for an industrial area, provision of irrigation water, prevention of flood damage and so on. In some cases there may be only one such purpose in a particular scheme; in others it may be a case of multi-purpose development. The details of cost-benefit analysis inevitably differ from project to project, and we can only cover a sample. We shall look at irrigation, flood control and hydro-electric schemes in turn, and in this way hope to catch the smell even if not the flavour of the ingredients. Finally, we shall have a few words to add on the particular characteristics of multi-purpose schemes.

(a) *Irrigation*

Since it is seldom possible to ascertain directly the price at which water could be sold upon the completion of a proposed irrigation project, and since this price would in any case give no indication of consumers' surplus, the *direct* benefits of a project have to be estimated by:

(i) forecasting the change in the output of each agricultural project, leaving out those outputs which, like the cattle feed, are also inputs;

(ii) valuing and summing these changes;

(iii) deducting the opportunity cost of the change in all farming inputs other than the irrigation water;

in order to get, as a result, the value of the net change in agricultural output consequent upon the irrigation of the area.

We now discuss each of these steps in turn.

(i) Forecasts of additional output, whether sold in the market or consumed on the farm, can be made in countries with well-developed agricultural advisory services. But this is only the beginning of the story. Even if there were no delay in the response of farmers to new conditions, it will often be the case that the full effects of irrigation will take some years to be felt. Since, in addition, farmers will take time to adapt, it is clear that what is required here is not just a simple list of outputs but a schedule showing the development of production over time. Yet this is too complicated in practice, and usually the best that can be done is to make estimates for one or two benchmark dates and extrapolate or, alternatively, postulate a discrete lag in the response of farmers.

The forecast is difficult as well as complicated (in principle), because it is the behaviour of a group of people that is involved, behaviour which may depend upon peasant conservatism, superstition, political tensions and so on just as much or more than it depends upon any nice agronomic calculus. Thus, an Indian study (Sovani and Rath [79, p. 138]) reports that the peasants in an area irrigated by the Hirakud dam erroneously believed that planting a second crop on the valley-bottom land would lead to waterlogging and salinisation. The authors explicitly assumed that in the first ten years after irrigation began the area would settle down to irrigated agriculture with the least possible change in techniques and capital investment.

The probability that farmers will not follow an income-maximising course of action is one reason why a farm-management or programming approach may be of little use—except in setting an outside limit to outputs. Another is that the requisite information may be lacking. Thus, it is frequently necessary either to substitute or supplement the projections based upon the assumption of maximising behaviour with projections based upon the assumption that the behaviour of other farmers elsewhere constitutes a useful precedent. The effect of irrigation in A is then forecast by comparing an irrigated area B either with B before irrigation or with an unirrigated area, C. There is obviously scope for judgment (and bias) here.

(ii) The amount the farmer gets for his crops may differ markedly from their value to the community where agriculture is protected or subsidised, as in the United States or the United Kingdom (Eckstein, [20, p. 200], Renshaw [68]). In fact, some United States calculations have allowed for this by making an arbitrary 20% deduction in the prices of major commodities in surplus or receiving federal support. This is one example of the point that when the conditions for optimal resource allocation are not fulfilled in the rest of the economy market prices may prove a poor guide to project costs and benefits. Another general problem on which we have already touched arises when the increment in the output of any crop is large enough to affect its price, so that there is no unique price for valuation purposes. There is the further point that output should be valued at a given price-level, consistent with the valuations of other benefits and of costs, but that future changes in price relativities need to be taken into account. Thus, price projections are required, and once again there is scope for judgment, as anything from simple extrapolation to highly sophisticated supply and demand studies may be utilised. Finally, there is the old problem, much aired in social accounting literature (*e.g.*, Prest and Stewart [66]) about the appropriate valuation of subsistence output.

(iii) The principles for valuing farm inputs are the same as those for valuing outputs, while the forecast of input quantities is clearly related to the forecast of output quantities. In an elaborate income-maximising analysis inputs and outputs would be simultaneously determined, while in a simpler approach inputs per acre of irrigated land or per unit of output will be taken as being the same as on comparable irrigated land elsewhere. In either case, costs include the opportunity earnings, if any, of any additional farmers who come to work in the irrigated area.[1]

[1] One particular difficult problem is the price to be assigned to water itself, which may not be a free good, if pre-emption for irrigation cuts down the amount available for, say, industrial purposes (cf. Eckstein [20, p. 218]).

The *secondary* benefits which have sometimes been regarded as appropriately included in irrigation benefit calculations reflect the impact of the project on the rest of the economy, both via its increased sales to farmers and via its increased purchases from them. We have already discussed the appropriateness of including these benefits. More important is the technological interdependence which is likely to be found in many irrigation schemes, such as when the effects on the height of the water-table in one area spill over to another district.

Any irrigation project will have a number of *minor* effects not obviously covered in the categories so far discussed. As these will vary from case to case, and no general list is possible, some examples may be of use. They are taken from an *ex-post* study of the Sarda Canal in India [63]:

> Canal water is also used for washing, bathing, watering cattle.
>
> Silt is deposited at the outlet heads, which necessitates constant and laborious cleaning of the channels.
>
> Some plots of land have been made untillable by unwanted water.
>
> The canal divides the area (and sometimes individual fields) into two parts, but has few bridges, so that much time is wasted in circumnavigating it.

Many such effects will be unquantifiable, but must nevertheless be remembered in any analysis.

(b) *Flood Control*

Ever since the River and Harbor Act of 1927 the United States Army Corps of Engineers has had the responsibility of preparing plans for improving major rivers for flood control purposes—as well as irrigation, hydroelectric power and navigation. On the flood control side, the major benefits which have been categorised in this—and other—work have been the losses averted. Losses of this sort can refer to different types of assets—property, furnishings, crops, etc.; or to different types of owners—individuals, business firms, government and so on. In all these cases the general principle is to estimate the mathematical expectation of annual damage (on the basis of the likely frequency of flood levels of different heights) and then regard such sums as the maximum annual amounts people would be willing to pay for flood control measures.

Other benefits which must be taken into account are as follows:

(i) Avoidance of deaths by drowning. We shall deal with the general principles relevant in such cases in connection with health improvements.

(ii) Avoidance of temporary costs, *e.g.*, evacuation of flood victims, emergency sand-bag work, etc.,[1] risks of sanitation breakdowns, epidemics, etc.

[1] In so far as this work is done by volunteers in their leisure time (*e.g.*, Cambridge students during the floods in the Fens in 1953), the cost involved raises the same issues as the saving of leisure time resulting from road improvements (see below, pp. 184 and 185).

(iii) Possibilities of putting flood land to higher uses if the risk of inundation is eliminated.[1]

The costs involved in flood control calculations are relatively straightforward. Obviously, the initial costs of the flood-control works and their repair and maintenance charges must be included. The most difficult point in any such compilation is likely to be the cost of land acquisition for reservoirs, etc. In the absence of anything remotely approaching a free land market in a country such as the United Kingdom there is bound to be an arbitrary element in such items.

There are some obvious reasons why private investment principles are insufficient in the case of flood-control measures. Protection for one inhabitant in a district inevitably implies protection for another, and so one immediately runs into the collective goods problem; protection for one district may worsen flood threats to another, and so this inevitably brings up technological externalities; finally, flood works often have to be on a large scale and of a complex nature, and so this brings up non-marginal and imperfect competition problems. So one simply has to try to estimate willingness to pay for flood protection by the roundabout devices described above. There is no simple short-cut appeal to market principles.

(c) *Hydro-electric Power Schemes*

The standard way of measuring the value of the extra electricity generated by a public hydro-electric scheme is to estimate the savings realised by not having to buy from an alternative source. This sounds simple, but in fact raises all sorts of complicated issues: we shall look at these by, first, considering the simple alternative of a single hydro-electric source versus a single private steam plant, and secondly, by considering the implications of adding another source to a whole supply system.

In the first case the general point is to say that benefits can be measured by the costs of the most economical private alternative. As Eckstein shows at some length [20, Ch. VIII], this raises a number of issues, *e.g.*, a private sector station will not be working under competitive conditions, and so its charges may not coincide with opportunity costs; private sector charges will not be directly relevant to public sector circumstances in that they will reflect taxes, private sector interest rates, etc.; as we need the pattern of future, as well as current, benefits, we have to allow for the effects of future technological changes in reducing alternative costs, and hence benefits, through time. A further point arises when a new hydro-electric station provides a proportionately large net addition to the supply in a region. In this case the alternative-cost principle would produce an over-estimate of benefits, and we are forced back to a measure of what the extra output would sell for plus

[1] To avoid double-counting, the loss of income through damage to property, etc., has to be calculated at the lower level of use prevailing before the flood measures.

the increased consumers' surplus of its purchasers. Presumably a survey of the potential market for the power will provide some of the needed information, but the difficulties of making reliable estimates are clearly enormous.

We now turn to the case where a new hydro-electric station has to be fitted into a whole system.

The amount of power produced by a new hydro-electric station and the times of year at which it will be produced depend not only upon the physical characteristics of the river providing the power but also upon the cost characteristics of the whole electricity supply system and upon the behaviour of the electricity consumers. The supply system constitutes a unity which is operated so as to minimise the operating costs of meeting consumption whatever its time pattern happens to be. Hence the way in which the hydro-electric station is operated may be affected by alterations in the peakiness of consumption, the bringing into service of new thermal stations and so on.

If we now try to apply the principle of measuring benefits by the cost savings of not building an alternative station it follows from the system interdependence just described that the only meaningful way of measuring this cost saving is to ascertain the difference in the present value of total system operating costs in the two cases and deduct the capital cost of the alternatives. A simple comparison of the two capital costs and the two running costs, that is to say, will only give the right answer if the level and time pattern of the output of each would be exactly the same. In general, therefore, a very complicated exercise involving the simulation of the operation of the whole system is required (Turvey [84]), as, for that matter, may be the case for other water-resource analysis (Maass [48]).

Finally, there is another point, emphasised by Krutilla and Eckstein [43]. Even if two or more hydro-electric stations are not linked in the same distribution and consumption network, there may be production interdependence. The clearest example is that when upstream stations in a river basin have reservoirs for water storage, this is highly likely to affect water flows downstream, and hence the generating pattern of stations in that area. If technological interdependence of this type is not internalised by having both types of station under the same authority it will be necessary to have some system of compensatory arrangement if we want to cut down resource misallocation.

(d) *Multi-purpose Schemes*

In practice, many river developments have a number of purposes in mind —not only those we have dealt with above but also transport improvements, etc., as well. Obviously, the range of choice now becomes much wider. Not only does one have to look at the cost-benefit data for, say, different sized hydro-electric stations, but one also has to take different combinations of, say, irrigation and navigation improvements. The calculations will also be more complicated, in that the possibilities of interdependence are clearly multiplied, and so the warnings we have already uttered about the feasibility of some calculations will be even more applicable. We shall have no more to say at this stage on multi-stage projects, but simply make the final point that these reflections are highly apposite in the case of projects such as the Morecambe Bay and Solway Firth barrage schemes (providing for industrial and domestic water supplies, transport improvements, land reclamation, improved recreation facilities, etc.), which are receiving a good deal of attention at the time of writing (in 1965).

2. *Transport Projects* [1]

(a) *Roads*

A great deal of work has now accumulated on the principles and methods of application of cost-benefit techniques in this field,[2] ever since the first experiments in the State of Oregon in 1938. We shall illustrate the arguments by references to the work done on the M1 in the United Kingdom (Coburn, Beesley and Reynolds [14], Reynolds [70], Foster [27]), this being a typical example of what one finds in this field.

The calculation of net annual savings was classified under four heads: (i) those relating to diverted traffic; (ii) those to generated traffic; (iii) savings in non-business time; and (iv) the effects of the growth of G.N.P. Under (i) (diverted traffic) estimates were made of the likely net savings of the traffic diverted from other routes to the M1, *i.e.*, positive items, such as working time savings of drivers, vehicle-usage economies, petrol savings,[3] accident reductions, etc., together with negative items in respect of additional mileages travelled on faster roads and maintenance costs of the motorway.[4]

In respect of generated traffic the argument is that the opening of the motorway would in effect reduce the " price " (in terms of congestion and inconvenience of motoring) and enable demand which had hitherto been frustrated to express itself in motorway usage. As it must be assumed that benefits per vehicle-mile to frustrated consumers are of less consequence than those to actual consumers (if not, they would not remain frustrated), they were rated as half as great as the latter in the M1 calculations.

Savings in non-business time were the third main ingredient. This calculation involves many complications, to which we shall return in a

[1] Although we shall not discuss air transport specifically, it might be noted that the cost–benefit technique has been applied to government aviation expenditure (Fromm [30]).

[2] For a general survey see T. E. Kuhn [44].

[3] Valued at factor cost. We have discussed the logic of this point above (p. 165). See also J. Lesourne [46, Ch. 4].

[4] It will be noted that no credit is given for the effect of road improvements in triggering off new industrial development. Such an effect is: " an additional net benefit . . . only to the extent that three conditions are fulfilled: (1) the specific investment would not have been made in the absence of the highway improvement; (2) it utilizes resources that otherwise would have remained unemployed; and (3) it does not displace economic activity that otherwise would have taken place " (Mohring and Harwitz [58, p. 55].

moment. The fourth component was the introduction of a trend factor, to allow for the long-term growth of G.N.P. and the effects on the demand for road travel—an obvious ingredient of any calculation, whether relating to private or public investment. The upshot of the combined calculations was that the rate of return was of the order of 10–15%.

A number of comments can be made on these calculations. First, there are the obvious statistical shortcomings which are recognised by everyone, including the authors. Second, there are a number of minor omissions, such as allowances for police and administrative costs, the benefits accruing to pedestrians and cyclists, etc., the advantages of more reliable goods deliveries (Foster [27], pp. 268 ff.). Thirdly, there are some inconsistencies in these particular calculations, in that on some occasions a long-period view seems to be taken (*e.g.*, when calculating the savings resulting from reductions in road vehicle fleets) and on others a short-period one (*e.g.*, in assessing the benefits of diversion of traffic from the railways). Much more important than these points are the savings due to accident reduction and to economies in travel time, where important logical and practical issues arise. On the first of these, the economic benefits of a fall in the amount of damage to vehicles and to real property, the work done by insurance companies, the work of the police and the courts are simple enough. It is the loss of production due to death or, temporarily, to accident or illness which raises complications. However, these complications are exactly the same as those raised in cost-benefit studies of health programmes, and so it will be convenient to leave discussion of this general topic until we reach that heading.

This leaves us with the problem of valuing time savings; as these savings often form a very high proportion of total estimated benefits of road improvements, they are extremely important. Unfortunately, these calculations have not so far been very satisfactory.

Whatever the valuation procedure followed, it is necessary to assume that one time saving of sixty minutes is worth the same as sixty savings each lasting one minute, since estimates of the value of time savings of different lengths are unobtainable. On the one hand, it is clear that some short-time savings are valueless, since nothing can be done in the time saved. On the other hand, however, there are cases where the extra time makes possible some activity which would otherwise be precluded, as, for instance, when arriving a little earlier at a theatre means that one does not have to wait until the interval to gain one's seat. Similarly, the value of an hour gained may depend partly upon when it is gained. *Faute de mieux*, such variations have to be ignored and an average treated as meaningful.

It is customary to distinguish between working time saved and leisure time saved, valuing the former at the relevant wage-rate, *e.g.*, drivers' wages in the case of buses and lorries. The argument is simply that this is what the worker's time is worth to his employer. As Winch has pointed out [89, p. 73], this raises certain difficulties: if the driver does the same work as before, the gain is a matter of his having more leisure, while if he works the same hours as before and does more work, the value of his marginal net product may fall. The first point matters only if leisure time is valued differently from working time, as Winch points out, but the second is awkward, if only in principle.

The various methods that have been proposed for valuing leisure time all rest upon the observation of choices which involve the substitution of leisure for some other good which, in contrast to leisure, does have a market price. Leisure can be substituted:

(i) for wages, net of tax, by workers;

(ii) for transport expenditure, by those who travel in their own time and are able to choose between alternative speeds of travel either directly (as drivers) or indirectly (*e.g.*, train versus bus);

(iii) for housing and transport expenditure, by people who can choose the location of their dwelling in relation to that of their place of work, and hence determine the length of the journey to work.

Each of these approaches has its difficulties. One difficulty which is common to all of them is that the substitution rarely involves just leisure and money; for example:

(i) A man may refuse to work an extra hour for an extra £1, yet value leisure at less than £1 because extra work involves missing a bus.

(ii) The driver who pays a toll and alters the running cost he incurs in order to get to his destination faster by using a toll-road is buying not only a time-saving but also the pleasure of driving along a restricted access highway. (A separate and trickier problem is that he may not know the true effect of the change in route and speed upon his car's running costs.)

(iii) A house nearer work may be in a less or more attractive environment.

These problems are surveyed in Winch [89]; Mohring [57] presents the theory underlying the approach via land values and shows how difficult it is to apply in practice; and Moses and Williamson [59] discuss the related problem of passengers' choice between alternative modes of transport and list American applications of the approach via toll-road utilisation. A recent piece of research in the United Kingdom (Beesley [2]) produces valuations of time savings on journeys by public transport on the basis of comparing different combinations of cash and time outlays for given journeys; by substituting this result into the comparison of public and private transport opportunities, an estimate of the valuation of time savings by private transport is obtained. It might be noted that those investigations yield markedly lower estimates than those quoted on previous occasions in the United

Kingdom (*e.g.*, Foster and Beesley [28], *Report of Panel on Road Pricing* [55]). So, at the very least, one can say that there are major unknowns which may or may not prove tractable to further analysis.

So far we have made no mention of the many American studies of the impact of road improvements on by-passed shopping centres, on the value of adjacent property and on the pattern of land use. This is because, as Mohring and Harwitz [58, pp. 132–3] explain, these "studies suffer from either or both of two shortcomings: (1) they have concentrated on measuring benefits to specific population groups, and have done so in such a way that *net* benefits to society as a whole cannot be estimated from their results; and/or (2) they have concentrated on measuring highway-related changes in the nature and locus of economic activity and have not isolated those aspects of change that reflect net benefits."

We have concentrated on the application of cost-benefit analysis to a major motorway construction. The same general principles apply in other types of road investment, ranging from the "simple" kind of case such as the Channel Tunnel or the Forth Bridge [1] to the far more complex network problems such as the whole transport system of a metropolitan area. If one wishes to include the *Buchanan Report* [56] notion of "environment" [2] in the calculus for urban road improvements the estimation process is likely to become very complex and laborious, if indeed it is feasible at all. The Report's own attempt to give an empirical filling to the idea is perfunctory in the extreme,[3] but Beesley and Kain [4] have proposed the principle of "environmental compensation" as an operational way of taking some account of environmental benefits and disbenefits in allocating budgeted expenditure on urban roads.

Finally, one might take note of the work of Bos and Koyck [7]. They construct a complete general equilibrium model of a simple economy with three geographical areas and four goods. This involves a series of demand equations, technical equations, supply equations and definitional equations. They show that a reduction in transport costs between two of these areas will raise national income by much more than the customary estimate of benefits, *i.e.*, the saving of transport costs of existing traffic between these areas plus half the cost of saving for the generated traffic. The essential point is that there is a much fuller allowance for ramifications, *e.g.*, they not only allow for the effects on goods transported but also on goods not transported. This system, of course, requires knowledge of all the demand and supply equations in the economy, so is scarcely capable of application by road engineers. It does, however, serve to remind us of the limitations of partial analysis.

[1] See J. M. W. Stewart "For Whom the Bridge Tolls," *New Saltire Magazine*, August 1962.

[2] "The idea of a place, an area or even a street which is free from the dangers and nuisances of motor traffic" (*op. cit.*, p. 37).

[3] The illustration on p. 214 [56] of the applications of cost-benefit analysis in the context of the Report's principles is based on purely hypothetical data.

(b) *Railways*

Railways have received a great deal less attention than roads from cost-benefit analysts, perhaps because they have, relatively if not absolutely, been a contracting sector of the transport industry in many countries. However, there have been two railway projects which have attracted attention in the United Kingdom in the last few years, and brief reference to them may be sufficient to illustrate the general principles.

In their well-known study of the new Victoria underground line in London, Foster and Beesley [28] followed much the same principles as those employed in cost-benefit studies on the roads. The main benefits were time savings, cost savings (*e.g.*, private vehicle operating costs), extra comfort and convenience, and a variety of gains to Central London resulting from an effective widening of the catchment area. These benefits were distributed among the traffic diverted to the Victoria line, the traffic not so diverted and generated traffic. But by and large, gains by generated traffic were unimportant compared with the other two categories; and of the various categories of savings, time savings amounted to almost half the total. When compared with the totality of costs involved in constructing and maintaining the line over a fifty year period it was found that there was a "social surplus rate of return" [1] of something of the order of 11 %, the precise figure depending on the rate of interest chosen. The reasons why this rate of return is much greater than any financial or accounting return were said to be two-fold: first, that London Transport's policy of averaging fares over different modes of travelling from one place to another meant that potential money receipts would underestimate benefits, and second, that potential revenue was reduced by the fact that road users are not charged the full social cost of the resources they absorb.

Although the proposals in the Beeching Report [10] for closing down sections of the United Kingdom main-line railway system were not couched in cost-benefit terms, various commentators (*e.g.*, Ray and Crum [67]) have looked at these aspects. The financial savings of the measures in view can be classified under four heads: improved methods of working, increased charges to some particular users (*e.g.*, National Coal Board), the savings from closing commuter lines and the savings from rural closures. The first of these clearly represents a social as well as a financial saving, and need not detain us further. The second is more debatable; raising charges does not as such save any real resources, but it is possible that it would stimulate some savings of cost, and so to that extent would involve a social gain. In so far as the closure of commuter lines leads to further road congestion in large cities, the social saving is likely to be very small indeed, if anything at all. Finally, the closure of rural lines involves questions such as redundancies of specialist labour in out-of-the-way areas, extra road maintenance, more road accidents,

[1] Defined as "total benefits less costs other than interest charges as a return on the capital invested, averaged over the whole period of operation and construction."

lengthier journeys, etc. We are not concerned with the details of such calculations, but it might be noted that the overall result of Beeching would seem to be a substantial saving in real terms, even if not quite as large as the financial one. This does, however, leave out many intangibles, such as the more indirect and longer-term effects on particular regions, *e.g.*, the North of Scotland; and no one, to our knowledge, has suggested any unique and convincing way of quantifying and incorporating such repercussions in the analysis.

To summarise, the principles developed in the analysis of road improvements can fairly readily be applied to railway investment and in the assessment of the overall consequences of railway closures. As before, time savings are an important item in many cases, and to the extent that we are still very ignorant of how to crack this hardest of nuts, we are still in a position of intellectual discomfort.

(c) *Inland Waterways*

A good deal of work has been done in the United States on the estimation of benefits from new canals or from rendering an existing river channel navigable. It has been discussed especially by Eckstein [20] and Renshaw [68, 69]. This is of interest both for its own sake and for the light it throws on other transport fields.

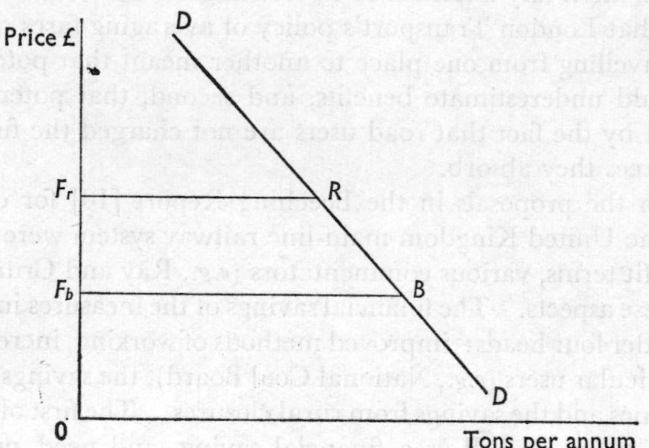

Fig. 2.—Inland Waterways.

Let us start with some points first made by Dupuit [19] and raised diagrammatically by Renshaw [68, 69]. Let *DD* in Fig. 2 be the demand curve for transport of a given commodity along a specified route and OF_r be the present rail freight rate. Then F_rR will be the existing volume of traffic. If a canal were built and the barge freight rate were OF_b traffic would expand to F_bB and the gain to shippers would be F_rRBF_b. This can be approximated by multiplying the existing volume of traffic F_rR by the unit freight saving

F_rF_b, and this is the procedure followed in practice, *e.g.*, by the United States Corps of Engineers.

We now bring in complications.

1. The gain to shippers will not measure social gain unless freight rates adequately reflect marginal social costs. The main reason why this may not be so is that railways are frequently subject to regulation. Thus, if the freight receipts of the railway from the traffic in question exceed its avoidable costs, part of the gain to shippers is merely a transfer from the railway's owners, and must be deducted to obtain a measure of the social benefit from the canal.

2. The single demand curve of the diagram is a legitimate construction only when neither canal nor railway are part of a network and only when they both link exactly the same points. If neither of these conditions is fulfilled a more complicated construction is required, since total system rail traffic and total system barge traffic are both functions of both rail and barge freight rates (including shippers' terminal costs). The net gain to shippers who direct traffic from rail to a canal joining points *A* and *B* will differ from the simple product of the freight rate differential between *A* and *B* and the number of tons of freight diverted to the canal because:

(i) There may be a saving or gain in transport costs beyond *A* and *B*. Consider, for example, traffic from *A* to *C*; this may previously have gone by rail all the way without going through *B*.

(ii) There may be a saving or gain in costs other than freight. Thus, if canal is slower than rail more working capital will be required.

(iii) The railway may cut its freight rate in response to competition from the canal, so reducing the amount of traffic diverted. This is discussed by Eckstein [20] with examples.

Taking these three complications into account we find that the social benefit from the canal (gross of its costs) equals:

The saving in railway system costs
Less barge costs
Less increase in shippers' other costs
Plus the value to shippers of generated traffic on the canal.

This amount will be less than the product of the diverted traffic volume and the rail–canal freight rate differential unless the consumers' surplus on generated canal traffic outweighs any excess of railway rates over avoidable costs, any deficit between canal freight rates and barge costs and any increase in shippers' other costs. Thus, except where traffic generation is expected to be large, multiplying the rate differential by traffic diversion may exaggerate benefits.

An example of the application of these techniques in a particular case relates to a cross-Florida barge canal.[1] The following figures were produced:

$000 per annum.

Item.	Corps of Engineers.	Consultants' evaluation.
Amortisation, interest, maintenance . .	5,960	8,235
Transportation savings	6,980	1,102
Commercial fishing boats' benefits . .	70	0
Contractor's floating equipment benefits .	30	0
New vessel delivery benefits . . .	110	0
Recreational boating benefits . . .	110	0
Flood control benefits	240	0
Enhancement of waterfront land values .	590	0
Benefit–cost ratio	1·20	0·13

To what extent the divergence is due to the facts that the Corps likes to build canals and that the consultants were retained by the railroads, and to what extent it is due to the intrinsic impossibility of making accurate estimates is left entirely to the reader to decide!

3. *Land Usage*

(a) *Urban Renewal*

The application of cost-benefit analysis to proposals for redevelopment projects in towns has been discussed by Rothenberg [71] and by Lichfield [47], both of whom have provided partial examples. The problem is complicated by the large number of types of people or institutions involved in urban development. Thus, the public acquisition of all private property in a slum area which is then redeveloped may involve more than one public agency, the dispossessed property owners, dispossessed tenants, owners and tenants of property adjacent to the redevelopment area, owners and tenants in other areas affected by the search for alternative accommodation on the part of the dispossessed tenants, potential developers and tenants of the cleared area and, finally, the population of the town at large, both as taxpayers who meet some of the cost and (more indirectly) in so far as they suffer any adverse social consequence from the slum.

Lichfield is primarily concerned to show how all the costs and benefits to all affected parties can be systematically recorded in a set of accounts. The arguments in favour of proceeding this way instead of by simply listing and evaluating the net amount of each type of cost or benefit are threefold. First, starting on an all-inclusive gross basis and then cancelling out to obtain net social benefits and costs insures against omissions. Second, the financial consequences of any project are sometimes important, and it may need to be redesigned in the light of the distribution of benefits and costs so as to compensate parties who would otherwise stand to lose from it, securing their

[1] United States Senate hearings on Public Works Appropriations, 1963; Civil Functions, Department of the Army, Part 2, p. 1881.

support for it. The notion of compensation is familiar enough in welfare economics; here is a case where it can be important in practice. Third, whether or not financial transfers are used to affect the final distribution of net gains, that distribution will often be relevant to choice. In practice, that is to say, for good or bad reasons, the attitude of a county council or similar body towards a scheme will depend upon who gains as well as upon how much they gain. As the client of the cost-benefit analyst, it will therefore want to know more than just the total net figures.

Rothenberg discusses those types of benefits from urban development projects which involve slum clearance (mentioning other, aesthetic, considerations in a footnote). The first is the " internalisation of market externalities," which we discuss in a moment, the second is the effect on real income distribution and the third consists of the reduction in fire risks, crime and other social consequences of slum living.

By internalising market externalities, Rothenberg is thinking of the improvement of efficiency in resource allocation which can be achieved when a neighbourhood is regarded as a unit where previously each of the separate owners in it had paid no regard to the adverse effects upon other owners' property of the inadequate maintenance of his own. Leaving aside a property tax complication which arises in the United States, Rothenberg's basic suggestion is that the social gain is measured by the increase in the total site value of the redevelopment area (" the value of the increased productivity of the land on the redevelopment site ") corrected for any change in locational advantages brought about by redevelopment plus any increase in the value of properties adjacent to the redevelopment area resulting from its physical improvement (*i.e.*, technological externalities). The nature of the locational advantages is not very clear, and the convenient assumption that the sum of locational effects in the town as a whole is zero requires a good deal of justification.

Another difficulty relates to the increment of site values. The relevance of site values after slum clearance is obvious enough, since these values are the capitalised values of the rents to be had from the new buildings which are most appropriate, less the present value of the costs of erecting and maintaining those buildings. But the relevance of site values in the absence of a redevelopment scheme is not so clear.

A second difficulty with Rothenberg's expositions is that the illustrative example of his technique is an *ex-post* one. This introduces problems which are irrelevant to the *ex-ante* calculations that are required if the technique is ever to be of use. How different an actual past change in land value would have been if things had been different, that is to say, is no concern of the man making forward-looking estimates. His problem is to estimate how much the site would sell for if not only it but also all the surrounding sites were to be redeveloped. The way to answer this question is surely to start with an estimate of the rental or selling value of new accommodation in the improved area and then deduct for building costs. But does this not require the art of the valuer as much as the science of the economist or econometrician?

(b) *Recreation*

The problem of estimating and valuing recreational gains or losses due to projects has received a good deal of attention in the United States, where much of the discussion has been usefully surveyed by Clawson [12]. An example of the problem is provided by the conflict between the provision of hydro-electric power and the preservation of the salmon runs in the Pacific Northwest (though this involves commercial fishing as well as sports fishing), while the gain to pleasure-boating from harbour improvements constitutes another case.

The principle is clear enough: what is needed in any particular case, on the benefit side, is measurement of the demand curve for access to the recreational facility in question. In practice, however, the choice has often lain between getting a figure by the wrong method and not getting one by the right method. Thus, Crutchfield [15] lists four invalid techniques that have been used in the case of sports fishing.

(*a*) The argument that recreational facilities should not, in principle, be measured in money terms and that some level of provision should thus be arbitrarily set regardless of competing demands.

(*b*) Expenditure on providing and using the fishery. This merely measures the size of the sport fishing industry, but provides no indication of the loss that would be sustained if it disappeared.

(*c*) Imputing to sport fishing the market value of the fish caught, which implies that the angler is simply out to get some food.

(*d*) Valuing anglers' fishing time at the earnings the anglers could have acquired by working. This implies, among other things, that every hour spent in any kind of recreation is equally valuable.

The method proposed by Clawson [12] and Trice and Wood [82], though statistically dubious, in practice does at least attempt to get at an imputed demand curve. The basic idea is to deduce the amount of usage at different "prices" from data of differential travel (and other) costs actually incurred in utilising recreational facilities. If visitors to a recreation area come from a series of concentric zones one can reasonably postulate that anyone coming from the nearest zone enjoys a consumer's surplus which can be measured by the difference between his travel costs and those incurred by a man coming from the farthest zone. (There is an implicit assumption that the inner-zone resident derives as much satisfaction from a visit as the outer-zone man, but in a situation where approximations have to be made this does not seem too wild a one.) It is understood that this notion is due basically to Hotelling, and that use has been made of it in an Upper Feather River basin study. Unfortunately, it ignores the point that part of the consumers' surplus derived from proximity may be swallowed up in residential rent.

variables [48]. Whether this is because of an overriding desire for security, or because debts accumulated during prosperity years are being paid off during recession, or for other reasons, remains to be established.

The final area in which much additional work can be expected is one which underlies all other areas of household behaviour, and which should have received primary attention long ago, namely, the measurement problem. Consumer surveys and budget studies have multiplied enormously during the post-war period, both in this country and elsewhere.[1] These studies have been conducted in much the same manner as earlier ones and undoubtedly contain much the same errors.[2] These errors are not small. The few studies that have been made appear to indicate that, more than almost any type of economic statistics, data obtained from consumer surveys or budget studies are subject to substantial errors. As a rule, expenditures tend to be understated somewhat (some substantially, such as tobacco and liquor), income tends to be understated more and saving tends to be understated most of all [107, pp. 113–50] [123, pp. 51–72]. Such errors are not uniform among different households or among population groups, though little basis exists for evaluation of their magnitude or effects; their influence on estimates of expenditures for population groups is essentially an unknown quantity. Above all, it is clear that past estimates of saving, whether obtained as a residual between income and expenditures or directly, are seriously in error, as are undoubtedly estimates of the distribution of assets and debts among the population [61].

Only one large-scale methodological study of data collection techniques has been undertaken in recent years, on means of improving the accuracy of savings data, under the sponsorship of the Inter-University Committee for Research on Consumer Behavior with financial assistance from the Ford Foundation and the U.S. Department of Agriculture. Initial publications of the study bring out clearly the substantial magnitude of the error problem, suggesting that biases in past surveys affect not only averages but distributions, and that the biases are large enough to render virtually meaningless the usual measures of sampling variation [108].

Under the circumstances it is amazing how little attention is being given to the improvement of data-collection techniques, and how much empirical analysis is focused on attempting to explain what may be no more than errors of observation.[3] Occasional studies of different aspects of the problem

[1] For a description of some of these studies see Jean M. Due [34]; also Eleanor Snyder [147], and the bibliography by James Morgan [127].

[2] A striking case in point is the new series of expenditure surveys of the U.S. Bureau of Labor Statistics. Originally, these surveys were to be preceded by methodological studies, but because of budget limitations these studies were eliminated, although they had been begun. As a result, data are being collected in the same manner as in the past, and with the same unknown errors.

[3] Thus, see comments by Margaret Reid [145]. Many of the findings of empirical studies reported at the *Conference on Consumption and Saving*, some of which were heatedly discussed, could have been due to errors of observation.

(c) *Land Reclamation*

A Dutch paper [41] describes the use of cost-benefit analysis for evaluating land-reclamation schemes. The particular points singled out are the insistence that one must not overlook related investment expenditure (*e.g.*, for the manufacture of raw materials for use on reclaimed land or for processing) and the corresponding returns, the use of foreign exchange shadow prices for such calculations as the expected saving in imports, allowances for harm done to fisheries and for benefits to road traffic and a general recognition of the widespread nature and importance of intangibles ("indeterminables" in Dutch–English). This is in no sense a complete listing of the relevant variables, but may be sufficient to savour the flavour of the dish.

4. *Health*

The major purpose of health programmes is to save lives and reduce illness, and on this score there is some overlap with flood-prevention and road-improvement measures. There are no special problems which relate to the estimate of the costs of such programmes, and the special problem of quantifying their effects is a matter for engineers and doctors rather than for economists. The interest of the latter is thus concentrated on the problem of valuing the benefits per life saved or per illness avoided, and this is all we shall consider here. And even within this limited area, we shall devote most of our time to the former. Our task is aided by the work of Weisbrod [86], and the useful surveys of Mushkin [62] and Klarman [42]. It might be further noted that this subject is a well-established one, having attracted the attention of Irving Fisher many years ago [26].

Before exploring the conceptual problems, it should be noted that some of the differences between authors in the way they estimate benefits stem from differences in the availability of statistics rather than from differences in what the authors would like to measure if they could. Thus, some of the simplifications in Reynolds' classic paper [70] on the cost of road accidents were surely dictated by statistical exigencies rather than by considerations of high principle. This paper at least has the merit that after calculating the average costs in 1952 of various consequences of accidents (death, injury, property damage, insurance, administrative costs) the author went on, in an appendix, to show how his results could be used to estimate the purely economic benefits that would have accrued from new pedestrian crossing regulations and from adequate rear lighting on all vehicles and cycles.

A death avoided means that a loss of production may be avoided. Thus the present value of this is an economic benefit to be credited to the measure responsible for saving life. The first step in estimating it is to ascertain what the average person whose life is made safer will earn over the rest of his life. This depends upon age at death, the probability of survival to each higher age, the proportion of people at each age who will both be in the labour force and employed and their contribution to production at each age.

(*a*) Age at death of those whose lives would be saved can be assumed to equal the average age of all those who die from whatever it is, unless the proposed life-saving expenditure obviously discriminates between age groups.

(*b*) The probability of survival to each age can be calculated from a life table for the group at risk, which should be amended to take account of any projected changes in its age-specific death-rates.

(*c*) Participation rates have to be forecast. It is generally agreed that the appropriate unemployment percentage to assume is that corresponding to "full employment." [1]

(*d*) The earnings of a person are usually taken as a measure of the value of his marginal product, average product being obviously too high. Since it is future earnings which are relevant, the trend of growth in earnings should be allowed for if the analysis starts with figures of current earnings.

In practice, Weisbrod was able to construct estimates only for all men and all women and not for any particular group at risk, on account of data limitations. He and Reynolds both took earnings in a recent year without making any addition for future productivity increases.

The question whether housewives' services should be included as lost production has produced some discussion. Since there can be no question but that the loss of these services does impose a cost upon the survivors, it would sometimes bias choice to disregard the services of housewives in calculating production loss. As Klarman [42] points out, the distribution of diseases between the sexes is not uniform, so that the relative economic benefits of different health programmes will be affected by the weight given to housewives' services. What is really at issue, therefore, is how to measure their value, not whether to measure it. One possibility is to estimate their opportunity cost, *i.e.*, what housewives could earn in paid jobs (net of taxes and extra expenses), since this provides a minimum estimate of what the services are worth to the family. Alternatively, replacement cost, *i.e.*, the cost of a housekeeper, could be used. Weisbrod [86] develops a very ingenious measure along these lines, where the value of a housewife's services is an increasing function of the number of other persons in her family. Neither measure can be accurately estimated in practice.

An even larger question is that of consumption. If society loses the production of the decedent, does it not also gain by not having to supply his

[1] As Selma Mushkin puts it: "One obvious reason for using the simplifying assumption of full employment is that, unless we do, we cannot arrive at any definite concept of what the resource gain is. Apart from this, however, the fact that production losses resulting from poor health cannot be realized in an unemployment situation should be attributed to unemployment, not to ill health. Unemployment has its own cost, which in effect may cancel out reductions in the cost of sickness, but for analytical purposes it is necessary to distinguish between the two. We therefore measure the gains of disease eradication or cure in the assumed absence of costs of unemployment, recognising, however, that unemployment itself may have an effect on the incidence of illness" [62, p. 138].

own consumption? The answer is a matter of definition. If society is defined to exclude the decedent, the loss is confined to the wealth he would have accumulated and the taxes he would have paid less the transfers he would have received, and would be borne partly by his heirs and partly by the Government on behalf of all other taxpayers. It thus constitutes the amount which society so defined would find it worthwhile to pay to save his life (leaving aside all non-materialistic considerations for later discussion). Now the society whose representatives decide whether or not to undertake a measure which would save lives includes those people who may lose their lives if the proposed measure is not undertaken. Hence, so the argument might run, society is relevantly defined as including the prospective decedent, and his consumption is part of the social loss contingent upon his death.

Those, like Weisbrod, who take the line that consumption should be deducted have to face the problem of estimating it, and Weisbrod does so with commendable ingenuity [86, Appendix I]. He argues that marginal rather than average consumption is relevant, and measures this as the change in family consumption with a change in family size, given income. Using family budget data, he calculates for each age bracket a weighted mean of the marginal consumption of persons in mean-income families of all sizes. It is only fair to add that he is far from dogmatic about the virtues of this approach.

Whether or not consumption is deducted, the economic value of a life saved varies according to a variety of factors, including age (it rises during childhood and falls after a certain age because of the twin influences of life earning patterns and discounting). Other things being equal, therefore, these calculations are worth undertaking only if we believe that more resources should be devoted to saving a more "productive" life than a less "productive" life—*e.g.*, the average man in preference to the average woman of the same age, a white Protestant American in preference to a coloured one, the average Englishman rather than the average Scot, a young worker rather than a baby.

To put the question this way outrages many people's feelings who do not see that the "other things" which are here assumed "equal" include one's estimate of the moral worth and human value of the different people and of the sorrow caused by their death. Without taking any position, therefore, we pass on to consider the non-economic value of a human life. By this we mean merely the amount which it is worth sacrificing in economic terms to save a life. It is less than infinity (since there are avoidable deaths), it exceeds zero (since money is spent to save lives) and it is worth ascertaining (in so far as consistent decision-making implies such a value).

The problem has been discussed by two French authors (Thedié and Abraham [81]) with a certain Gallic elegance which does not entirely conceal the (necessary) arbitrariness of their procedure. They speak of "affective" loss and distinguish: affective injury to the family, affective injury to the rest of the nation, *pretium doloris* and *pretium vivendi*, the last two corresponding to the prospective decedent's aversion to suffering and death respectively. Court judgments, they consider, " should . . . make it possible in each country to obtain an average opinion as regards the sums to be spent to avoid the various affective losses."

Estimates of the benefits to be had from reducing illness, relating to particular diseases, offer no new problems of principle but involve great statistical difficulties. Mushkin [62] discusses some of the principles, making the useful distinction between the effects of disability (*e.g.*, loss of working time) and debility (*e.g.*, loss of capacity while at work). Weisbrod [86] and Klarman [42] also raise valuable pointers. But the fundamental difficulty—and this affects the loss through deaths arguments too—is that of the multiplicity of variables—when there are manifold influences at work on life-expectancy, productivity and the like, how can one hope to sort out the unambiguous influence of a particular health programme or any other single causative factor?

Finally, mention should be made of a different approach to all those problems, even though, as far as we are aware, it is not one which has been pursued. This stresses that the problem is essentially the *ex-ante* one of deciding how much to spend in reducing various kinds of risk. Since people in their private capacities do incur costs to reduce risks to which they and their children are exposed, it is conceivable that their valuation of diminutions in risk could be inferred from their behaviour.

5. *Education*

Although there is a rapidly growing literature on the economics of education, not all of it falls within our purview. Thus, attempts to include human capital as a factor of production in quantitative analyses of the sources of economic growth scarcely qualify as cost-benefit analysis, despite their present-day interest. We are primarily concerned with studies which might assist policy-makers in choosing where and how to increase expenditure on education. These studies concentrate on the costs of education, including imputed earnings foregone and on those benefits of education which take the form of higher incomes. The statistical necessity for these limitations is obvious, and so most authors who have dealt with the subject have felt obliged to discuss the items which have been omitted. Blaug [5], Bowman [9] and Weisbrod [87], for example, have provided elegant accounts of some of the unmeasured benefits.[1]

Here we confine ourselves to what can and has been measured. Since

[1] *E.g.*, Weisbrod [87] classifies external benefits into residence-related (*e.g.*, mothers who are able to go out to work when children are at school), employment-related (*e.g.*, mutual benefits conferred by employees in a factory) and those which accrue to society in general. The width of the last category obviously depends on the angle of view: international benefits (allowing for migration) are greater than national, and the latter in turn greater than regional, for the same reason.

successive authors all improve and refine upon the work of their predecessors we need refer only to three recent contributions, those of Becker [1], Lee Hansen [33] and Hunt [39]—at least so far as recent American work is concerned.

Becker summarises his work as follows:

> " In chapter V attention is focused on the social gain from college education as measured by its effects on national productivity. The major difficulty here, one that always plagues economists, is in measuring the benefits and costs to society that are not captured or borne by college-educated persons. All that could be done was to derive—on the basis of crude information—lower and what is best labelled ' possible ' upper limits to the social rates of return, limits that unfortunately are wide apart. The more reliable lower limits thus derived do not differ much from the private rates of return, but the upper levels are almost double the latter. In the same chapter it is shown that private rates of return on college education exceed those on business capital. The evidence is insufficient to decide whether this, or the converse, is true of the social rates."

Hansen, building on earlier writings by Miller, Houthakker, Schultz and others, calculates internal money rates of return for successive stages of education. These rates of return are those which make the present value of the cost and return streams equal and are calculated both for social and for private money costs and returns. Social costs include:

> " (1) school costs incurred by society, that is, teachers' salaries, supplies, interest and depreciation on capital; (2) opportunity costs incurred by individuals, namely, income foregone during school attendance; and (3) incidental school-related costs incurred by individuals, for example, books and travel. Private resource costs include the same three components except that in (1) above tuition and fees paid by individuals are substituted for society's costs which are normally defrayed through taxation " (*op. cit.*, p. 130).

Returns are estimated from cross-section data of the incomes of individuals classified by age and education. The differences between the cross-section income streams of people with varying levels of education are attributed to the differences in education levels. (Before-tax figures are taken as social returns and post-tax figures as private returns.) By postulating that these observed relationships will endure for half a century or so, and by adjusting for the incidence of mortality, time streams of the extra incomes due to different levels of education are thus obtained. It may be noted, incidentally, that we are not only dealing with a very long pay-off period but also with a situation where returns may be negative in the early years (Blaug [5]).

The obvious holes in this procedure have not escaped our authors, but it may be as well to list some of these difficulties. First, there is the danger in using a current cross-section analysis to predict a future time series. Second, there is the question whether incomes reflect marginal productivity sufficiently well to be used as a measure of social returns. Both of these problems are examined by Blaug [5]. Third, there is the complication suggested by Weisbrod [87, pp. 109 ff.] that the value of extra education includes the value of the option which it confers to obtain still further education. From a social point of view, the principle of the matter is clear: to extend someone's education from a leaving age of, say, sixteen, to one of seventeen either will or will not be followed by a further extension to eighteen. If it is, we must relate the cost of two years' extra education to the returns from two extra years; if it is not, only the costs and returns of the single extra year are relevant.

A fourth major difficulty in the estimate of returns to extra education is perhaps the most formidable of all: that income depends on other variables besides age and education. This leads us straightaway into the complications of multivariate statistical analysis. Becker [1] points out that he has partly met the problem by calculating separate rates of return from college education for white male graduates, non-whites, women and rural persons. He also takes up the particular problem arising from the correlation between ability and education, adducing " limited quantitative evidence . . . (which) suggests that this correlation explains only a small part of the apparently large return." Hunt [39] has used multiple-regression techniques to ascertain the effect upon the earned incomes of some 9,000 male college graduates in 1947 of a large number of variables, including measures of (or proxies for) ability, expenditure per pupil, size of college, parents' education, type of occupation and region. The results are then applied to calculate rates of return from additional college expenditure per undergraduate pupil and from graduate education. The confidence intervals of these estimates are very wide, but at least it is made abundantly clear that correction for other determinants of income is very necessary.

All the difficulties in rate-of-return calculations just discussed have recently been examined by Blaug [5]. He provides a most useful list of various factors which tend to produce biased estimates of the rates of return and points out that the bias is mostly downward.

Research into rates of return in education has not been entirely confined to academic education. Thus, Borus [6] has recently examined the retraining of unemployed workers. He obtained data from interviews with 373 Connecticut workers involved in retraining and used multiple-regression techniques to compare the experience of those who used their training with that of those who did not. He examined benefits and costs to the workers, to the Government and to the economy as a whole. Like others, he " solves " the choice of discount rates by taking two limiting cases, a rate of 5% (the rate at which a worker might lend his savings) and one of 15% (a borrowing rate for workers).

6. *Other Fields*

Cost-benefit techniques have been applied in a number of other fields, but there are only two which we shall mention specifically—Research and Development, Defence. Coverage of these two areas under one single heading should not be taken to mean either that we think they are unimportant or that there is not much work of interest to survey, or that the problems are identical under each heading. The point is simply that no new issues of general principle seem to arise, and so from our point of view they can be held to exemplify further some of the topics we have already discussed.

There is a rapidly burgeoning literature on the economics of research and development, and some specifically relates to the cost-benefit calculus associated with it (see, for instance, Griliches [31], Nelson [64], Williams [88], Scherer [75]). But in reading it, one is struck by two things: one is the uncertainty and unreliability of cost estimates for particular research programmes and the second is the extraordinarily complex nature of the benefits resulting therefrom. Anyone living in the United Kingdom is very familiar with the belated discoveries by government departments that particular programmes of development (especially military ones) have cost far more than anticipated.[1] And although there are some examples of quantitative assessments of benefits—among which Griliches' paper is absolutely outstanding—one cannot help feeling that the multiplicity of benefits and their diffusion among recipients will normally be such as to prevent precise quantification.

On defence, there has been a considerable literature, ever since that most public of all unpublished works—the proposals by Lerner for running the United States part of the Second World War on market principles.[2] It is customary (McKean [54], Hitch and McKean [38]) to single out three ways in which cost-benefit techniques can be applied. First comes the allocation of resources between major missions, *e.g.*, conventional *v.* nuclear armaments. Second, there is the choice between different weapon systems to achieve any given mission, *e.g.*, land-based *v.* sea-borne nuclear weapons. Third, there is the assessment of the relative merits of different military research and development programmes. The third of these has been covered as part of research and development in general, and so we need say no more about it. As for the first and second, we seem to end up in a " one hoss-shay " kind of situation where costs but not benefits are susceptible to economic analysis. There is obviously no objective way of comparing different military aims; Scherer's proposal [75] to assemble the brass-hats together and apply a sophisticated ranking technique (to projects, not people!) to sort out the priorities arising from their collective wisdom is one which is hardly likely

[1] It could presumably be argued that the range of uncertainty is reduced by virtue of the fact that programmes never seem to cost less than anticipated; but that is of more intellectual than financial comfort.

[2] A. P. Lerner, " Design for a Streamlined War Economy "; for a summary see Hitch and McKean [38], pp. 222–4.

to appeal to the military themselves or to their political masters. This means that we are really left with the second category only—that of finding the least-cost method of reaching a particular target or fulfilling a particular task. This is obviously very important, but it cannot be said to be an exercise in all the ramifications of cost-benefit analysis. No doubt there have been many exercises of this kind, but in the nature of things they are not publicly available.[1]

IV. Conclusions

Wide divergences of view have been expressed about the role and usefulness of cost-benefit analysis. Thus, at one extreme we have the following:[2]

> "We have begun to grope our way towards a practical concept of economic planning which may prove in a few year's time to be as revolutionary in its policy implications as was the Keynesian revolution in economics thirty years ago. It also originated, many years ago, with a Cambridge economist: Keynes' contemporary Pigou. It is the concept of social costs and benefits. . . . This leads to the revolutionary concept that we can actually add up the social costs and benefits, in money terms, by asking what value people would themselves put on them. We can then express them as a rate of return on capital, as an ordinary capitalist would, and so determine our investment rationally, from the point of view of the community as a whole, just as the capitalist can now do from his private point of view."

Against this exaggerated view, Arthur Smithies concluded in 1955 [78] after a somewhat sceptical appraisal of the usual evaluation methods:

> "The foregoing discussion leads to two major conclusions: First, judgment plays such an important role in the estimation of benefit-cost ratios that little significance can be attached to the precise numerical results obtained. . . . Second, competition is likely to drive the agencies towards increasingly optimistic estimates; and far from resolving the organisational difficulties, computation of benefit-cost ratios may in fact make them worse" (*op. cit.*, pp. 344–5).

These quotations make it clear that one can view cost-benefit analysis as anything from an infallible means of reaching the new Utopia to a waste of resources in attempting to measure the unmeasurable. It is now our task to assess whether the divergences from the upper limit are likely to exceed those from the lower one, or vice-versa—a cost-benefit analysis of cost-benefit analysis, as it were.

There are obviously two very different sorts of limitations to the potential usefulness of cost-benefit—those of principle and those of practice. On the

[1] It should be noted that the example in Hitch and McKean [38, p. 155] is an illustrative application only. See also Schlesinger [76] for a fairly sceptical appraisal of the quantitative possibilities in this general area.

[2] P. Hall, *Labour's New Frontiers* (London: Andre Deutsch, 1964), p. 173).

whole, we shall concentrate on the former. Statistical deficiencies differ greatly from one country to another; they also have a habit of being remedied over time. It would therefore seem much more profitable at this stage of a general survey article to concentrate on the fundamental difficulties of principle which are likely to remain however much our statistical sources and techniques improve over time.

It is clear from our survey that the benefit side poses many more problems than the costs side, and so we shall largely concentrate on that. We have already made the distinction between the *enumeration* and the *evaluation* of benefits, and so this will serve as a convenient point of departure. As far at *enumeration* goes, when there are many diverse types of benefit from a project and/or many different beneficiaries it is difficult to list them all and to avoid double counting. This is one reason why it is so much easier to apply cost-benefit analysis to a limited purpose development, say, than it is to the research and development aspects of some multi-purpose discovery, such as a new type of plastic material, or new mode of transport, such as the Hovercraft.

On the *evaluation* of benefits, there are several layers of difficulty. First, there is the point that we are trying to measure surpluses, and this immediately takes us into the vast jungle (not to mention jungle warfare) of the measurability of utility, the validity of the simplifying assumptions (constant marginal utility of money to the individual as he moves along a small segmens of his demand curve) necessary to enable us to operate with Marshall's triangle, the comparability of utilities between persons and so on.

Second, one frequently needs to go beyond measurement of benefits on the basis of market prices and make allowances for imperfections, externalities and so on. This raises some extremely awkward problems, as has been very clearly demonstrated in some of the recent literature on externalities (Coase [13], Buchanan and Stubblebine [11], Davis and Whinston [17], Turvey [85]). Thus, to take the most hackneyed of all illustrations, the cost imposed by the smoky factory chimney on the nearby housewife's washing line should be measured on the basis of the *minimum* cost which the sufferer must incur to avoid it.

The third major problem of evaluation is that of choosing an appropriate discount rate. The ideal solutions which have been suggested require knowledge of the as yet unknown answers to questions relating to many aspects of the economy (*e.g.*, the general level of interest rates compatible with the desired growth rate of the economy).

The fourth difficulty—and this affects the enumeration as well as the evaluation of benefits—is that of allowing in any systematic fashion for uncertainty. When all is said and done, none of us can predict major political and military upheavals, to say nothing of natural disasters, and no amount of wishing such problems at the bottom of the sea or pretending that they are already there will be of much help in policy formation and judgment.

These are a formidable range of difficulties which might give the appearance of being a technical if not an actual knockout. But before we throw in the towel we have to ask some further questions. First of all, is there a better alternative? The practical problem is that decisions do have to be taken by public agencies. It can, of course, be said that one can sidestep the issue by requiring public agencies to operate on a " commercial " basis, leaving resource allocations to be resolved through the operation of the pricing system. Those who wish to support this kind of policy must believe that externalities, market imperfections, etc., have no importance whatever. It seems reasonable to ask them to demonstrate this.

An important advantage of a cost-benefit study is that it forces those responsible to quantify costs and benefits as far as possible rather than rest content with vague qualitative judgments or personal hunches. This is obviously a good thing in itself; some information is always better than none. Furthermore, quantification and evaluation of benefits, however rough, does give some sort of clue to the charges which consumers are willing to pay. It may well be a salutary check on the biases likely to creep into estimated costs and benefits by enthusiastic advocates of particular projects, that, wherever technically feasible, some charges should be imposed.[1] The discipline of the market-place is so easily and so readily forgotten in these situations that some empirical evidence about benefit projections is highly necessary. Insistence on some charging process may therefore be a sensible antidote to wilder excesses of particular lobbies. We must remember, however, that the extent to which the authorities impose these charges brings in distributional as well as efficiency calculations.

Needless to say, the problems of charging are very complex. In particular, there is the possibility that some methods of charging may reduce the benefits of the project below the maximum possible. Beesley and Foster [3] have shown this in their inquiry as to how the London Transport Board might finance the Victoria Line. They show, for example, that a general increase in all fares would roughly halve the annual net benefits of the line.

A similar practical point stressed by some practitioners of cost-benefit analysis is that it has the very valuable by-product of causing questions to be asked (*e.g.*, the justification of existing pricing policy) which would otherwise not have been raised.

Even if cost-benefit analysis cannot give the right answers, it can sometimes play the purely negative role of screening projects and rejecting those answers which are obviously less promising. This role is akin to that of a University or College entrance examination: that whether or not one can grade the prospective candidates reasonably well on the basis of previous examination performance, personal interview, etc., the special entrance examination at least gives one a cast-iron justification for rejecting the weaker

[1] For an excellent discussion of biases, see Fox and Herfindahl's assessment of the application of cost-benefit analysis in United States Corps of Engineers water-resource projects [29].

brethren. In much the same way, insistence on cost-benefit analysis can help in the rejection of inferior projects, which are nevertheless promoted for empire-building or pork-barrel reasons.

Thus, it sometimes turns out that even with an overestimate of benefits a project can be rejected. In such cases the extent of the overestimation does not matter.

The case for using cost-benefit analysis is strengthened, not weakened, if its limitations are openly recognised and indeed emphasised. It is no good expecting this technique, at any rate in its present form, to be of any use if a project is so large as to alter the whole complex of relative prices and outputs in a country. It is no good expecting those fields in which benefits are widely diffused, and in which there are manifest divergences between accounting and economic costs or benefits, to be as cultivable as others. Nor is it realistic to expect that comparisons between projects in entirely different branches of economic activity are likely to be as meaningful or fruitful as those between projects in the same branch. The technique is more useful in the public-utility area than in the social-services area of government. Comparisons between, say, different road projects are more helpful than those between, say, road and water projects; and both these are likely to be more helpful than applications in the fields of education, health, research and so on.

We leave the last words in our survey to those independent and disinterested arbiters—the cataloguers of the University Library, Cambridge, England. In their wisdom, they classify the major work edited by Maass [48], to which we have referred on a number of occasions, under the heading "Useful Arts."

Bibliography

Note: This is mainly the list of articles, books, etc., to which we have referred in the text and in no sense is a complete bibliography of the subject.

1. G. S. Becker, *Human Capital* (New York: Columbia University Press, 1964).
2. M. E. Beesley, " The Value of Time Spent in Travelling: Some New Evidence," *Economica*, Vol. XXXII, May 1965.
3. M. E. Beesley and C. D. Foster, " The Victoria Line: Social Benefits and Finances," *Journal of the Royal Statistical Society*, Vol. 128, Part 1, 1965.
4. M. E. Beesley and J. F. Kain, " Urban Form, Car Ownership and Public Policy: An Appraisal of Traffic in Towns," *Urban Studies*, Vol. 1, No. 2, November 1964.
5. M. Blaug, " The Rate of Return on Investment in Education in Great Britain," *The Manchester School*, Vol. XXXIII, No. 3, September 1965.
6. M. E. Borus, " A Benefit Cost Analysis of the Economic Effectiveness of Retraining the Unemployed," *Yale Economic Essays*, Vol. 4, No. 2, Fall 1964.
7. H. C. Bos and L. M. Koyck, " The Appraisal of Road Construction Projects," *Review of Economics and Statistics*, Vol. XLIII, February 1961.
8. H. R. Bowen, *Toward Social Economy* (New York: Rinehart, 1948).
9. Mary J. Bowman, " Social Returns to Education," *International Social Science Journal*, Vol. XIV, No. 4, 1962.

10. British Railways Board, *The Reshaping of British Railways* (The Beeching Report) (H.M.S.O., 1963).
11. J. M. Buchanan and W. C. Stubblebine, " Externality," *Economica*, Vol. XXIX, November 1962.
12. Marion Clawson, " Methods of Measuring the Demand for and Value of Outdoor Recreation," *Resources for the Future, Inc.* (Washington, D.C., 1959).
13. R. H. Coase, " The Problem of Social Cost," *Journal of Law and Economics*, Vol. III, October 1960.
14. T. M. Coburn, M. E. Beesley and D. J. Reynolds, *The London–Birmingham Motorway: Traffic and Economics*, Road Research Laboratory Technical Paper No. 46. D.S.I.R., H.M.S.O., 1960.
15. J. A. Crutchfield, " Valuation of Fishery Resources," *Land Economics*, Vol. XXXVIII, May 1962.
16. H. Dalton, *Principles of Public Finance* (4th edn. revised), (London: Routledge & Kegan Paul, 1954).
17. Otto Davis and Andrew Whinston, " Externalities, Welfare, and the Theory of Games," *Journal of Political Economy*, Vol. LXX, June 1962.
18. M. M. Dryden, " Capital Budgeting: Treatment of Uncertainty and Investment Criteria," *Scottish Journal of Political Economy*, Vol. XI, November 1964.
19. J. Dupuit, " On the Measurement of Utility of Public Works," *International Economic Papers*, Vol. 2 (translated from the French).
20. Otto Eckstein, *Water Resource Development* (Cambridge, Mass.: Harvard University Press, 1958).
21. Otto Eckstein, " A Survey of the Theory of Public Expenditure Criteria," in James M. Buchanan (ed.), *Public Finances: Needs, Sources and Utilization* (Princeton: Princeton University Press, 1961).
22. B. H. Farmer, *Ceylon. A Divided Nation* (London: Oxford University Press, 1963).
23. M. S. Feldstein, " Net Social Benefit Calculation and the Public Investment Decision," *Oxford Economic Papers*, Vol. 16, March 1964.
24. M. S. Feldstein, " The Social Time Preference Discount Rate in Cost Benefit Analysis," ECONOMIC JOURNAL, Vol. LXXIV, June 1964.
25. M. S. Feldstein, " Opportunity Cost Calculations in Cost Benefit Analysis," *Public Finance*, Vol. XIX, No. 2, 1964.
26. I. Fisher, " Report on National Vitality: Its Wastes and Conservation," *Bulletin of One Hundred on National Health*, No. 30 (Washington, 1909).
27. C. D. Foster, *The Transport Problem* (London: Blackie, 1963).
28. C. D. Foster and M. E. Beesley, " Estimating the Social Benefit of Constructing an Underground Railway in London," *Journal of the Royal Statistical Society*, Vol. 126, Part 1, 1963.
29. I. K. Fox and O. C. Herfindahl, " Attainment of Efficiency in Satisfying Demands for Water Resources," *American Economic Review*, Vol. LIV, May 1964.
30. G. Fromm, " Civil Aviation Expenditures," R. Dorfman (ed.) *Measuring Benefits of Government Investments* (Washington, D.C.: Brookings Institution, 1965).
31. Zvi Griliches, " Research Costs and Social Returns: Hybrid Corn and Related Innovations," *Journal of Political Economy*, Vol. LXVI, October 1958.
32. R. J. Hammond, *Benefit–Cost Analysis and Water Pollution Control* (Stanford, California: University Press, 1958).
33. W. L. Hansen, " Total and Private Rates of Return to Investment in Schooling," *Journal of Political Economy*, Vol. LXXI, April 1963.
34. E. K. Hawkins, *Roads and Road Transport in an Underdeveloped Country. A Case Study of Uganda*, Colonial Office, Colonial Research Studies No. 32 (London: H.M.S.O., 1962).

35. J. G. Head, " Public Goods and Public Policy," *Public Finance*, Vol. XVII, 1962.
36. J. R. Hicks, " Economic Theory and the Evaluation of Consumers' Wants," *Journal of Business*, Chicago, Vol. 35, July 1962.
37. J. Hirshleifer, J. C. de Haven and J. W. Milliman, *Water Supply, Economics, Technology and Policy* (Chicago: University of Chicago Press, 1960).
38. C. J. Hitch and R. N. McKean, *The Economics of Defense in the Nuclear Age* (London: Oxford University Press, 1960).
39. S. J. Hunt, " Income Determinants for College Graduates and the Return to Educational Investment," *Yale Economic Essays*, Fall 1963.
40. Inter-Agency River Basin Committee (Sub-Committee on Costs and Budgets), *Proposed Practices for Economic Analysis of River Basin Projects* (" The Green Book ") (Washington, D.C., 1950).
41. International Institute for Land Reclamation and Improvement, *An Assessment of Investments in Land Reclamation* (Wageningen, Holland, 1960).
42. H. E. Klarman, " Syphilis Control Problems," R. Dorfman (ed.) *Measuring Benefits of Government Investments* (Washington D.C.: Brookings Institution, 1965).
43. J. V. Krutilla and Otto Eckstein, *Multiple Purpose River Development* (Baltimore: Johns Hopkins Press, 1958).
44. T. E. Kuhn, *Public Enterprise Economics and Transport Problems* (Berkeley and Los Angeles: University of California Press, 1962).
45. A. P. Lerner, *The Economics of Control* (New York: Macmillan, 1944).
46. J. Lesourne, *Le Calcul Economique* (Paris: Dunod, 1964).
47. N. Lichfield, *Cost Benefit Analysis in Urban Redevelopment*, Research Report, Real Estate Research Program, Institute of Business and Economic Research (Berkeley: University of California, 1962).
48. A. Maass, M. M. Hufschmidt, R. Dorfman, H. A. Thomas, S. A. Marglin and G. M. Fair, *Design of Water Resource Systems: New Techniques for Relating Economic Objectives, Engineering Analysis, and Governmental Planning* (London: Macmillan, 1962).
49. S. A. Marglin, " The Social Rate of Discount and Optimal Rate of Investment," *Quarterly Journal of Economics*, Vol. LXXVII, February 1963.
50. S. A. Marglin, " The Opportunity Costs of Public Investment," *Quarterly Journal of Economics*, Vol. LXXVII, May 1963.
51. S. A. Marglin, *Approaches to Dynamic Investment Planning* (Amsterdam: North Holland, 1963).
52. Julius Margolis, " Secondary Benefits, External Economies, and the Justification of Public Investment," *Review of Economics and Statistics*, Vol. XXXIX, August 1957.
53. R. N. McKean, *Efficiency in Government through Systems Analysis* (New York: John Wiley & Sons, 1958).
54. R. N. McKean, " Cost-benefit Analysis and British Defense Expenditure," in A. T. Peacock and D. J. Robertson (eds.), *Public Expenditure, Appraisal and Control* (Edinburgh: Oliver and Boyd, 1963).
55. Ministry of Transport, *Panel on Road Pricing* (Smeed Report) (H.M.S.O., 1964).
56. Ministry of Transport, *Traffic in Towns: A Study of the Long Term Problems of Traffic in Urban Areas* (Buchanan Report) (H.M.S.O., 1963).
57. H. Mohring, " Land Values and the Measurement of Highway Benefits," *Journal of Political Economy*, Vol. LXIX, June 1961.
58. H. Mohring and N. Harwitz, *Highway Benefits: an Analytical Framework* (Northwestern University Press, 1962).
59. L. N. Moses and H. F. Williamson, " Value of Time, Choice of Mode, and the Subsidy Issue in Urban Transportation," *Journal of Political Economy*, Vol. LXXI, June 1963.

60. R. A. Musgrave, *The Theory of Public Finance. A Study in Public Economy* (New York: McGraw-Hill, 1959).
61. R. A. Musgrave and A. T. Peacock, *Classics in the Theory of Public Finance* (London: Macmillan, 1958).
62. Selma J. Mushkin, " Health as an Investment," *Journal of Political Economy*, Vol. LXX (Supplement), October 1962.
63. National Council of Applied Economic Research (New Delhi), *Criteria for Fixation of Water Rates and Selection of Irrigation Projects* (London: Asia Publishing House, 1959).
64. R. R. Nelson, "The Simple Economics of Basic Scientific Research," *Journal of Political Economy*, Vol. LXVII, June 1959.
65. A. C. Pigou, *The Economics of Welfare* (4th edn.) (London: Macmillan, 1932).
66. A. R. Prest and I. G. Stewart, *The National Income of Nigeria 1950–51*, Colonial Office Research Series (H.M.S.O., 1953).
67. G. F. Ray and R. E. Crum, "Transport: Notes and Comments," *National Institute Economic Review*, No. 24, May 1963.
68. E. F. Renshaw, *Towards Responsible Government* (Chicago: Idyia Press, 1957).
69. E. F. Renshaw, " A Note on the Measurement of the Benefits from Public Investment in Navigation Projects," *American Economic Review*, Vol. XLVII, September 1957.
70. D. J. Reynolds, " The Cost of Road Accidents," *Journal of the Royal Statistical Society*, Vol. 119, Part 4, 1956.
71. J. Rothenberg, " Urban Renewal Programs," R. Dorfman (ed.) *Measuring Benefits of Government Investments* (Washington, D.C.: Brookings Institution, 1965).
72. P. A. Samuelson, " The Pure Theory of Public Expenditure," *Review of Economics and Statistics*, Vol. XXXVI, November 1954.
73. P. A. Samuelson, " Diagrammatic Exposition of a Theory of Public Expenditure," *Review of Economics and Statistics*, Vol. XXXVII, November 1955.
74. P. A. Samuelson, " Aspects of Public Expenditure Theories," *Review of Economics and Statistics*, Vol. XL, November 1958.
75. F. M. Scherer, " Government Research and Development Programs," R. Dorfman (ed.) *Measuring Benefits of Government Investments* (Washington, D.C.: Brookings Institution, 1965).
76. J. R. Schlesinger, " Quantitative Analysis and National Security," *World Politics*, January 1963.
77. W. R. D. Sewell, J. Davis, A. D. Scott and D. W. Ross, *Guide to Benefit-Cost Analysis* (Resources for Tomorrow) (Ottawa: Queen's Printer, 1962).
78. Arthur Smithies, *The Budgetary Process in the United States* (Committee for Economic Development Research Study) (New York: McGraw-Hill, 1955).
79. N. V. Sovani and N. Rath, *Economics of a Multiple-purpose River Dam: Report of an Inquiry into the Economic Benefits of the Hirakud Dam*, Gokhale Institute of Politics and Economics Publication No. 38 (Poona, 1960).
80. P. O. Steiner, " Choosing Among Alternative Public Investments in the Water Resource Field," *American Economic Review*, Vol. XLIX, December 1959.
81. J. Thédié and C. Abraham, " Economic Aspect of Road Accidents," *Traffic Engineering and Control*, Vol. II, No. 10, February 1961.
82. A. H. Trice and S. E. Wood, " Measurement of Recreation Benefits," *Land Economics*, Vol. XXXIV, August 1958.
83. Ralph Turvey, " Present Value versus Internal Rate of Return—An Essay in the Theory of the Third Best," Economic Journal, Vol. LXXIII, March 1963.
84. Ralph Turvey, " On Investment Choices in Electricity Generation," *Oxford Economic Papers*, Vol. 15, November 1963.

85. Ralph Turvey, " On Divergences between Social Cost and Private Cost," *Economica*, New Series, Vol. XXX, August 1963.
86. B. A. Weisbrod, *Economics of Public Health: Measuring the Economic Impact of Diseases* (Philadelphia: University of Pennsylvania Press, 1960).
87. B. A. Weisbrod, " Education and Investment in Human Capital," *Journal of Political Economy*, Vol. LXX (Supplement), October 1962.
88. B. R. Williams, " Economics in Unwonted Places," ECONOMIC JOURNAL, March 1965.
89. D. M. Winch, *The Economics of Highway Planning* (Toronto: Toronto University Press, 1963).
90. F. Yates, *Sampling Methods for Censuses and Surveys* (London: Griffin, 1960).

*Printed in Great Britain by
Richard Clay (The Chaucer Press), Ltd.,
Bungay, Suffolk*

Printed in Great Britain by
Richard Clay (The Chaucer Press), Ltd.,
Bungay, Suffolk